Global Humanities
Studies in Histories, Cultures, and Societies

01/2015
On the Correlation of Center and Periphery

Global Humanities
Studies in Histories, Cultures, and Societies

01/2015

On the Correlation of Center and Periphery

Edited by Frank Jacob

Neofelis Verlag

Global Humanities – Studies in Histories, Cultures, and Societies
01/2015: On the Correlation of Center and Periphery
Ed. by Frank Jacob

German National Library Cataloguing in Publication Data
A catalogue record for this book is available from the German National Library:
http://dnb.d-nb.de

Cover Design: Marija Skara
Printed by PRESSEL Digitaler Produktionsdruck, Remshalden
Printed on FSC-certified paper.
ISSN: 2199-3939
ISBN (Print): 978-3-943414-68-4
ISBN (PDF): 978-3-943414-91-2

Global Humanities appears biannually.

Inhalt

Constructions

Editorial

In his structural theory of imperialism, Johan Galtung underlined the unequal division between center and periphery:

> The tremendous inequality, within and between nations, in almost all aspects of human living conditions, including the power to decide over those living conditions; and the resistance of this inequality to change. The world consists of Center and Periphery nations; and each nation in turn, has its centers and periphery.[1]

His theory followed other theories of imperialism, e.g., John A. Hobson's[2], which claimed that imperialism was an expression of industrialized nations' fear of international competition, which led to the exploitation of the colonial sphere and a growing antagonism between the great powers. Galtung observed this antagonism during the Cold War and the victimization of the so-called Third World, the global periphery[3], which was doomed to suffer from this conflict between superpowers.

For a long time the center-periphery model remained "a spatial metaphor which describes and attempts to explain the structural relationship between the advanced or metropolitan 'centre' and a less developed 'periphery', either within a particular country, or (more commonly) as applied to the relationship between capitalist and developing societies."[4] Sociological studies in particular focused on "economic underdevelopment and dependency."[5] However, other research questions were also increasingly relevant. What were the characteristics of the distinguishing process between center and periphery? What was exchanged and what was the nature of this exchange?[6] It also became clear, that "a purely relational center-periphery model is insufficient as a conceptual tool for understanding the historical dynamics of center-periphery

1 Johan Galtung: A Structural Theory of Imperialism. In: *Journal of Peace Research* 8,2 (1971), pp. 81–117, here p. 81.

2 John A. Hobson: *Imperialism: A Study*. London: Nisbet 1902.

3 Frank Jacob (ed.): *Peripheries of the Cold War*. Würzburg: Königshausen & Neumann 2015 (in print).

4 Gordon Marshall: Centre–periphery model. In: *A Dictionary of Sociology,* 1998. http://www.encyclopedia.com/doc/1O88-centreperipherymodel.html (accessed 12.01.2015).

5 Ibid.

6 E. Spencer Wellhofer: Core and Periphery: Territorial Dimensions in Politics. In: *Urban Studies* 26,3 (1989), pp. 340–355.

dominance."[7] Both spheres create independent variables, and even if Western capitalism still dominates the states of the so-called Third World[8], postcolonial studies in different disciplines have shown that the colonial periphery was not passive in this relationship. Many centers were highly influenced and impacted by the colonial periphery.[9] Some fields also highlight the need for a borderless approach, without any cultural prepossessions to study both spheres on an equal footing.[10]

The different humanities disciplines have a lot to gain by researching this correlation, especially with regard to interdisciplinary research projects. Research in various fields, e.g., urban studies[11], literary studies[12], or economic geography[13], has been based on the concept, but there is still sufficient room for a higher level of interdisciplinarity, especially in the 21st century, which is the most 'global' century in human history. Mass communication, mass media, and big data[14] are available almost everywhere. As a consequence, research has also become global, expressed through international conferences, research cooperation, and transnational projects. Opening this research to interdisciplinary approaches is not a new goal, but I believe the academic community can do more in this regard. Consequently, this new interdisciplinary journal was established to provide a broader insight into the different humanities

7 Jon Naustdalslid: A Multi-Level Approach to the Study of Center-Periphery Systems and Socio Economic Change. In: *Journal of Peace Research* 14,3 (1977), pp. 203–222, here p.203.

8 Paul James: Postdependency? The Third World in an Era of Globalism and Late-Capitalism. In: *Alternatives* 22 (1997), pp. 205–226, here p. 205.

9 Ania Loomba / Suvir Kaul / Matti Bunzl / Antoinette Burton / Jed Esty (eds): *Postcolonial Studies and Beyond*. Durham, NC: Duke UP 2005; Francis Barker / Peter Hulme / Margaret Iversen (eds): *Colonial Discourse / Postcolonial Theory*. Manchester: Manchester UP 1996. Sanjay Seth (ed.): *Postcolonial Theory and International Relations: A Critical Introduction*. London: Routledge 2013.

10 Blai Guarné: The World Is a Room: Beyond Centers and Peripheries in the Global Production of Anthropological Knowledge. In: *Focaal* 63 (2012), pp. 8–19.

11 Adam Grydehøj: Constructing a Centre on the Periphery: Urbanization and Urban Design in the Island City of Nuuk, Greenland. In: *Island Studies Journal* 9,2 (2014), pp. 205–222.

12 Robin MacKenzie: Centre and Periphery in Lawrence Norfolk's *The Pope's Rhinoceros* and Christoph Ransmayr's *Die letzte Welt*. In: *Orbis Litterarum* 67,5 (2012), pp. 416–436.

13 Jiaping Wu: Between the Centre and the Periphery: The Development of Port Trade in Darwin, Australia. In: *Australian Geographer* 42,3 (2011), pp. 273–288.

14 Kenneth Neil Cukier / Viktor Mayer-Schoenberger: The Rise of Big Data. http://www.foreignaffairs.com/articles/139104/kenneth-neil-cukier-and-viktor-mayer-schoenberger/the-rise-of-big-data (accessed 10.01.2015).

from an interdisciplinary perspective. By combining history, political and social studies, media studies, and literature, along with performative arts studies and other subfields of the humanities into a single journal with a global and transnational perspective, the disciplines will hopefully be enriched by a broader exchange of concepts and ideas.

This first volume, which deals with the correlation between Center and Periphery, is a first attempt at using diverse disciplines to analyze such a global issue. In the first section, Henner Kropp, Ingo Löppenberg, and Dina Mansour analyze forms of receptions which exist between the center and the periphery. Kropp deals with the image of Russian America in the Czarist Empire, while Löppenberg focuses on the Inuit in Imperial Germany. Mansour adds a perspective on the role of gender and religion within the Islamic context of modern Europe.

The second section deals with forms of exchanges between the two spheres. Oliver Schlenkrich and Christoph Mohamad-Klotzbach investigate the interrelationship between democratization and foreign aid flows from the center to the periphery, while Evangelidis Vasileios describes the development of technological progress by analyzing center-core exchanges. Finally, Jeffrey Shaw shows how philosophical and religious ideas of self-transcendence come into existence via the exchange between intellectuals from distinct cultures from different spheres.

The third section explores how stereotypes which arise from the geographical and cultural distance between center and periphery also lead to exploitation. Julia Harnoncourt highlights the exploitation of workers in peripheral Brazil. Liony Bauer continues with an analysis of the consequences of 'economic securitization' for the Roma minority in postwar Germany. The section concludes with a study by De-Valera N. Y. M. Botchway into the rewriting of colonial historiography in post-colonial Ghana.

The final part investigates the artificial construction of center and periphery stereotypes. Solveig Lena Hansen and Cathrin Cronjäger analyze how Jeanette Winterson transcended a spatialized Other, an artificial periphery, in *The Stone Gods*, and Kyle J. Wanberg offers a discussion of a theory of global aesthetics which could create a world literature, instead of one that is determined by the center based presumptions. Last but not least, Julia Brühne highlights the interpretation of Mexican border crossing, nostalgia, and identification in Robert Rodríguez's movie *Machete* (2010).

In conclusion, I would like to use this opportunity to thank the authors for their patience, the members of the scientific board for their support, as well as Denise Martinez and Tim Keogh for their invaluable help during the final days of editing. Special thanks are also due to Frank Schlöffel and Matthias Naumann for their belief in the project and their unlimited help during the whole process of conceptualization, planning, and editing.

New York, January 2015
Frank Jacob

Receptions

Halfway around the World

Russian America as a Part of the Russian Empire

Henner Kropp

When a Russian merchant established the first tiny permanent non-native settlement on the northwestern shores of the American continent in today's Alaska and initialized the history of *Russkaya Amerika* (Russian America), as the new colony was called, the character of the Russian Empire changed. For the first and only time in its history, Russia was now in the possession of an overseas colony. Thanks to the new colony, Russia now expanded over three continents, and was no longer solely a land empire.[1]

This article provides a very brief overview of the history of Russian America, with an emphasis on the aspects that illustrate the relationship between the colony and the Empire's capital, St. Petersburg. The core questions are the integration of the Russian colony into the imperial governmental system, the coincidence of entrepreneurial and governmental interests in St. Petersburg's attitude towards Alaska and the geographical and geopolitical circumstances under which the Russian colony was installed and maintained. As a result, other important facets like the territorial and political competition between Russia and other nations in the North Pacific, the interaction with the native population or the role of the Orthodox Church will only be briefly touched upon.[2]

Russians in Alaska and the Beginning of Russian America

Until the 18th century, the territory east of the Russian Pacific coast remained unexplored to European and Asian nations. Within a century, Russian

1 Guido Hausmann offers a distinction and terminological classification: Maritimes Reich – Landreich. Zur Anwendung einer geografischen Deutungsfigur auf Russland. In: Guido Hausmann / Angela Rustemeyer (eds): *Imperienvergleich. Beispiele und Ansätze aus osteuropäischer Perspektive. Festschrift für Andreas Kappeler.* Wiesbaden: Harrassowitz 2009, pp. 489–510.

2 The history of Russian America has been fervently discussed among historians. Unsurprisingly Russian historiographers have provided the largest contribution, but there are also numerous publications from the United States, Canada, and other countries. The most comprehensive study of the history of Russian America is provided by the three-volume publication by Nikolai Bolkhovitinov (ed.): *Istoriya Russkoi Ameriki, 1732–1867.* Moskva: Mezhdunarodnye otnosheniya 1997–1999.

merchants, Cossacks and promyshlenniki[3] had crossed the entire of Siberia at an enormous speed, but the ocean they reached in 1638[4] proved to be a resistant natural barrier. Roughly one hundred years later, The Great Northern Expedition (1733–1743), one of the most complex scientific ventures in Russian history thus far, was dispatched from St. Petersburg to finally gain more concrete geographic knowledge about the North Pacific. Despite an enormous number of scientific results – for example the exact position of the Alaskan Peninsula and its distance from the Russian shore – the expedition proved fatal for many of its members. Vitus Bering, the expedition's leader, died shipwrecked on an island in the Pacific, and few survivors made it back to Kamchatka.[5] With them they brought furs from a marine animal thus far unknown in Russia: the sea otter.

The fur trade had quickly developed into a major pillar of the Russian economy. As well as the enormous fortunes merchants earned, the fur trade was closely linked to the formation of the Russian Empire. Through the *yasak* – a fur tax people in annexed territories had to pay to the Russian administration – Russians gained control over enormous territories, and the need for more and more hunting grounds was the reason why the Russians pushed eastwards so quickly. The enthusiasm among Russian officials back in St. Petersburg was diminished by the backslash from the Great Northern Expedition, and their interest in the territory east of the Russian Pacific shores noticeably declined. This gap was willingly filled by the private merchant companies that played a major role in the history of Russian America.[6]

When merchants and investors learned about the sea otter and its extremely thick and therefore valuable fur on the Commander and Aleutian Islands,

3 Contracted men from Siberia hired to hunt for fur: first in Siberia, and later on the Aleutian Islands and in Russian America. As a result of their long travels, they were occasionally the first Russians to enter unexplored territory.

4 Boris Polevoi: Predystoriya Russkoi Ameriki (zarozhdenie interesa v Rossii k severo-zapadnomu beregu Ameriki). In: Nikolai Bolkhovitinov (ed.): *Istoriya Russkoi Ameriki, 1732–1867*, vol. I: Osnovanie Russkoi Ameriki, 1732–1867. Moskva: Mezhdunarodnye otnosheniya 1997, pp. 12–51, here pp. 17–18.

5 Folkwart Wendland: Das Russische Reich am Vorabend der Großen Nordischen Expedition, der sogenannten zweiten Kamtschatka-Expedition. In: Doris Posselt (ed.): *Die Große Nordische Expedition von 1733 bis 1743. Aus Berichten der Forschungsreisenden Johann Georg Gmelin und Georg Wilhelm Steller*. Leipzig / Weimar: Gustav Kiepenheuer 1990, pp. 332–384, here p. 359.

6 The historian Andrei Grinev sees this development as an important moment in the history of the Russian colony, because only the partial retreat of the government cleared the way for merchants. Andrei Grinev: Rol' gosudarstva v obrazovanii Rossiisko-amerikanskoi kompanii. In: Nikolai Bolkhovitinov (ed.): *Russkoe otkrytie Ameriki*. Moskva: ROSSPEN 2002, pp. 437–450, here p. 438.

they did not hesitate to equip hunting expeditions to these recently discovered islands. The first hunting expedition to the Aleutian Islands returned to the Russian mainland in 1744 with fabulous results,[7] and a new fur rush began. Island by island, the Aleutian Islands were seized by Russian fur hunters, and in the 1760s their ships dropped anchor off the Alaskan shore.[8] Only a handful of merchant companies had the fortune to compete in the highly cost intensive race for new hunting grounds, and by the 1780s only two companies remained. The Shelikhov-Golikov Company came up with a final plan to outdo its last competitor: through a permanent settlement on the Alaska Peninsula, the company's promyshlenniki would be able to extend the hunting season considerably and would not lose time through the journey back to mainland Russia for winter. In 1784, the company's owner, Grigorii Shelikhov, sailed to Kodiak (Kad'yak) Island, where he supervised the construction of the first permanent Russian settlement on American soil.[9] Shelikhov returned in 1786 to Siberia, where he hired Aleksandr Baranov as the new outpost's leader. The two men signed a contract in 1790, and in 1791 Baranov arrived in Alaska.

The Formation of the Russian American Company

The role of the tsarist government in the expansion to America and the distinction between governmental and private interests are complex and diverse subjects. The major influence and contribution of merchants has been mentioned above, but the Russian government undeniably played a significant role in the annexing of Siberia, Kamchatka, the Commander and Aleutian Islands, and Alaska itself. As well as The Great Northern Expedition and its importance for Russian expansion across the Pacific, the influence of the state was always present on a smaller scale. The merchant ships that were sent out from Eurasia to America were obliged to carry a state official on their journeys. These men, called *oko gosudarevo* (the eye of the government), oversaw the proper calculation and collection of the *yasak* and made sure that, after returning to a Russian port, 10% of the journey's takings was handed over to the state.[10] The scientific exploration and geographic coverage of the new Russian territories were also part of the government agenda, especially under

7 Andrei Grinev: *Kto est' kto v istorii Russkoi Ameriki*. Moskva: Academia 2009, p. 636.

8 Lydia Black: *Russians in Alaska, 1732–1867*. Fairbanks: University of Alaska Press 2004, p. 86.

9 Ibid., p. 107.

10 Grinev: Rol' gosudarstva v obrazovanii Rossiisko-amerikanskoi kompanii, pp. 438–439.

the reign of Catherine the Great. Her Siberian Governor, Fedor Soimonov, monitored the advancement of nautical schools to better prepare Russian captains and crews for shipping on the open sea,[11] and in 1765 and 1798 further expeditions were launched to the Arctic and Alaska.[12]

However, Catherine the Great hesitated to make formal or legal concessions to the Shelikhov-Golikov Company regarding the new territories in America. As a consequence, Russian America remained a tiny, not very prosperous, but highly cost-intensive project run by merchants. Shelikhov's proposal of a semi-governmental trade company with a monopoly on fur trade and hunting in the American territories – which would have been the final blow to eliminate his last remaining rivals – did not draw any approval in St. Petersburg. Catherine the Great dedicated her entire attention to the ongoing military conflicts with Turkey and Sweden in Europe, and increased political devotion to the easternmost reaches of the empire was the last burden the empress wanted to add to her political agenda. Also, the negative experience that her British counterpart recently had with his American colonies could explain why she refrained from conceding too much political influence and independence to the new colony.[13]

The picture changed when Catherine the Great died in 1796. Shelikhov's widow – he had died in 1795 – and her son-in-law Nikolai Rezanov, a nobleman with excellent connections to the tsarist court, reached their goal under Catherine's successor Paul I. In 1799, the tsar enacted an *ukaz* to charter the joint-stock company *Rossiisko-amerikanskaya kompaniya* (Russian American Company, RAC) and granted several rights to the desired monopoly for 20 years.[14] As a consequence, the new colony and its inhabitants now officially stood under the protection of the Russian crown, and Alaska became a de facto part of the Russian Empire.

To what extent the Russian government was willing to advance its territorial and political interests in the American continent is hard to determine. And the question of whether the merchant companies used the government for their economic ambitions or if the tsar found an easy way to gain control over new territories without high political risk remains unclear (and is still a controversial subject among historians). But undoubtedly the government never lost control over the American venture and tried to maintain its role as

11 Grinev: *Kto est' kto v istorii Russkoi Ameriki*, p. 499.

12 Black: *Russians in Alaska*, pp. 80–91.

13 Grinev: Rol' gosudarstva v obrazovanii Rossiisko-amerikanskoi kompanii, p. 444.

14 Black: *Russians in Alaska*, p. 225.

a careful observer for as long as possible. Aleksandr Petrov emphasizes that such a major venture could never have taken place without the concession of the state.[15] Andrei Grinev points out that the Russian government found an easy way to significantly extend the borders and influence of the Russian Empire while letting the merchants do the lion's share of the work.[16] And Martina Winkler argues that the merchants' strong influence certainly represents the pragmatic approach St. Petersburg had towards the expansion over the Pacific, and that the Russians were more interested in the American coast than the continent itself.[17]

Reaching and Supplying Russian America

Now that the Russian Empire stretched over three continents, the task of communication and infrastructural connection between the center and the periphery became more pressing than ever. Russian America was unique, though. Obviously the only way to reach Alaska from mainland Russia was by ship, and the Russian navy of the time had neither a long nor successful history, and was navigating on an unknown ocean. Reaching the colony as a traveler was an enormous effort, as a reliable and continuous supply of all the needed goods was an apparently impossible task under the contemporary infrastructural conditions.

All goods that could not be manufactured or grown in Alaska – which in the early decades of the colony applied to almost everything – had to be shipped from Siberia to America. Just the journey from Yakutsk, then a central trading city in Siberia, by horse to Okhotsk and from there by ship via the Aleutian Islands to Novo Arkhangel'sk, as the new colony's capital was named, took at least half a year;[18] the entire distance from St. Petersburg to Alaska was no less than 12,000 miles.[19] Not to mention that East Siberia was hard to supply from the European part of Russia and lacked many goods itself. As an effect, only one ship per year could be dispatched to Novo Arkhangel'sk from Okhotsk.[20]

15 Grinev: Rol' gosudarstva v obrazovanii Rossiisko-amerikanskoi kompanii, p. 448.

16 Ibid., p. 440.

17 Martina Winkler: Another America. Russian Mental Discoveries of the North-west Pacific Region in the Eighteenth and Early Nineteenth Centuries. In: *Journal of Global History* 7 (2012), pp. 27–51, here pp. 33–34.

18 James R. Gibson: *Imperial Russia in Frontier America. The Changing Geography of Supply of Russian America, 1784–1867*. New York: Oxford UP 1976, pp. 57–60.

19 Ibid., p. 44.

20 As a further consequence, mail, newspapers and information about political developments

And if, due to a poorly trained crew, a lack of experience among the captains and officers, or the not always seaworthy boats, a ship sank – as happened to the *Mikhail* in 1801 – the absence of food and other supplies became an enormous problem.[21] The wet climate and lack of fertile soil prevented efficient farming and livestock breeding and made independent self-supply of the colony impossible.[22] And ultimately fur hunting, not the development of a sufficient infrastructure or other time-intensive tasks like farming or fishing, was the main reason why the Russians had settled in Alaska.

Not surprisingly, the colony only grew very slowly. In 1799, when the RAC was founded, only 225 Russians lived in Alaska. This increased to 470 in 1805 and around 500 in 1817.[23] The harsh climate and the remoteness of the American colony were the major reasons for the RAC's significant problems in hiring workers from Siberia, as it was particularly hard to convince well-trained or highly motivated men to either leave their families behind or take them with them to an unfamiliar and hostile environment.

The launching of the first Russian circumnavigation from Kronstadt (St. Petersburg), the only other option to reach Novo Arkhangel'sk by ship from mainland Russia, was supposed to provide significant relief. Obviously, this venture was very cost intensive and demanding, and similar plans and attempts had been given up in the recent past. In 1803, two ships – the *Neva* under the command of Yurii Lisyanskii and the *Nadezhda* under the command of Adam Johann von Krusenstern, who was also in charge of the overall command – departed from Kronstadt. Via Finland, Great Britain, Spain, Brazil and the Sandwich Islands (Hawaii), the journey led to Alaska, and after a stop in the Chinese port of Canton, the ships went back to St. Petersburg, where they arrived in the summer of 1806.[24] Despite the prestigious effect the journey had for the Russian navy, it quickly transpired that circumnavigation could not be the proper solution for the colony's supply problem: it was simply too expensive. The costs for the cargo the RAC bought in St. Petersburg at market prices had multiplied when the ships arrived in Novo

in Europe only reached the colony after a huge delay; letters usually only arrived in the colony a year after they had been written in St. Petersburg.

21 Alexander Alekseev: *The Destiny of Russian America 1741–1867*. Kingston, ON / Fairbanks: The Limestone Press 1990, p. 124.

22 Gibson: *Imperial Russia in Frontier America*, pp. 4–6.

23 Ibid., pp. 7–11.

24 Peter Tikhmenev: *A History of the Russian American Company*. Seattle / London: University of Washington Press 1978, p. 79.

Arkhangel'sk due to expenses for the ship and crew and the losses caused by rats and spoilage during the long journey. Even the fact that the ships brought the desired furs or other valuable goods from the Far East with them back to St. Petersburg did not bring the venture even close to being profitable. For example, the journey of the *Kutuzov* from 1820 to 1822 cost 700,000 rubles, but the ship only brought cargo worth 200,000 rubles back to mainland Russia.[25]

Far from St. Petersburg: Some Features of the Development of Russian America in the 19th Century

Summarizing the condition of the colony and its specific goals at the beginning of the 19th century does not provide a clear picture. As discussed above, governmental and entrepreneurial goals and influence merged together, and are not easy to identify as one or the other. What sounds like a harmonic symbiosis led occasionally to misunderstandings and problems. For example, contact with other European nations in America, mainly the British Hudson Bay Company, the Spanish colonists in California and US-American traders from the East Coast, had both positive and negative aspects. On the one hand, the Russian colonists in Alaska benefited from the visits of foreign vessels and trade with their captains, at least temporarily easing their supply situation. On the other hand, the avoidance of political miscommunications and disgruntlement in America was the overriding goal of the St. Petersburg government, and it was always anxious to see the interaction between Russian American colonists and other nations. The native population in Alaska was another group the colonists had to deal with. From the very beginning, the contact between Russians and the native population was a key factor for the development of the young colony.

The indigenous people of the Aleutian Islands, called Aleut, lived scattered over the islands and could offer only very little resistance against the Russian intruders, who more and more frequently headed for their islands in the second half of the 18th century. The Russian ship crews took hostages after their arrival on an island and forced the tribe to hunt sea otters for them.[26] In the rare case of resistance against this oppression, the Russians did not hesitate to use violence and strike down any opposition, for example, during the

25 Gibson: *Imperial Russia in Frontier America*, p. 87.

26 Erwin Buchholz / Gert Buchholz: *Rußlands Tierwelt und Jagd im Wandel der Zeit.* Gießen: Wilhelm Schmitz 1963, pp. 28–29.

uprising on Unalashka Island in 1764.[27] But the Aleut people also developed into an indispensable source of labor, especially due to their skilled hunting methods and the lack of Russian men to cover all necessary work. Slowly but surely the relationship improved, and under the decisive ministration of the Russian Orthodox Church, the Aleut grew more and more integrated in the Russian colony. And when Russian men and Aleut women began to marry, their children formed a Creole class as a cultural bridge between Russians and Aleut.[28]

When the Russians started to settle in mainland Alaska, they occupied the territory of another tribe, the Tlingit. The Tlingit were a much stronger opponent than the Aleut; their living environment was not separated by water like the Aleutian Islands, making it much easier to defend and providing much more substantial nutrition.[29] Their resistance to the Russians on their coast presented a significant security threat to the colony, and the Russians' fear of further Tlingit attacks after they destroyed the colony's capital on Sitka Island in 1802 became a major challenge to Russian life that Aleksandr Baranov and his successors had to confront.[30]

The enduring problem of ensuring reliable and sufficient supply to the colony was the other main concern for the Russian colonists. The contact with foreign traders mentioned above turned out to be neither constant nor without political difficulty. Baranov and especially Rezanov envisioned expanding the territory of the Russian colony southwards, where a warmer climate supposedly favored successful farming. However, a cautious approach was required so as not to provoke conflicts with other nations present in the Pacific. The Sandwich Islands and the Californian territory were the major areas of interest for the colony's governors in Novo Arkhangel'sk. Russian agitation on the Sandwich Islands came to an abrupt end after the German RAC-employee Georg Anton Schäffer almost caused a new war on the archipelago during his time on the islands from 1815 to 1817; however, the approach in California turned out to be more promising.

27 Black: *Russians in Alaska*, pp. 89–90.

28 Both the development of Russian-Aleut relations and the role of the Russian Orthodox Church in the Russian colony are covered in detail in Bolkhovitinov (ed.): *Istoriya Russkoi Ameriki, 1732–1867*. Ilya Vinkovetsky also devotes a major part of his most recent publication to the same topics: *Russian America. An Overseas Colony of a Continental Empire, 1804–1867*. Oxford / New York: Oxford UP 2011.

29 Vinkovetsky: *Russian America*, pp. 20–21.

30 Tikhmenev: *A History of the Russian American Company*, p. 66.

During the first decade of the 19th century, the Russians had already approached the Californian coast for sea otter hunting, as Baranov had received reports about the attractiveness of the land and the abundance of sea otters.[31] Rezanov, who had come to the colony in 1805, advanced the Russian ambitions in California further and visited the Spanish governor in San Francisco to prepare the opening of a Russian outpost. Fort Ross was built in 1811 and, until its disposal in 1841, provided at least a minor contribution to the supply of the main colony in Alaska.

Russia's Retreat and the Sale of the Colony

After the RAC's disastrous experiences on the Sandwich Islands, the shipwreck of another expedition at the delta of the Columbia River,[32] and the expansion into California, St. Petersburg dedicated top priority to avoiding further turbulence in the North Pacific and leading the Russian colony towards quieter times in the 1820s. Contracts with the US-American and British governments were signed to ease the political tensions that had grown continuously during the previous decades due to the competition among the nations in the North Pacific.[33] The Russian government made far-reaching concessions: Despite ceding the supply of the colony to the Hudson Bay Company, it was willing to determine the borders of Russian influence in Alaska, a commitment St. Petersburg had been avoiding for a long time. In 1825, a contract was signed between the Russian and British governments to define Prince of Wales Island as the southern border of Russian influence in Alaska. By refraining from further expansion in North America, the political brisance of the Russian colony was lowered, a development that was highly appreciated by the government in St. Petersburg.

But the continued over-hunting of the sea otter also became noticeable, and the decline in the economic attractiveness of the colony was more and more obvious. St. Petersburg was plagued by what the Russian Empire was supposed to do with a colony that was still a factor of political uncertainty and

31 Aleksei Istomin: Ideya russkoi kolonizatsii Kalifornii i prodvizhenie russkikh v etot krai, 1803–1812 gg. Osnovanie kreposti Ross. In: A. A. Istomin / Dzh. R. Gibson / V. A. Tishkov (eds): *Rossiya v Kalifornii*, vol. I. Moskva: Nauka 2005, pp. 31–47, here pp. 33–34.

32 Simultaneous with the first Russian expedition to California in 1806, a ship was also dispatched to the Columbia River. After the shipwreck, the remaining members of the crew barely made it back to Alaska, and the idea of a Russian outpost in that spot was abandoned. Aleksei Istomin: Ideya russkoi kolonizatsii Kalifornii, pp. 38–40.

33 Tikhmenev: *A History of the Russian American Company*, p. 66.

was no longer profitable. Russia's defeat in the Crimean War and the subsequent reforms led to a tough decision by Alexander II and his closest advisers: The Russian Empire had to get rid of Alaska before it was taken by force.[34]

Through diplomatic dodges, the sale of Alaska was mooted to the US government via the Russian embassy in Washington. When the Russian offer became public, both the press and US-politicians had a mixed attitude towards the possible purchase of Alaska. While some emphasized primarily economic advantages – fishing and whaling, advancing the Manifest Destiny, excellent trading in the Pacific and Asia – others noted the perceived worthlessness of the Alaskan soil and possible foreign policy tensions, especially with Great Britain.[35] Only after some debate did the US-government agree to buy Alaska for $7.2 million in 1867.

In St. Petersburg, the sale of the colony caused mixed reactions as well. In particular, members of the Russian navy, for whom Russian America had become an important outpost and an attractive step on the career ladder, protested heavily but vainly.[36]

Conclusion

The relationship between the Russian colonists in Alaska and the government in St. Petersburg is characterized by ambivalence and uncertainty among the tsars and other political decision makers. On the one hand, the Russian political leadership undoubtedly had an interest in a Russian expansion towards the North American continent. Enormously risky and highly expensive ventures like the Great Northern Expedition or the circumnavigations from Kronstadt are evidence of a deep desire to be among the nations who competed for influence in the North Pacific. Despite the enormous impact private merchant companies had on the Russian approach to America, the significance of the government's role cannot be denied.

On the other hand, the Russian government lacked the final determination to establish Russian influence as a long term political factor on the northwestern

34 This approach is favored by the historian Aleksandr Petrov. The sale of Russian America remains a hotly debated topic among Russian historians. Elena Skvortsova: *Kak i zachem na samom dele Rossiya prodala Alyasku.* http://sobesednik.ru/rassledovanie/20140406-kak-iz-zachem-na-samom-dele-rossiya-prodala-alyasku (accessed 29.05.2014).

35 Howard I. Kushner: *Conflict on the Northwest Coast. American-Russian Rivalry in the Pacific Northwest, 1790–1867.* Westport, CT: Greenwood 1975, pp. 143–148.

36 Tikhmenev: *A History of the Russian American Company*, pp. 166–167.

coast of America. The tsars' ultimate goal was to increase the economic and prestigious benefits for the Russian Empire while avoiding political conflict. Why did the Russian Empire not defend their ambitions there more resolutely? Why was the decision to surrender the colony made so easily? A closer look at the political events in Europe from the late-18th to the mid-19th century makes clear that the Russian military and political forces were tied to this region for a long time. Under the reign of Catherine the Great, when Shelikhov approached the empress with his idea of a semi-private trading company to gain control over Alaska, her entire attention was dedicated to the ongoing wars with Sweden and Turkey. Only a decade later, Napoleon overthrew the political order in Europe and made a shift in political attention impossible. And in the mid-19th century, the Crimea and the Black Sea became the more important political arenas for the Russian Empire during its conflict with the Ottoman Empire, France and Great Britain. The fate of Russian America was sealed by the center, not by the periphery, and the Russian colonists in Alaska had barely any influence on the future of their colony.

The Russian government could not afford a confrontation in the remotest part of its empire. The colony needed to be a politically quiet but economically profitable and prestigious enterprise. But the Russian presence on the northwest coast of America would have needed a much more committed and risky engagement to overpower political rivals and establish a more reliable connection to mainland Russia – a price the St. Petersburg government was unwilling to pay.

Their Knowledge about Arctic Nature

The Utility of Indigenous Knowledge for German Polar Exploration and Knowledge of the Inuit in Imperial Germany

Ingo Löppenberg

It was cold at the Cumberland Sound, but the German scientists were too excited and curious to feel it. They had prepared an easy task – at least in their eyes – for the Inuit who were helping them erect their arctic scientific station. Now the scientists watched what the Inuit did, secretly taking notes. The Germans did not understand the language of the Inuit and could not help them, but this was not necessary because the workers quickly realized what to do. They recognized the signs on the wooden pillars, German letters, and began to erect the house very quickly. The Germans were impressed. They had not believed that "savages" would be able to complete the task so easily. This direct contact clearly demonstrated that old images of the Inuit as wild tribes with a low culture and no developmental possibilities were wrong.[1]
During the First International Polar Year in 1882/1883, two German scientists encountered Inuit in their homelands for the first time. Neither of the previous German polar expeditions in 1868 and 1870 had offered the opportunity to study Inuit in their natural environment, nor had the 1880 Hagenbeck "Völkerschau" (ethnological display) with two Inuit families in Berlin. This was a major task for the young academic discipline of ethnology, established by their important German advocate, Adolf Bastian.[2] In this

1 Heinrich Abbes: Die deutsche Nordpolar-Expedition nach dem Cumberland-Sunde I. In: *Illustrirte Zeitschrift für Länder- und Völkerkunde* 46,20 (1884), pp. 294–298, here p. 296.
I would like to thank the Gerda Henkel Foundation, which has made it possible to work on my forthcoming PhD thesis: "Im Namen Seiner Majestät – Expeditionen im Kalkül preußischer Wissenschaftspolitik 1815–1880". Some related ideas are presented here. I would also like to thank Jens Peters for his critical remarks and his help with the English language.

2 Adolf Bastian was born in Bremen in 1826. After studying medicine, he worked for eight years as a surgeon on different merchant vessels around the globe. After returning to Germany, he published his travel accounts and his first ethnological study. Finally, he was appointed as a docent in Berlin 1866, after he had explored South East Asia for five years. In 1873, he was nominated as director of the Museum für Völkerkunde in Berlin. He died, a restless traveler and scientist, in 1905 in Trinidad and Tobago. For further information and literature on Bastian, see Peter Bolz / Susan Kamel / Manuela Fischer (eds): *Adolf Bastian and His Universal Archive of Humanity. The Origins of German Anthropology*. Hildesheim: Olms 2007. A scientific biography on Bastian is still missing.

paper I will examine the influence of the direct contact between German scientists in the field – here the arctic regions in Canada – with the object of their ethnographic interest and how this experience modified their previously stereotypical ideas. I will demonstrate that travel was the main research practice for the emerging disciplines of anthropology and ethnology, because none of the earlier travel literature, artifacts, or contact with Inuit during the exhibition in Berlin could provide the necessary scientific data. This is contrary to many other histories of the emergence and development of German anthropology, which has received much attention in recent years.[3] Andrew Zimmermann, for example, claims that the "turn to the field" of ethnology "was a response to their dissatisfaction" with data "brought together by amateurs" around 1900.[4] In contrast, I would argue that the earlier travel experiences had a more important impact on the development of ethnological research. Also, in recent years the practical turn has seen science historians focus on the research practices used by scientists to craft knowledge. Some basic studies have dealt with the history of fieldwork and collecting sciences[5], but little is known about the ethnographic fieldwork of German scientists, especially in polar regions.[6] My essay is intended to contribute to the growing number of studies dealing with the practical turn in science history. It is time to raise some new questions about this topic, thus I will focus on whether and how instructions given by ethnologists taught researchers in the field

3 Andrew D. Evans: *Anthropology at War. World War I and the Science of Race in Germany*. Chicago / London: The University of Chicago Press 2010; Uwe Hoßfeld: *Geschichte der biologischen Anthropologie in Deutschland*. Stuttgart: Franz Steiner 2005; Matti Bunzl / H. Glenn Penny (eds): *Worldly Provincialism. German Anthropology in the Age of Empire*. Ann Arbor: University of Michigan Press 2003; Andrew Zimmermann: *Anthropology and Antihumanism in Imperial Germany*. Chicago: University of Chicago Press 2001.

4 Zimmermann: *Anthropology and Antihumanism*, p. 217.

5 Robert E. Kohler: Finders, Keepers. Collecting Sciences and Collecting Practice. In: *History of Science* 45,150 (2007), pp. 428–454; Bruno J. Strasser: Collecting Nature. Practices, Styles, and Narratives. In: Robert E. Kohler / Kathryn M. Olesko (eds): *Clio Meets Science. The Challenges of History*. Chicago: University of Chicago Press 2012, pp. 303–340; Henrika Kuklick: Personal Equations. Reflections on the History of Fieldwork, with Special Reference to Sociocultural Anthropology. In: *Isis* 102,1 (2011), pp. 1–33; Kristian H. Nielsen / Michael Harbsmeier / Christopher J. Ries (eds): *Scientists and Scholars in the Field. Studies in the History of Fieldwork and Expeditions*. Aarhus / Kopenhagen: Aarhus UP 2012.

6 Cornelia Lüdecke: Kalte Exotik – Eskimos im Blickpunkt der deutschen Ethnologie um 1880. In: Hedwig Roderfeld (ed.): *23. Internationale Polartagung der Deutschen Gesellschaft für Polarforschung, Münster, 10.–14. März 2008. Programm und Zusammenfassung der Tagungsbeiträge*. Berlin: Geo-Union Alfred-Wegener-Stiftung 2008, pp. 51–52; William Barr: *The Expeditions of the First International Polar Year 1882–83*. Calgary: Arctic Institute of North America 2008, pp. 85–106, 347–356.

and shaped the analysis of the collected data. What were Heinrich Abbes and Karl Richard Koch's aims for their scientific texts? How where they connected to ethnological discussions in Germany? What kind of information did the two travelers bring back to their readers in Germany? And what possible connections between the Inuit and European travelers and settlers were established by the two scientists?

To answer these questions I will first summarize the genesis of the idea of the savage Inuit during the Enlightenment and how it was disseminated. I will then give a brief overview of the Humboldtian tradition and its function for the emergence of German Anthropology, referring to the works of Adolf Bastian, the famous founder of this discipline. Next I will investigate the importance of direct contact for gathering new data about the Inuit. Artifacts in the Prussian Kunstkammer and the living Inuit shown in Berlin during Hagenbeck Völkerschau proved insufficient for the purposes of scientific research. Furthermore, I will reflect on how this direct contact shaped the notions of German scientists and – through their publications – of the German population at large. As primary objects of interest, I have chosen two scientists from the German group for the International Polar Year 1882/83, Abbes and Koch, and their different published observations. I will particularly focus on the moments of their first encounters, their methods of observing Inuit and the different forms of their publications. Finally, I will show what Abbes and Koch thought about the Inuit after direct contact, what it was possible to learn from them and what kind of future the Inuit have.

Arctic People and European Scholars during the Enlightenment and the Early Modern Period

The scholars of the Enlightenment loved travel books. For most of them, it was their only chance to leave their armchairs and explore the world outside of Europe. They also loved real travel, but these journeys only brought them to their colleagues throughout Europe. Next to letters, travel was more an instrument of knowledge exchange than a type of research. Only the voyages of discovery sent by the European powers of Spain, Great Britain, France, and Russia had scientific purpose, but this was secondary to gaining economic and political power.[7]

7 Charles W. J. Withers: *Placing the Enlightenment. Thinking Geographically about the Age of Reason.* Chicago / London: The University of Chicago Press 2007; Rob Iliffe: Science and Voyages of Discovery. In: *The Cambridge History of Science*, vol. 4: Eighteenth-Century Science, ed. by Roy

The northern regions around the Arctic Polar Sea which attracted the scholars' curiosity were mostly Greenland, a Danish colony; Canada, initially a French but since 1763 a British colony; and the Northern shore of Russia. During expeditions and missionary travels in these regions, a lot of travel literature was produced and analyzed by the armchair scientists. Most of these open with a statement that all of the peoples living in northern regions have nothing in common with Europeans except people living in Sweden, Norway, and Finland. August Ludwig Schlözer, a German polyhistorian, clearly separated Greenland from Europe: "I count Greenland to America and the Greenlanders are really Eskimos".[8] This geographic separation was combined with a cultural separation founded on the old climate theory. According to this theory, people in cold regions were, without exception, unable to create civilized communities and had to live on a basic level as hunters or fisherfolk. Immanuel Kant repeatedly promoted these ideas in his works.[9] Some scholars like Georges-Louis Leclerc de Buffon repeated old myths, for example that Eskimos were anthropophagi and drank whale oil instead of water. He wrote that they ate their food raw and would wash themselves with their urine.[10] Another scholar, Isaak Iselin, wrote that the Eskimos were childish with no inclination for hard work. It was claimed that all of them were slow in mind but very sexually active, with no concept of manners.[11] That is why these intellectuals called them savages. All of these kinds of stereotypes, which

Porter. Cambridge: Cambridge UP 2003, pp. 618–645; Marie-Noëlle Bourguet: The Explorer. In: Michel Vovelle (ed.): *Enlightenment Portraits*. Chicago / London: University of Chicago Press 1997, pp. 257–315.

8 Cit. Hendriette Kliemann: *Koordinaten des Nordens. Wissenschaftliche Konstruktionen einer europäischen Region 1770–1850*. Berlin: Berliner Wissenschaftsverlag 2005, p. 176: "Grönland rechne ich zu Amerika, wirklich sind auch die Grönländer die Eskimaur." Every English translation in this article was made by the author himself. The original German text will be given in the footnotes. For a general overview, see Harry Liebersohn: Anthropology before Anthropology. In: Henrika Kuklick (ed.): *A New History of Anthropology*. Malden / Oxford / Victoria: Blackwell 2008, pp. 17-31.

9 Kliemann: *Koordinaten des Nordens*, pp. 63–70.

10 Thomas Nutz: *„Varietäten des Menschengeschlechts." Die Wissenschaft vom Menschen in der Zeit der Aufklärung*. Köln / Weimar / Wien: Böhlau 2009, pp. 300–301.

11 Ibid., p. 301. See also Maike Schmidt: „Unter dem rauhesten Himmelsstrich". Grönland in der Reiseliteratur und Geschichtsphilosophie des 18. Jahrhunderts. In: Maximilian Bergengruen / François Rosset / Markus Winkler (eds): *Beyond Empirical Sciences. Literature and Travel Report in the 18th Century and around 1800*. Freiburg: Academic Press Fribourg 2012, pp. 41–54, and Mike Frömel: *Offene Räume und gefährliche Reisen im Eis. Reisebeschreibungen über die Polarregionen und ein kolonialer Diskurs im 18. und frühen 19. Jahrhundert*. Hannover: Wehrhahn 2013, especially pp. 235–242.

dealt with ordinary life, eating, working, and sexual activities, were mentioned by the savants because they made it very easy for the reader to see the difference between a European and an Eskimo.

Of course, not all European scholars promoted this kind of image. One exception was Johann Reinhold Forster, father of Georg Forster. He was on the second expedition with James Cook, and his direct contact with indigenous people in the Pacific as well as his piety may explain why he wrote about people living in the arctic: "Complaints about their disloyalty and cruelty are unfounded [...]. They are tender to their children, fulfill the duties of fatherhood and support their families with great courage and a steadfastness which would scare off many a thousand Europeans."[12]

But instead of following such wise voices, various public media promoted the negative stereotypes and preserved them for many years. Among these were conversation lexica like the *Brockhaus* – part of many a bourgeois household. For example, the article *Amerika* states: "Even though he has developed into only two races, the human in A[merica] is very different and peculiar. One of these races is that of the people of the extreme North, commonly named Eskimos, [...] a weak kind of people, standing on the lowest step of culture."[13]

Another example was the magazine *Pfennig-Magazin*, a German copy of the famous English *Penny-Magazine*. In an 1834 article dealing with the Eskimos being visited by English Expeditions in the search of the North-West Passage, the reader could read that all females were "very ugly".[14] (Fig. 1)

Their houses were allegedly filled with a harsh smell so "that a European could not stay there for long", and despite of all their abilities to live in this

12 Johann Reinhold Forster: *Geschichte der Entdeckungen und Schiffahrten im Norden. Mit neuen Originalkarten versehen.* Frankfurt an der Oder: Strauß 1784, p. 557: "Die Klagen über ihre Treulosigkeit und Grausamkeit sind unbegründet [...]. Sie haben Zärtlichkeit für ihre Kinder, erfüllen die Pflichten des Vaters und Versorgers der Ihrigen mit großem Muthe und einer Standhaftigkeit, die viele 1,000 Europäer abschrecken würde."

13 Amerika. In: *Allgemeine deutsche Real-Encyklopädie für die gebildeten Stände*, vol. 1: A bis Bl. 8. ed. Leipzig: Brockhaus 1833, pp. 230–235, here pp. 232–233: "Am verschiedenartigsten und eigenthümlichsten zeigt sich in A. der Mensch, obwohl er nur zwei Hauptrassen bildet. Die eine machen die Völker des äußersten Nordens aus, die man gewöhnlich mit dem Gesamtnamen Eskimo bezeichnet, [...], ein schwacher Volkshaufen , der noch auf der untersten Stufe der Bildung lebt." See also Indianer. In: *Allgemeine deutsche Real-Encyklopädie für die gebildeten Stände*, vol. 8: Höfken bis Kirchenbann. 10. rev. and ext. ed. Leipzig: Brockhaus 1853, pp. 210–216, which contains much more and drastic kinds of stereotypes.

14 Die Eskimos in den Ländern an der Hudsonbai. In: *Das Pfennig-Magazin der Gesellschaft zur Verbreitung gemeinnütziger Kenntnisse*, 26.07.1834, pp.515–517, here p. 516: "Die Weiber sind sehr häßlich [...]."

Fig. 1: Unknown: Inuit in North America. In: *Das Pfennig-Magazin der Gesellschaft zur Verbreitung gemeinnütziger Kenntnisse*, 26.07.1834, p. 520.

cold region and their craftsmanship, it was clear to the author that "in mental matters, [they] occupy a very low level".[15]

Travel literature and its use in newspaper articles and encyclopedias provided the main sources for any scientific studies concerned with people in and outside of Europe. But the dawn of Humboldtian Science made the old literature unusable, because it did not meet a crucial criterion: authenticity.

Making Traditions and Crafting Data

Authenticity was the main virtue of what is called Humboldtian Science. According to Susan F. Cannon, this type of science, named after Alexander von Humboldt, contains four elements. The first is authenticity, defined as an "insistence on accuracy […] for all instruments and all observations"[16]. This means it was no longer possible to rely only on second- or third-hand observations. The scientist needed to go to the data. Alongside this there ran a deep distrust of old theories and "the theoretical mechanisms and entities of the past"[17]; the task became to observe and experience "the immense variety of real phenomena" in order to create new "laws dealing with the very complex

15 Ibid., p. 517: "[…] daß ein Europäer schwerlich lange darin ausdauern kann." "In geistiger Hinsicht stehen die Eskimos auf einer sehr niedrigen Stufe".

16 Susan F. Cannon: Humboldtian Science. In: Ead. (ed.): *Science in Culture. The Early Victorian Period.* New York: Science History Publications 1978, pp. 73–110, here p. 104.

17 Ibid.

interrelationship of the physical, the biological, and even the human."[18] This kind of science required a special gaze, a "Humboldtian Gaze," which Lorraine Daston defined as "a way of seeing that was at once morphological and numerical, aesthetic and scientific, local and global."[19] All of this could only happen through travel. And this new approach to scientific expeditions made it necessary to invent new instruments and methods of gathering, analyzing, and presenting data and scientific facts.

This invention of a new kind of science had a great influence on the emerging new sciences dealing with humans. The 19th century saw the development of three new disciplines. One of these was anthropology, the study of the human physical body. It required a lot of measurements and new instruments to exactly reproduce the different parts of a human being. The scientists preferred parts of the skeleton, especially skulls, instead of flesh, which was not very practical for any measurements except mass. In Germany, the most important advocate of anthropology was Rudolf Virchow.[20] The second of the new sciences was prehistory. It focused on prehistoric remains like excavated artifacts and skeletons. Virchow was involved in this discipline, too.[21] Finally, the third discipline was ethnology, which "aimed at the comparative study of the culture and psychology of the world's peoples as an alternative means of exploring human history."[22] The founder and most important advocate of this discipline in Germany was Adolf Bastian. Bastian, like Virchow, was a physician, had travelled around the globe and had lived for several years in East and Southeast Asia.[23] He was deeply influenced and "inspired" by Alexander von Humboldt. He dedicated his first work, *Der Mensch in der Geschichte*[24], to him, and his intensive analysis of Humboldt's *Kosmos*[25] led him to the conclusion that Humboldtian Science was the key to any further

18 Cannon: Humboldtian Science, p. 104.

19 Lorraine Daston: The Humboldtian Gaze. In: Moritz Epple / Claus Zittel (eds): *Science as Cultural Practice*, vol. I: Cultures and Politics of Research from Early Modern Period to the Age of Extremes. Berlin: Akademie 2010, pp. 45–60, here p. 45.

20 Evans: *Anthropology at War*, pp. 6–27; Zimmerman: *Anthropology and Antihumanism*, pp. 86–107.

21 Evans: *Anthropology at War*, p. 29.

22 Ibid., p. 28.

23 Ibid.

24 Adolf Bastian: *Der Mensch in der Geschichte. Zur Begründung einer psychologischen Weltanschauung*, 3 vol. Leipzig: Wigand 1860.

25 Alexander von Humboldt: *Kosmos. Entwurf einer physischen Weltbeschreibung*, 5 vols. Stuttgart: Cotta 1845–1862.

development of ethnology as a science and gaining knowledge about human nature.[26]

Bastian based his method of ethnological research on the then-dominant concept of "inductive empiricism"[27], wherein all conclusions must be based on clear and certain facts produced via standardized research practices which had to be practiced and internalized by every scientist. This was also a demand of the Humboldtian Gaze, because this was the only way to make data comparable.[28] Finally, only a comparison of all data observed around the globe and brought home would make it possible to describe humans in their natural environments and their cultural way of life and to identify "the psychological unity of the entire human species".[29] But the ongoing expansion of European culture and Christianity caused this pure way of life of the natural people outside Europe to disappear. In Bastian's eyes, it was time to act and to give clear instructions for ethnological research.

As soon as he got a chance, Bastian set to work. He wrote a chapter in the book *Anleitung zu wissenschaftlichen Beobachtungen auf Reisen* (*Instructions for scientific observations on travels*)[30], where he outlined how an observer could gain ethnological facts. The first step was to make contact with people interested in trading. Bastian listed all kind of objects an ethnological museum would need. He made it clear that trading was a kind of introduction in order to make friendly initial contact, and that the artifacts were data, too. The next step was conversation with and careful interrogation of the natives. He listed several questions the observer had to ask, beginning with simple things like "What is the name of the tribe?" followed by more complex conversations, for example about funeral rites. The observer should then start a vocabulary and count or estimate the number of people. One problem for Bastian was that an observer would disturb the natural way of life. He demanded that the observer should not ask leading questions and that some rituals and traditions must be listened to and observed in secret. Physical observations were

26 H. Glenn Penny: *Objects of Culture. Ethnology and Ethnographic Museums in Imperial Germany*. Chapel Hill: University of Northern Carolina Press 2002, pp.18–23, here p. 19; H. Glenn Penny: Traditions in the German Language. In: Kuklick (ed.): *A New History*, pp. 79-95, here p. 85.

27 Evans: *Anthropology at War*, p. 65.

28 Daston: The Humboldtian Gaze, p. 58.

29 Evans: *Anthropology at War*, p. 65.

30 Adolf Bastian: Allgemeine Begriffe der Ethnologie. In: Georg von Neumayer (eds.): *Anleitung zu Wissenschaftlichen Beobachtungen auf Reisen. Mit besonderer Rücksicht auf die Bedürfnisse der kaiserlichen Marine*. Berlin: Robert Oppenheim 1875, pp. 516–533.

to be made after the observer had acquired the people's trust. Perhaps Bastian hoped this would make them easier to acquire.[31]
There were two other options for ethnological studies in 19th century Germany. The first one was the study of ethnological objects in museums. In Berlin, ethnological collections arose from the old private collections of the Hohenzollern kings. In 1810, this collection was again reorganized under its director Jean Henry and taken over by Leopold von Ledebur in 1830. After the Neues Museum was built, the collections were incorporated into its rooms. In 1869 Adolf Bastian was von Ledebur's assistant, and he became the director of the collection after his mentor's retirement in 1876. He quickly launched several projects to build his own museum and to buy new objects for it.[32] The collection had several Inuit artifacts, mostly weapons and clothes, but also some models of their houses and boats. The major part of this collection came from Greenland, but some objects also came from Labrador and the Aleutians. They had been sold or donated by consuls and ship captains. However, not all of them had survived, and some likely had been thrown away because they were made of common seal bowels and had started to decay.[33] These objects were much more authentic than any travel literature, but preservation was a major issue. And, as Bastian noted, objects without knowledge of how they were made or how and why they were used were less useful than objects combined with observations.
The other method of data acquisition available in 19th century Germany did not present the same problems. It was possible to observe the creation and use of artifacts in "Völkerschauen". This attraction of presenting living humans from outside of Europe was very popular in Berlin, and the scientists seized their chance. Carl Hagenbeck, a salesman from Hamburg, engaged different groups of people around the globe and presented them in the Berlin Zoological Gardens. In 1880, Adrian Jacobsen, who was also a trader of ethnological artifacts for Bastian, brought two Inuit families to Berlin. Both families performed their skills in kayak driving and some rituals and wore their traditional clothes. One family was willing to let Virchow take their measurements.

31 Bastian: Allgemeine Begriffe der Ethnologie, pp. 530–533.

32 Peter Bolz: From Ethnographic Curiosities to the Royal Museum of Ethnology. Early Ethnological Collections in Berlin. In: Bolz / Fischer / Kamel (eds): *Adolf Bastian and His Universal Archive of Humanity*, pp. 173–190. See also H. Glenn Penny: Bastian's Museum. On the Limits of Empiricism and the Transformation of German Ethnology. In: Bunzl / Penny (eds): *Worldly Provincialism*, pp. 86–126.

33 Leopold von Ledebur: Aus der Ethnologischen Sammlung des Königlichen Museums zu Berlin. In: *Zeitschrift für Ethnologie* 1 (1869), pp. 193–204, here pp. 193–198.

However, they all quickly succumbed to smallpox.[34] In the end, the observations and measurements of the Inuit family were disappointing and of course not authentic in this artificial environment. To achieve real authenticity meant studying humans and their way of life in their natural environment; thus it was necessary to travel to the Arctic. Virchow and Bastian would soon get a new chance to get fresh data from travelling scientists in the region.

Meeting in the Contact Zone

After two successful North Pole Expeditions, Chancellor Bismarck refused to pay for a third one. In his eyes, there was no need for the fledgling German Empire to send expeditions into this cold region without any commercial advantages. But Virchow and the Conference for International Polar Research (hastily founded by Georg von Neumayer) started to promote new research undertakings. Virchow talked to the German Reichstag, and it was possible to form a coalition with the Chief of the Imperial Admiralty Albrecht von Stosch to exert pressure on the Chancellor. Eventually, they succeeded in securing 300,000 Reichsmark from the Reichstag's budget.[35]

The German expeditions of the first International Polar Year would comprise two major expeditions – one to the Cumberland Sound and one to South Georgia – and one auxiliary expedition to Labrador. Their main tasks were to perform daily meteorological and magnetic measurements, but other Humboldtian disciplines like zoology, botany, and geography also received attention. However, the instructions did not mention any ethnological research. Nonetheless, two German scientists conducted this research and published several articles and essays about their observations. These two men were Karl Friedrich Koch, who was supposed to go to Labrador mainly to observe polar lights, and Heinrich Abbes, who was engaged as a mathematical assistant.

Koch's travel account contains only a few notes on ethnological observations. His main function was to install some meteorological stations at the missionary houses on Labrador and then to follow his own interests in polar lights.[36] During his travel by ship, Koch made his first contact with the Inuit.

34 Zimmerman: *Anthropology and Antihumanism*, pp. 22–23; Hilke Thode-Arora: Das Eskimo-Tagebuch von 1880. Eine Völkerschau aus der Sicht eines Teilnehmers. In: *Kea. Zeitschrift für Kulturwissenschaften* 2 (1991), pp. 87–115.

35 Reinhard Krause: Das Erste Internationale Polarjahr (IPY) 1882/1883. Die Entwicklung der Beteiligung Deutschlands. In: *Polarforschung* 77,1 (2007), pp. 17–36.

36 K. R. Koch: Geschichte der supplementären Expedition unter Dr. R. K. Koch nach Labrador. In: Georg von Neumayer (ed.): *Die Internationale Polarforschung 1882–1883. Die deutschen*

At that moment, all his stereotypical images collided with reality and started to change. A boat with Inuit reached their ship, and Koch was amazed how so many people could fit into such small vessels. But he was slightly disappointed because the men and women wore European clothes, and the women seemed to be "very proud of them".[37] After a little while, a woman changed "the European skirt and presented herself in her national costume".[38] Once again Koch was disappointed. Perhaps it was real Inuit style, but the material was obviously European.

Koch traveled a lot on Labrador and visited all the missionaries to build up the meteorological stations and train people in their use. He got several chances to observe the Inuit's way of life on Labrador. His account of these observations started with myths concerning the migration of Inuit from Greenland to Labrador. Then he gave a description of their culture, following the seasons. In the winter, the Inuit lived near to the missionaries. At their stations, the Inuit were introduced to European science: they could use a microscope and had access to European magazines read by the missionaries. Often, they all sang and made music together, sometimes German folk songs. To Koch this was a sign of superior mental abilities, as was their great interest in geography. Koch mentioned that the Inuit were very good at reading and drawing maps.[39] The hunting season on Labrador started around March. After weapons, the most important tool was the sledge. On some excursions, Koch got the chance to drive a sledge together with an Inuit.[40] He learned how to handle this craft and how to manage all the dogs pulling it. He summarized the different animals (reindeer, salmon, common seal) and the respective techniques developed by the Inuit to hunt them. In this context, Koch mentioned laziness as a negative characteristic. To his European mind, it was hard to understand why the Inuit had developed no way of storing their food and lived without any ambitions.[41] In Koch's account of the Inuit, only rare elements of Bastian's instructions can be found. There are no physical

Expeditionen und ihre Ergebnisse, vol. 1: Geschichtlicher Theil. Berlin: A. Asher 1891, pp. 145–189. See also Gaston R. Demarée / Astrid E. J. Ogilvie: The Moravian Missionaries at the Labrador Coast and their Centuries-long Contribution to Instrumental Meteorological Observations. In: *Climatic Change* 91,3–4 (2008), pp. 423–450, here p. 445.

37 Koch: Geschichte, p. 149: "auf die sie noch besonders stolz zu sein schienen."

38 Ibid.: "sie zog den europäischen Rock aus und präsentierte sich uns nun in ihrer Nationaltracht".

39 Ibid., p. 174.

40 Ibid., pp. 180–186.

41 Ibid., pp. 175–179.

observations and only a few myths. But his intensive contact during the long period of his stay on Labrador and his life with the Inuit at the stations and on his excursions fulfilled the key criterion of authenticity. He also traded some objects made by the Inuit. There are no descriptions of them, but Koch brought some carvings of walrus ivory back to Germany.[42]

In the end, Koch was impressed by the Inuit. After he had lived with them more than a year, "force of habit" enabled his European eyes to differentiate between beautiful and normal faces among the Inuit women.[43] He declared that "nobody has a right to compare an indigenous people, who have to fight the struggle of survival daily, with the standard of European civilization and European comforts and luxury."[44] Of course, he knew that the Inuit on Labrador had a hybrid culture and that they had not preserved a pure form of their customs like Inuit from further north. But that was also a chance for them. Several times, Koch mentioned in his account that the Inuit population on Labrador was shrinking, while more and more settlers from England and Canada were arriving. Many of them took an Inuit woman as a wife and produced a "Mischvolk", a cultural and biological mix of Europeans and Inuit. To Koch, this was a big chance. It prevented Inuit culture from becoming extinct and enabled the Europeans to settle in this region. They could only survive together.[45]

In contrast to Koch, Heinrich Abbes wrote a real study of his ethnological observations, which was published in the second volume of *Die Deutschen Expeditionen und ihre Ergebnisse*.[46] But in this study, no first contact is mentioned.

42 Ulrike Beisiegel (ed.): *Die Sammlungen, Museen und Gärten der Universität Göttingen*. Göttingen: Universitätsverlag Göttingen 2013, p. 32.

43 K. R. Koch: Die Küste Labradors und ihre Bewohner. In: *Deutsche Geographische Blätter* 7,2 (1884), pp. 151–163, here p. 153: "Macht der Gewohnheit".

44 Ibid.: "[…] da man kein Recht hat, an ein Naturvolk, das tagtäglich den harten Kampf ums Dasein führen muß, den Maßstab europäischer Civilisation und europäischen Komforts und Luxus zu legen." After Koch returned 1883 to London, he was "simultaneously amazed and depressed" by the lot of people and the European civilization (ibid., p. 163: "erstaunt und bedrückt").

45 Ibid., p. 180.

46 Heinrich Abbes: Die Eskimos des Cumberlandgolfes. In: Georg von Neumayer (ed.): *Die Internationale Polarforschung 1882–1883. Die Deutschen Expeditionen und ihre Ergebnisse*, vol. II: Beschreibende Naturwissenschaften in einzelnen Abhandlungen. Hamburg: Deutsche Seewarte 1890, pp. 1–61. Another account of the Inuit was from Leopold Ambronn: Bemerkungen über den Cumberland-Sund und seine Bewohner. In: *Deutsche Geographische Blätter* 6 (1883), pp. 347–357. He was deputy leader and astronomer on the expedition. He described that the Inuit made several of the carvings drawn by Abbes as gifts for the scientists. He mentioned a scene which showed the importance of Bastian's demand for secret observations. When

It is possible to find such a description in Abbes' account for the *Illustrierte Zeitschrift für Länder- und Völkerkunde*. It was common to publish some of the scientific observations in popular magazines because of the extra money earned this way. In the magazine, Abbes wrote that the first two Inuit came on board the German ship *Germania* with the Scottish first mate of a whale hunting ship. They were supposed to be navigators for the German captain at the Cumberland. One of the Inuit, an old one named Noktukkerle, started to dance and sing for the German scientists, while the young one named Koak was not very happy about this. The Germans were fascinated by their strange clothes and the unfamiliar sound of the songs.[47] Soon after the Germans had left the ship and started constructing their station, some Inuit families and other tribesmen arrived. They presented the Germans with a common seal and a reindeer and were gifted in exchange with bread and tobacco. The Germans followed Bastian's instructions, and they were able to convince some of the Inuit to stay near to the station. Abbes learned the language of the Inuit very quickly and could also speak English, which some of the Inuit were able to speak via contact with European whale hunters. Therefore he was designated the official spokesman of the expedition and thus had the opportunity to gather further observations in direct contact.[48]

He started his study with a description of the Inuit's physical appearance, highlighting the typically small bodies, their hairstyles and the shapes of their heads and eyes. Abbes took this as a sign of an Asian heritage but declared this was just a hypothesis, underlined by linguistic studies. After, he wrote about the early history of contact between Vikings and the Inuit, the settlements of missionaries on Greenland, and the discoveries by English and American ships in the Canadian arctic region. He mentioned that all of these travels had been "useless for the ethnographic knowledge of this region."[49] Only the observations by the team at the German Polar Station and the fieldwork of Franz Boas – i. e. only direct contact during a longer stay – provided new data. Abbes declared that his observations were made only at the station with Inuit working for or visiting them. He gave examples of situations where

Ambronn watched an Inuit playing a game with small wooden plates ("perhaps similar to our dominoes"), he wanted to know what this was and how it was played. But nothing could persuade the Inuit to talk about it. Ibid., p. 357: "vielleicht ähnlich unserem Domino".

47 Abbes: Die deutsche Nordpolar-Expedition, p. 295.

48 Ibid., p. 297.

49 Abbes: Die Eskimos des Cumberlandgolfes, p. 6: "[…] ohne irgendwelchen Nutzen für die Kenntniß der Ethnographie des Landes."

Fig. 2:
Heinrich Abbes: Table 1, from id.: Die Eskimos des Cumberlandgolfes. In: Georg von Neumayer (ed.): *Die Internationale Polarforschung 1882–1883. Die Deutschen Expeditionen und ihre Ergebnisse*, vol. II: Beschreibende Naturwissenschaften in einzelnen Abhandlungen. Hamburg: Deutsche Seewarte 1890, between pages 60–61.

it was possible to observe individual characteristics of the Inuit. To demonstrate how the Inuit liked to use irony and sarcasm, he reported a scene where a German tried to stabilize a pole with small stones. As a result, the pole remained unfixed. An Inuit watched the German's attempts for a while. Then he started to help him and laid down small pieces of cork. After that, he burst out laughing and went away.[50]

The Inuit living near the station made it possible for Abbes to watch how they made their houses from ice. He gave a detailed description and a very lively drawing of it in his study. (Fig. 2)

50 Ibid., p. 57.

Abbes was impressed by the Inuit's abilities and ideas to make living in these houses comfortable and clean, which was contrary to the quoted *Pfennig-Magazin* article.[51]

Direct contact and observations made it possible to fulfill one of Bastian's key instructions, not only to acquire artifacts but also to watch how they were made and used. Abbes brought back a lot of drawings of different weapons and ritual objects. He described how the weapons were used during a hunt for whales or ducks.[52] Abbes then demonstrated how important Bastian's demand was. He declared that a man would be allowed to settle down and build a house of his own when he was able to hunt a seadog by himself.[53] This connection of the description of an object's correct use and the results, combined with the culture of everyday life, was the highest exemplar of Humboldtian authenticity.

Also connected to Bastian's instruction was Abbes' section about Inuit myths, which he had heard from the Inuit living at the station. He compared and completed them with recently published myths by other authors. He wrote about the Inuit's religion and their belief in life after death, he summarized their legends about the heritage of men, their own history, and the creation of the earth. He also provided some information about their language, but no long lists of vocabulary.[54] Once again, he clearly followed Bastian and his demand for data.

At the end of his work, Abbes gave a clear recommendation. He wrote that some Inuit objects, like their wooden snow-goggles, which could not become fogged like European models made from black glass or wire, would be very useful for any further Polar expeditions.[55] He then stated,

> Their knowledge about Arctic nature could be useful for research in many areas, and maybe they could be trained with only a little effort for basic elementary observations. The proven loyalty, responsibility and devotion of the Inuit would be the best

51 Abbes: Die Eskimos des Cumberlandgolfes, p. 21–24.

52 Ibid., p. 29–32. See also Heinrich Abbes: Die Eskimos des Cumberland-Sundes I. In: *Illustrirte Zeitschrift für Länder- und Völkerkunde* 46,13 (1884), pp. 198–201; Heinrich Abbes: Die Eskimos des Cumberland-Sundes II. In: *Illustrirte Zeitschrift für Länder- und Völkerkunde* 46,14 (1884), pp. 213–218. In this popular account of his ethnological observations, Abbes linked his drawings more directly to the text than was possible in his study. All these drawings were printed in Abbes: Die Eskimos des Cumberlandgolfes, between pp. 60–61. Figure 2 can be found in Abbes: Die Eskimos des Cumberland-Sundes I, p. 199.

53 Abbes: Die Eskimos des Cumberlandgolfes, p. 32.

54 Ibid., p. 40–54. A list can be found in Abbes: Die Eskimos des Cumberland-Sundes II, p. 218.

55 Abbes: Die Eskimos des Cumberlandgolfes, p. 30.

> guarantee against the repeat of sad catastrophes which have dominated the history of arctic research.[56]

This opinion was shared by W. Giese, leader of the German expedition to the Cumberland Gulf. In his travel account, he pointed out that the Inuit had helped the Germans with their experience in surviving in the arctic region. They taught the Germans techniques to build snow houses and to dig in frozen snow and ice. He also wrote very positively about the abilities of Okeitung, who lived near the station and travelled with Giese in the region. He and his family were also the main sources for Abbes' ethnological description.[57]

Like Giese, Abbes pointed towards Franz Boas' ethnological account for further information about the Inuit.[58] Boas is well known in the literature, and his achievements were recommended by contemporaries and followers. His method for living with the Inuit in the Cumberland Gulf region during 1883–1884 was of course much more in accordance with Bastian's instructions than the studies by Koch and Abbes.[59] But all three of these early ethnologists mostly followed the methods and data tasks prescribed by Bastian and Humboldtian Science. However, in the end, only Boas would continue to work on ethnological matters. For Koch and Abbes, it was only an episode; for Boas, it would become his life's calling.

56 Ibid., p. 61: "Ihre Kenntniß der arktischen Natur könnte der Forschung in vieler Beziehung von Nutzen sein und mit geringer Mühe ließen sie sich vielleicht zur Unterstützung des elementaren Beobachtungsdienstes anlernen. Vor Allem aber würde man in der erprobten Treue, Zuverlässigkeit und Aufopferung der Eskimos die beste Bürgschaft gegen eine Wiederholung der traurigen Katastrophen besitzen, an welchen die Geschichte der arktischen Forschung nur allzu reich ist."

57 W. Giese: Die Expedition nach dem Kingua-Fjord, deren Verlauf und Rückkehr. In: von Neumayer (ed.): *Die Internationale Polarforschung*, vol. I, pp. 41–91, here pp. 71–72.

58 Ibid., p. 72. Unlike Boas, Giese believed that their opportunity to acquire information about Inuit culture had been limited. Abbes: Die Eskimos des Cumberlandgolfes, p. 8, shared this opinion because really living with the people was superior to living near the Inuit in a European science station.

59 Franz Boas: *Baffin-Land. Geographische Ergebnisse einer in den Jahren 1883 und 1884 ausgeführten Forschungsreise.* Gotha: Justus Perthes 1885; Matti Bunzl: Franz Boas and the Humboldtian Tradition. From Volksgeist and Nationalcharakter to an Anthropological Concept of Culture. In: George W. Stocking Jr. (ed.): *Volksgeist as a Method and Ethic. Essays on Boasian Ethnography and the German Anthropological Tradition.* Madison / London: The University of Wisconsin Press 1996, pp. 17–78; Ludger Müller-Wille: *The Franz Boas Enigma. Inuit, Arctic and Science.* Montréal: Baraka 2014; Norman Francis Boas: *Franz Boas 1858–1942. An Illustrated Biography.* Mystic: Seaport Autographs 2004.

Conclusion

The negative stereotypes of the Enlightenment created and repeated by several well-known and respected scholars were brought to the German audience via media like encyclopedias and cheap magazines during the early modern period. The impact of the Humboldtian Sciences with their demand for authenticity made it possible for several scientists to invent and establish their own methods of research, standardized and published in handbooks of instructions. Adolf Bastian did this for German ethnology. When the time was right, he and Virchow, one of Germany's most important advocates for a strong German science governance after 1880, helped to realize expeditions to arctic regions with the help of other scientists. Only in this cold periphery was it possible for some scientists trained in the Humboldt gaze and Bastian's instructions to observe the Inuit within their natural environment, which changed the old negative stereotypes. They proved that scientific travel and stations were the most important research techniques for data creation outside of the lab. The scientists also reported how useful the Inuit's survival and travelling skills could be for further expeditionary and stationary exploration of the arctic. The Inuit way of life could be a model for Europeans. It was transferred through the scientists from this periphery back to Germany. This recognition was later shared by Robert E. Peary, the first man at the North Pole and Roald Amundsen, the first man at the South Pole. Amundsen's counterpart Robert F. Scott, who used European methods like machines and ponies, died during his attempt. Insights from the periphery of the Arctic were processed in the European center, transformed traditional approaches to gathering data, and were later applied to new research on another periphery: Antarctica.

Stirring the "Mix"

Gender and Religion within Islamic Contexts in Europe

Dina Mansour

Introduction

The separation between 'state' and 'religion' has been long established in Europe and most parts of the Western world with the state acting as a neutral agent upholding the emblems of citizenship and rights. In most countries of the Islamic and Arab world, on the other hand, national constitutions have conferred the state a religion and stipulated that laws are either to abide by or not to contradict this stipulated 'state religion'. Minorities who defy religious or social traditional norms in their country of origin are not only faced as a consequence with acts of institutional and social discrimination, but even more so, have their very lives threatened.

This same dilemma found across many parts of the Islamic and Arab world has been 'exported' and is often witnessed within Arab/Islamic migrant communities[1] across the European Union (EU). Literature[2] addressing the integration of migrants in Europe often overlooks the social and political dynamics *within* migrant populations themselves that affect or even hinder their integration and assimilation in their host country. Research in the field has often focused and critically analyzed national or regional policies across the EU under the pretext of respect of 'cultural relativism'. This has largely condemned a category of migrants to be overlooked and be largely stereotyped: women of an Arab and/or Islamic migrant background who defy the 'exported' social, cultural and religious norms of their countries of origin. Honor killing, forced genital mutilation/cutting (FGM/C), early and/or arranged marriage, forced veiling and domestic violence are only some of the 'exported' practices that women living within migrant communities are

1 With 'Arab/Islamic' and for the purposes of this paper the author is referring to the Middle East and North African region including Turkey and Iran.

2 See Robert Miles / Dietrich Thränhardt: *Migration and European Integration: The Dynamics of Inclusion and Exclusion.* London: Pinter 1995; Andrew Geddes / Adrian Favell: *The Politics of Belonging: Migrants and Minorities in Contemporary Europe.* Aldershot: Ashgate 1999; Andrew Geddes: *Immigration and European Integration: Towards Fortress Europe?* Manchester: Manchester UP 2000; Ayhan Kaya: *Islam, Migration and Integration: The Age of Securitization.* Houndmills: Palgrave Macmillan 2009.

sometimes forced to endure. Policies on the national and European level, on the other hand, are often criticized for not being tolerant enough to such practices.

This article aims at examining the existing limitations in understanding intragroup dynamics *within* migrant populations within the EU that result in creating what can be termed as 'minorities within minorities'. Examining the case of migrant women of an Arab and/or Islamic background in the EU will vividly demonstrate the vulnerable situation of this category of women who defy and distance themselves from their close-knit circles of family and community. Generally, the intragroup dynamics within both communities – that of the host and their country of origin render them often in limbo – neither tolerated nor integrated.

This short paper, which aims to be part of a larger study,[3] will be reporting the results of a pilot survey aimed at exploring factors governing identity formation, intragroup dynamics and the sense of integration and belongingness of this category of women in the EU. The aim of this survey is to shed light on the importance of understanding the dynamics that may hinder or encourage integration as well as shed new light on the concepts of identity, minority and culture when it comes to migration policies and politics.

Defining the Scope

The scope of this topic – the dynamics impacting the integration of first and/or second generation migrant women of Arab and/or Islamic background in the EU – bridges multiple academic disciplines.[4] Most significantly, it bridges the fields of sociology, psychology, economics, law and political science. In addressing these themes incisively, this article employs an interdisciplinary approach that focuses on three main areas: (1) identity formation/identity politics; (2) minority rights/human rights; and (3) clash-dialogue of civilizations/Islam and the West.

Identity politics

A rising theme in political and academic discourses alike since the 1970s, identity politics became mainly connected with the shared experiences of

3 The author aims at conducting a large-scale survey to further examine this topic and integrate it into a larger research project. A pilot survey, whose results are referred to in this paper, has been conducted in the period of May 5–15, 2014.

4 See Robert J. Pauly: *Islam in Europe: Integration or Marginalization?* Aldershot: Ashgate 2004.

social division, exclusion, discrimination and the denial of equal rights of targeted social groups, mainly minority groups.[5] This is largely due to the fact that identity politics emerged as a theme of large-scale political movements (e.g. the Civil Rights Movement and the second wave of the feminist movement) that called for equality in treatment and rights that were denied on the basis of their 'shared' identity. Encompassing 'society' on the one hand and the 'state' on the other, targeted social groups had to face both social and political/institutional exclusion that tapped them within the concept of the "other". Today, the question of identity, however, is slowly changing, especially when it comes to the European context.[6] Identity politics is no longer constrained to the "other" or part of the "clash of civilization" discourse *per se*, but it is rather expanding to encompass the perception of the "self". The question, therefore, is what constitutes an identity? Largely described by social scientists as an "empty vessel", the concept of 'identity' itself has been widely criticized for its ambiguity and for being a catch-all term fillable with almost any content.[7] Hence, it is largely viewed as a concept that is difficult to employ as a tool for analysis, especially since there is no common agreement among social scientists on the boundaries of the definition. Beyond ethnicity and other physically distinguishable properties, the concept is to a large part dependent on the perception of common characteristics, beliefs, ideologies or in short, on the perception of a common 'culture'. This brings the concept under the potential bias of 'perception' by both those observing and possessing a 'supposed' identity.

Despite the problems of definition and methodology associated with 'identity,' identity politics emerged as a discourse akin to social justice and minority rights, which cannot be separated from law and politics. On the other hand, identity politics fails – as in the case of this study – to highlight intragroup differences and conflicts. Hence, failing to acknowledge differences *within* groups adds to the tension among groups.[8] Moreover, ignoring intragroup

5 Richard D. Parker: Five Theses on Identity Politics. In: *Harvard Journal of Law & Public Policy* 29 (2005), pp. 53–59; Cressida Heyes: Identity Politics. In: *The Stanford Encyclopedia of Philosophy*, ed. by Edward N. Zalta. Spring 2012 Edition. http://plato.stanford.edu/archives/spr2012/entries/identity-politics/ (accessed 11.07.2014).

6 John Erik Fossum: *Identity-politics in the European Union*. Oslo: ARENA 2001.

7 Jeremy MacClancy: *Expressing Identities in the Basque Arena*. Oxford: James Currey 2007, pp. 26–43; Helen M. Macbeth / Jeremy MacClancy: *Researching Food Habits: Methods and Problems*. New York: Berghahn 2004, p. 64.

8 Kimberle Crenshaw: Mapping the Margins: Intersectionality, Identity Politics, and Violence against Women of Color. In: *Stanford Law Review* 43,6 (1991), pp. 1241–1299, here p. 1242.

differences creates minority groups within already existing minority groups that are often left unrepresented within social and political dynamics of their larger communities. This creates what can be termed as "minorities within minorities". When it comes to identity politics and the definition of minorities, however, 'culture' lies at the core of both themes. Like 'identity', 'culture' is by no means a static concept, but it is predominantly "eclectic, dynamic, and subject to significant alteration over time"[9] and space. "Traditional cultural beliefs are also neither monolithic nor unchanging."[10] This adds to the difficulty of defining the parameters of an identity that can be said to be largely defined by a common culture.

Directly or indirectly associated with "othering" and recognizing difference, are issues of discrimination, social conflict and exclusion. Discrimination is based on the creation of hierarchies among so-called 'identity blocs' within one given society, which is accompanied by the association of particular qualities to each identity bloc. A socially constructed 'point of reference' linked to the group representing the majority and/or those with the most political power then becomes the benchmark against which the treatment of other groups is determined and measured.[11] History stands witness to the fact that social structures of power have played a direct role in structuring inequality and in creating invisible 'points of reference'.[12] Discrimination on account of race, ethnicity, gender, sex, belief or political/ideological affiliation is not a recent phenomenon, but what is apparent, however, is that discrimination is "likely to persist so long as there are human cultures and subcultures, which is likely to mean as long as people are raised in families."[13] Difference, which is at the core of discrimination, is linked to power and the distribution of resources. What follows then in any social structure is for inequality to become normalized.[14] This makes identities, either perceived or constructed,

9 Bonny Ibhawoh: Between Culture and Constitution: Evaluating the Cultural Legitimacy of Human Rights in the African State. In: *Human Rights Quarterly: A Comparative and International Journal of the Social Sciences, Philosophy, and Law* 22,3 (2000), pp. 838–860, here p. 841.

10 Ibid.

11 See Martha Minow: Foreword: Justice Engendered. In: *Harvard Law Review* 101 (1987), p. 10; Martha Minow: *Making All the Difference: Inclusion, Exclusion, and American Law*. Ithaca, NY: Cornell UP 1991.

12 Minow: *Making All the Difference*, p. 51.

13 Anthony Appiah: But Would That Still Be Me? Notes on Gender, "Race", Ethnicity, as Sources of "Identity". In: *The Journal of Philosophy* 87,10 (1990), pp. 493–499.

14 Lani Guinier / Gerald Torres: *The Miner's Canary: Enlisting Race, Resisting Power, Transforming Democracy*. Cambridge, MA: Harvard UP 2003.

particularly important, especially in stipulating laws against discrimination and in guaranteeing equal treatment and rights within one society. In fact, since international human rights law came to highlight the individual within the body of international law, defining the limitation of a legal person lies at the very core of signifying or denying certain rights and responsibilities.[15] This necessarily means that the very notion of rights actually stipulates interconnectedness with the individual and the society in which it can be claimed. In other words, it designates and even necessitates interconnectedness with difference.

Both the International Covenant on Civil and Political Rights (ICCPR) and the International Covenant on Economic, Social and Cultural Rights (ICESCR) have explicitly expressed the importance of respecting the basic norms of non-discrimination and equality, which are at the core of the body of international human rights law as a whole. Article 2(2) of the ICESCR and Article 2(1) and 26[16] of the ICCPR have both emphasized the importance of ensuring and respecting the core principles of non-discrimination and equality without which the rights set forth in the conventions at hand are to be jeopardized. It is worth noting that "the non-discrimination basis of international human rights law supports the view that such rights are applicable to 'all individuals within [a State's] territory and subject to its jurisdiction'."[17] Thus, as a general rule, each of the rights stipulated in the ICCPR and the ICESCR, which are by far the most fundamental human rights conventions after the Universal Declaration of Human Rights (UDHR), must not only be respected but also effectively guaranteed without discrimination.[18]

Minority Rights

A 'minority' can generally be defined as a group of individuals that possess characteristics – by virtue of either race, ethnicity, gender, nationality, culture, belief or political/ideological affiliation – that differentiates them from the

15 Simeon O. Ilesanmi: Human Rights Discourse in Modern Africa: A Comparative Religious Ethical Perspective. In: *The Journal of Religious Ethics* 23,2 (1995), pp. 293–322, here p. 297.

16 Sarah Joseph / Jenny Schultz / Melissa Castan: The International Covenant on Civil and Political Rights. Cases, Materials and Commentary. In: *British Yearbook of International Law* 73 (2003), pp. 367–369.

17 Ibid.

18 HRC General Comment No. 15 on "The Position of Aliens under the Covenant", UN doc. CCPR/C/21/Rev. 1, 19.05.1989, § 2.

majority.[19] The UN defines a 'minority' as a community that (a) is settled either compactly or dispersedly on the territory of a state; (b) is smaller in number than the rest of the population of the state and whose members are citizens of that state; (c) has ethnic, linguistic or cultural features that differentiates it from the rest of the population and who are guided by the will to safeguard these features.[20]

Within the European Union context, however, 'minorities' have often been associated with either "national" or "ethnic" minorities. Both concepts suffer from ambiguity and fail to reflect the changing demography, particularly as a result of increasing international migration. Within the European context, the most common term used is '*Volksgruppe*' (German for part of a people) or "ethnic group". This generally refers to communities divided by national borders that share the same ethnicity, exhibit similar cultural preferences, or are of the same ethnic origin. Such 'minorities' are sometimes also referred to as "national minorities". Both terms are problematic on the empirical level since they are likely to primarily refer to individuals or groups who share a similar racial or ethnic background or those born in, or are the citizens of, another country. Evidently, this can leave out large communities that may fall within the general definition of a minority or lead to discrepancies or the omission of data that could correctly reflect reality.[21] As a consequence, the current definition of what constitutes a 'minority' is widely criticized for being ambiguous, limited, biased and by no means reflective of the existing demographic reality within the EU. Without a proper definition, a large part of the population that may fall under separate identity groups are not properly understood and included in policy debates. There is always the risk that they fall under a stereotypical bias perception that may presuppose them to discrimination and deny them their most basic rights.

At the EU level the protection of 'national minorities' has been on the agenda of the Council of Europe since its foundation, and consequently resulted in the adoption of a number of texts since 1949. One of the most comprehensive treaties, the Framework Convention, which entered into force in

19 John Packer / Kristian Myntti: *The Protection of Ethnic and Linguistic Minorities in Europe*. Åbo: Institute for Human Rights, Åbo Akademi University 1993, pp. 54–55.

20 Thomas Benedikter: Legal Instruments of Minority Protection in Europe – An Overview. In: *Minorities in Europe – Society for Threatened People*, Nov. 2006. http://www.gfbv.it/3dossier/eu-min/autonomy-eu.html (accessed 11.05.2014).

21 Martin Kahanec / Anzelika Zaiceva / Klaus F. Zimmermann: *Ethnic Minorities in the European Union: An Overview*. Bonn: IZA 2010, p. 5.

February 1998 and to which thirty-nine states are party, does not contain a definition of what constitutes a 'national minority'. Hence, defining to whom this treaty applies is left to the discretion and margin of appreciation of each member party.[22]

Considerable literature does exist on international migration, especially within economics, psychology, political science and sociology.[23] Yet, though largely referred to as constituting a minority within the EU, without a proper understanding of what constitutes a 'minority', the immigrants will not be properly included in policy and legal debates. More importantly, the intragroup social and political dynamics *within* minority groups would be left up to stereotyping and would remain unstudied.

Islam and the West

The entrenchment of Muslim communities in Europe over the last two and a half years has engendered debates on the national and regional levels about the place of Islam within and outside Western Europe.[24] Debates over cultural perceptions, social norms, practices and traditions have recently come to the forefront of public debates regarding the place of this ever-growing community. As explained above, on the legal and policy level, the EU lacks a proper definition for what constitutes a 'minority' that extends beyond the historical European context – one that properly reflects recent international migration trends.

During the Cold War scholars and practitioners of international relations viewed the world through a bipolar lens of a Western and Eastern bloc. Today differences within what once constituted two clashing blocs lie at the core of

22 Promoting the Full and Effective Equality of Persons Belonging to Minorities: Framework Convention for the Protection of National Minorities. In: *National Minorities – Council of Europe*. http://conventions.coe.int/Treaty/en/Treaties/html/157.htm (accessed 11.06.2014).

23 See e.g. Philippe Fargues: *The Demographic Benefit of International Migration: Hypothesis and Application to the Middle Eastern and North African Contexts*. Washington: The World Bank 2006; Jonathon W. Moses: *International Migration: Globalization's Last Frontier*. London: Zed 2006; Michael P Smith / Adrian Favell: *The Human Face of Global Mobility: International Highly Skilled Migration in Europe, North America and the Asia-Pacific*. New Brunswick, NJ: Transaction 2006; Martin Geiger / Antoine Pécoud: *The Politics of International Migration Management*. Houndmills: Palgrave Macmillan 2010; Brian R. Opeskin / Richard Perruchoud / Jillyanne Redpath-Corss (eds): *Foundations of International Migration Law*. Cambridge: Cambridge UP 2012; Karen O'Reilly: *International Migration and Social Theory*. Houndmills: Palgrave Macmillan 2012; Rahel Kunz: Governing International Migration through Partnership. In: *Third World Quarterly* 34,7 (2013), pp. 1227–1246.

24 See Pauly: *Islam in Europe*.

post-Cold War political and policy debates. One pioneer work in this regard has been offered by Samuel Huntington in his provocative work "The Clash of Civilizations and the Remaking of World Order". Huntington's work has not only emphasized the importance of culture on the process of political development and democratization, but it has, moreover, "extended this kind of argument about norms, values and attitudes to the world stage."[25] Following Huntington's argument, ideology and culture (not economics) are to lie at the core of identity formation and are to dominate not only intrastate relations, but also international relations between states. He further aggregates all dominant cultures in the world under two main 'civilizations' thus adopting a bipolar confrontational view similar to that of the Cold War era. The two classified 'civilizations' he focuses on are: the Western versus the Islamic civilizations. Accordingly, he argues that the new fault lines "between civilizations will be the battle lines of the future."[26] What he fails to do, however, in his pioneering study is to divert from providing a "thin description" of the cultures encompassing what he grouped under each so-called 'civilization' into a "thick description"[27] that aims to go beyond a stereotypical perception of the "other". This directly or indirectly contributes to a stereotypical and aggregate perception of cultures of the Arab/Islamic world that feed into debates concerning migrants in Europe, especially in post-9/11 political debates. Debates on the national and regional levels aimed at representing Arab and/or Islamic migrant communities have recently called for the 'cultural relativism' argument in calling for mutual understanding and dialogue rather than the 'prophesized' clash by Huntington. The 'cultural relativist' argument, though supported by well-intended political and human rights practitioners and scholars, indirectly fails intragroup minorities that defy 'relativism' and choose to assimilate socially and culturally in their specific host countries. Freeman notes that the establishment of communities of minorities in states often results in clashes of identities that are rooted in both religious and overarching cultural differences between majorities and minorities and within minorities themselves.[28]

25 William A. Darity: *International Encyclopedia of the Social Sciences*, 2nd Edition, Political Culture. New York: Macmillan 2007.

26 Samuel P. Huntington: The Clash of Civilizations? In: *Foreign Affairs* 72,3 (1993), pp. 22–49, here p. 22.

27 Clifford Geertz: *The Interpretation of Cultures: Selected Essays*. New York: Basic 1973.

28 Pauly: *Islam in Europe*, pp. 24–25.

As such, deviating from the Huntington perception of an aggregate understanding of identity formation on the individual as opposed to the community level within Arab/Islamic migrant communities would help us to better understand intragroup dynamics and provide better political representation in the form of policies for those communities. This is crucial in moving from clash to dialogue and finally to intercultural balance and acceptance.

Intragroup Differences: Penetrating Stereotypes

The aim of the present article is not to provide a feminist or gender-based approach in analyzing the situation of women of a migrant Arab and/or Islamic background in the EU. As already argued, literature within international migration, economics, psychology, sociology and political science have shed light on the situation of migrant populations in general and women in particular in the EU in terms of labor conditions, domestic violence, family formation and integration, among others. Yet, the aim of this article is to shed light on the situation of a particular category of migrant women that can be categorized under 'minorities within minorities'.

In practice, identity formation within migrant communities is dependent on a multitude of layers and a web of networks (see Fig. 1). The 'self' is to the greatest extent affected by firstly 'family' and secondly the 'community' that

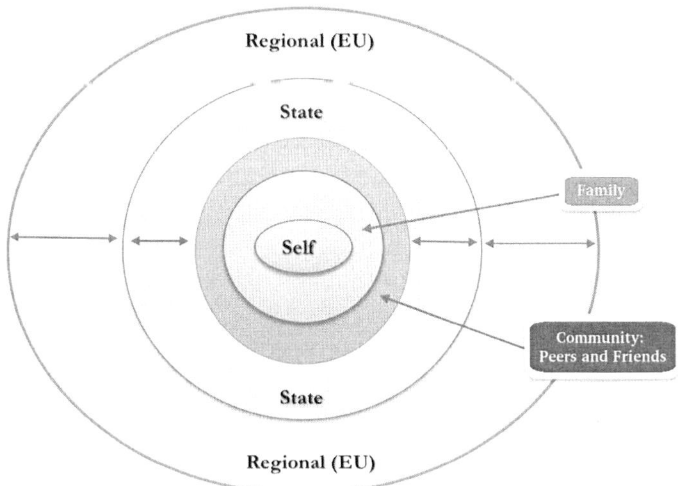

Fig. 1: Mapping the layers defining and affecting the formation of an 'identity' within migrant communities in the EU.

in turn encompasses friends and peers. Both the 'state' and supranational/ regional levels (here the 'EU' level) affect the 'self' to a much lesser extent through laws and policies.

Within more traditional migrant communities, the close-knit levels of family and community form a closed web aimed at monitoring and safeguarding the social norms, traditions and culture of their country of origin. As much as such a close-knit network provides a safety net that would protect more vulnerable groups within a particular migrant population, it can, however, also completely isolate them from the political and social environment of the host country thus hindering their integration and assimilation and rendering them completely dependent on the community to which they belong. They end up literally living within the shadows of their country of origin with the host country acting as a mere vessel. This situation is particularly observed among Turkish first, second and even third generation migrant communities in Germany.[29] Within Arab and/or Islamic migrant communities, which mostly mirror their country of origin, the position of the woman is particularly vulnerable. In such a patriarchal social structure, it can be assumed that education, social class and financial independence may provide women more freedom to determine the closeness to their family and community. From a relationship of complete dependence or providing a safety net, education, social class and financial independence would provide the woman more freedom, choice and room to integrate within the host country. At the same time, though a minority that deviated from a larger minority group, it is still faced with stereotyping by the larger community of the host country. Religion, traditions and social norms are highly regarded within Arabic/Islamic societies, and migrant communities usually form a collective close-knit network that would guarantee their safeguard. With religion interfering in almost all aspects of life and politics in much of the Arab and Islamic world, it is largely reported among Arab and Muslim migrant communities that religion

29 Carol Pfaff: Turkish in Contact with German: Language Maintenance and Loss among Immigrant Children in Berlin (West). In: *International Journal of the Sociology of Language* 90,1 (1991), pp. 97–130; Ruth Mandel: Shifting Centers and Emergent Identities: Turkey and Germany in the Lives of Turkish 'Gastarbeiter'. In: Dale F. Eickelman / James P. Piscatori (eds): *Muslim Travellers. Pilgrimage, Migration, and the Religious Imagination*. Berkeley: University of California Press 1991, pp. 153–171; Ruth Mandel: *Cosmopolitan Anxieties: Turkish Challenges to Citizenship and Belonging in Germany*. Durham: Duke UP 2008; Claudia Diehl / Michael Blohm: Rights or Identity? Naturalization Processes Among 'Labor Migrants' in Germany. In: *International Migration Review* 371 (2003), pp. 133–162. A notable example here are cases of second or even third generation migrants of a Turkish background, who were born in Germany, yet remain unable and even resist learning the language of the host country well into adulthood.

remains to be regarded as a main pillar of their culture. Cultural practices (e.g. FGM, arranged/early marriages, forced veiling) that do not conform to the European norms and values regarding the treatment of women continue to be practiced. Attempting to challenge or even deviate from the cultural and religious norms of the community would in some instances even put women at risk of retaliatory measures from both family and community, the most notable of which being what is known as 'honor killings'. With kinship being at the center of Arab and Islamic family relationships, the personal choices of women of an Arabic/Islamic background often transcend from being viewed as a personal to a family/community matter. Arab kinship structure, in particular, is mostly described as being one of 'patrilineal endogamy', where marriage choices are viewed as a partnership not between individuals but rather as an association between two families.[30] In most countries of the Arab region, women have very little choice in such decisions, where in Egypt, for example, around 41 % of all women interviewed in the women-status module section of the Egyptian Demographic Health System (reportedly 7,123 women) claimed that they did not know their husbands at all before marriage, and less than a quarter of the women interviewed reported 'choosing' their husbands freely.[31]

Qualitative interviews conducted as part of a larger research by the Social Care Research Unit at King's College between December 2011 and February 2012 on 66 low-skilled Turkish migrants in London aged 55 and above of both genders generally show that the community not only acted as a safety net but has, in some instances, even shielded its members from the English society, culture, and state.[32] Hence, it didn't allow much incentive to integrate nor learn about the language or culture of the host country. As one woman puts it, "I began to work in a [Turkish] garment workshop. I did not have to speak English because everyone here [in the UK] spoke Turkish" (Female, age 75). Another says, "[w]e lived here [UK] for a long time but we had worked entirely with Turkish people as tailors. We do not know much about the English community" (Female, age 75). Such an isolated status did

30 Shereen Hussein / Jill Manthorpe: Women from the Middle East and North Africa in Europe: Understanding Their Marriage and Family Dynamics. In: *European Journal of Social Work* 10,4 (2007), pp. 465–480, here pp. 468–469.

31 Ibid, pp. 469–470.

32 The interviews, which have been conducted in Turkish, by Shereen Hussein and Sema Oglak, aimed at examining the process of aging, the impact of network hierarchies, and access to social care among Turkish migrants in London. The detailed results of this research have been presented at the Turkish Migration Conference on May 30 and June 1, 2014.

not allow for women to know of their rights or the protections guaranteed to them by the state. As one explains, "[w]e don't know what are our benefits or rights due to language barriers" (Female, age 74). It can also be said that it largely alienated them from the native population, where one woman says, "I feel more comfortable, safe and secure with Turkish people" (Female, age 60).[33]

To examine the situation of high-skilled migrant women of an Arab and/or Islamic background living in the EU, a pilot survey has been conducted on a selected sample of 11 women in the period of May 5–15, 2014.[34] The sample has been conducted anonymously online following the snowballing method. Respondents were asked a variety of 25 questions on education, identity, integration, and family and peer affiliation and pressure. Though non-representative, the purpose of the survey was to acquire first-hand information on the situation of a sample of well-educated women of a migrant Arab and/or Islamic background and examine if they can be said to constitute a 'minority within a minority'. The results may lay down the foundation for a more expansive research endeavor in the future across the EU. The preliminary results of the pilot survey can be summarized as follows:

Over 72% of those surveyed were between the ages of 18 and 35 and over 27% between the ages of 35 and 50. The large majority of the respondents, who agreed to take the survey, had an Iranian background, and two of the respondents were of a 'mixed' European-Arab and/or Islamic background. When asked whether they perceive themselves as being integrated in their host countries, over 72% said that they feel integrated, 9% were undecided and 18% said that they did not feel integrated. At the same time, when asked if they consider themselves 'European', over 72% said that they didn't, whereas over 27% said that they did. Unlike the case of the above qualitative research, which targeted low-skilled women migrants, this survey targeted well-educated women, where 80% confirmed that they migrated to the EU for study-related reasons. When asked for the reason why they do not consider themselves 'European', most respondents referred to cultural differences between their countries of residence and origin as being the major

33 Shereen Hussein / Sema Oglak: Aging, Identity and Place: The Experience of Turkish Migrants in the United Kingdom. Turkish Migration Conference, London, UK, May 30–June 1, 2014.

34 The sample has been selected on the basis of education, gender and place of residence. Only women currently residing (and have been residing for over one year) in the EU and are well-educated were asked to undertake this survey.

factor. One respondent said, "I am coming from a different culture; I respect [the] European culture, but I am proud of where I come from enough not to consider myself [of] another nationality. Although I am merged in both." Another said, "I lived about 26 years in Iran; in a very different environment and culture, which is not easy to forget." Yet, an average of over 80 % of the respondents confirmed their belief in the principles of secularism (separation of state and religion), human rights and the equality of women. When asked whether they feel more comfortable in engaging in social activities with members of communities of their countries of origin, over 54 % of the respondents confirmed that they feel more "at home" with members of their own communities. The justifications given by respondents in this regard were varied, as follows:

> With Europeans, I feel that I have to be careful about my behavior because they may easily judge me. With other non-European cultures, I feel more comfortable, especially with people from my own country, because I know how things work and what is considered appropriate behavior.
>
> [This is] mostly because of the language, and I am not familiar with the cultural background of the Europeans.
>
> I don't feel like I have that much in common with the majority of immigrants from my same country of origin.
>
> I feel equally comfortable with both Austrians and Iranians, and also all other kinds of nationalities. With Vienna being a very international city, I had a very multicultural way of life, and I have always appreciated this. I never choose friends or company only for the fact that they have the same origin, I try to find fitting characters.

With regards to the question regarding family formation and the choice for marriage, the majority of those surveyed (over 54 %) stated that they would marry a European without any social, religious and cultural conditions; over 18 % stated that they would do so under the condition that they share each other's religious beliefs; and over 27 % stated that they wouldn't, as they would prefer someone of the same (cultural and/or religious) background. None of those surveyed stated that their decision is motivated by the fear of judgment from the family or community.

Conclusion

The aim of this paper is to highlight the importance of intragroup dynamics within migrant groups in the EU that produce what can be termed as 'minorities within minorities'. The case of women of a migrant Arab and/or Islamic background in the EU who choose to challenge the cultural and religious traditions of their countries of origin and with it, the control of the close-knit circle of the family and community, calls for a better understanding of the dynamics *within* migrant populations in the EU. Without a revised vision on the dynamics governing identity formation within migrant communities in the EU and a definition of 'minorities', which reflect the changing demographic makeup, policies would remain dissociated from reality.

At the same time, the 'cultural relativist' approach in dealing with migrant groups of a different cultural background does render vulnerable minorities within those groups assailable to practices that may violate their basic human rights. The results of the pilot survey outlined in this paper open the door for a more extensive fieldwork and empirical research aimed at exploring more closely the factors that push women to deviate from their close-knit network of family and community and defy highly regarded norms and traditions. This would allow for the better articulation of policies on the national and regional levels that would better guarantee integration and assimilation. With the 'self' being at the center, the process of identity formation within migrant communities (as depicted in Fig. 1) consists of a multitude of layers starting from the layers with the strongest effect, i. e. the 'family' and 'community', and ending with the 'state' and 'supranational/regional' levels. Neglecting the center-periphery relationship affecting the identity formation of migrant communities will push policies to a surface that will never touch the very heart and core of such communities.

Exchanges

Open and Closed Electoral Autocracies in the (Semi-)Periphery from 1996 to 2010

Democratization and Foreign Aid Flows

Oliver Schlenkrich / Christoph Mohamad-Klotzbach

Introduction

During the "Third Wave" of Democratization[1], several countries on the so-called periphery became more and more democratic. This trend has been confirmed by other recent studies.[2] These studies focused on democracies, comparing the quality of the "old" established ones with the "young" and newer ones. One of the results was the development of new terms such as "defective democracies"[3], "deficient democracies"[4] or "hybrid regimes"[5]. However, there are still many authoritarian regimes on the periphery. Although Juan Linz[6] developed a typology of authoritarian and totalitarian regimes during the 1970s, it is only in the past few years that extensive authoritarian research has begun to be conducted.[7] This research shows that there are different

1 Samuel P. Huntington: *The Third Wave. Democratization in the Late 20th Century*. Norman: University of Oklahoma Press 1993.

2 Keith Jaggers / Ted R. Gurr: Tracking Democracy's Third Wave with the Polity III data. In: *Journal of Peace Research* 32 (1995), pp. 469–482; Hans-Joachim Lauth / Oliver Kauff: Demokratiemessung. Der KID als aggregiertes Maß für die komparative Forschung. Empirische Befunde der Regimeentwicklung von 1996 bis 2010. In: *Würzburger Arbeitspapiere* 2 (2012), pp. 1–35.

3 Wolfgang Merkel / Hans-Jürgen Puhle / Aurel Croissant / Claudia Eicher / Peter Thiery: *Defekte Demokratien*, vol. 1: Theorien. Opladen: Leske + Budrich 2003.

4 Hans-Joachim Lauth: *Demokratie und Demokratiemessung: Eine konzeptionelle Grundlegung für den interkulturellen Vergleich*. Wiesbaden: VS Verlag für Sozialwissenschaften 2004.

5 Larry J. Diamond: Thinking About Hybrid Regimes. In: *Journal of Democracy* 13,2 (2002), pp. 21–35.

6 Juan Linz: *Totalitarian and Authoritarian Regimes*. Boulder, CO: Lynne Rienner 2000.

7 Barbara Geddes / Joseph Wright / Erica Frantz: New Data on Autocratic Regimes. 2012. http://dictators.la.psu.edu/pdf/pp10.pdf (accessed 21.04.2014); Barbara Geddes: What Do We Know About Democratization After Twenty Years? In: *Annual Review of Political Science* 2 (1999), pp. 115–144; Axel Hadenius / Jan Teorell: Authoritarian Regimes: Stability, Change, and Pathways to Democracy, 1972–2003. Working Paper No. 331. Kellogg Institute 2006. http://kellogg.nd.edu/publications/workingpapers/WPS/331.pdf (accessed 06.02.2014); Axel Hadenius / Jan Teorell: Pathways from Authoritarianism. In: *Journal of Democracy* 18,1(2007), pp. 143–156; Steffen Kailitz / Patrick Köller (eds): *Autokratien im Vergleich* (= *PVS Special Issue* 47). Baden-Baden: Nomos 2013; Andreas Schedler: *Electoral Authoritarianism. The Dynamics of Unfree Competition*. Boulder, CO: Lynne Rienner 2006; Jan Teorell: *Determinants of Democratization. Explaining Regime Change in the World, 1972–2006*. Cambridge: Cambridge UP 2010.

institutional settings and mechanisms of rule in authoritarian regimes. Thus, they "draw on different groups to staff government offices and different segments of society for support. They have different procedures for making decisions, different ways of handling the choice of leaders and succession, and different ways of responding to society and opponents."[8]

In this study, we analyze two ideas: First, we look at the thesis of Axel Hadenius and Jan Teorell[9], who argue that different types of authoritarian regimes have different chances of democratization. They show that multiparty systems have a higher possibility of becoming democracies than, for example, military regimes. This leads to the following questions: Can we reproduce their findings for the period 1996–2010 if we combine their data with the Combined Index of Democracy (CID), which offers a better instrument for measuring regime quality? Do all multiparty systems have the same chance of democratization or is it appropriate to differentiate between them? We prove not all multiparty systems – we call them electoral autocracies[10] – have the same chance of democratizing and there is no direct path to functioning democracy. However, there is a path from open electoral autocracies to deficient democracies.

Second, we want to test this newly established typology by looking at the countries in the so-called semi-peripheral and peripheral areas of the world.[11] This terminology, which is based on research into World-System Analysis by Immanuel Wallerstein, was very prominent in the 1970s and 1980s in disciplines like History and Political Science (especially in International Relations), and has experienced a "rebirth" during the last few years.[12] Again, two questions arise: What different types of autocracies exist in the semi-periphery and periphery? And what amount of foreign aid – a key variable in the center-periphery relationship – flows to these authoritarian regime types? We can

8 Geddes: What Do We Know About Democratization, p. 121.

9 Hadenius / Teorell: Authoritarian Regimes; Hadenius / Teorell: Pathways from Authoritarianism.

10 Schedler: *Electoral Authoritarianism*.

11 For definitions see Part 3 of this Paper.

12 Immanuel Wallerstein: The Rise and Future Demise of the World Capitalist System: Concepts for Comparative Analysis. In: *Comparative Studies in Society and History* 16,4 (1974), pp. 387–415; Immanuel Wallerstein: *The Capitalist World-Economy*. Cambridge: Cambridge UP 1979; Immanuel Wallerstein: *World-Systems Analysis. An Introduction*. 5th ed. Durham / London: Duke UP 2007; Rob Clark / Jason Beckfield: A New Trichotomous Measure of World-system Position Using the International Trade Network. In: *International Journal of Comparative Sociology* 50,1 (2009), pp. 5–38; Rob Clark: World-System Position and Democracy, 1972–2008. In: *International Journal of Comparative Sociology* 53,5–6 (2012), pp. 367–399.

show that open electoral autocracies gain significantly more foreign aid than most of the other authoritarian regime types.

The Combined Index of Democracy and Authoritarian Regime Types

In the last few years, datasets for authoritarian regimes have been developed. Barbara Geddes, Joseph Wright, and Erica Frantz[13] distinguish three types of pure autocracy (personalist regimes, military regimes, and single-party regimes) over a period from 1946 to 2010, whereas José Antonio Cheibub, Jennifer Ghandi, and James Raymond Vreeland[14] distinguish between military dictatorships, civilian dictatorships, and monarchies over the time from 1946 to 2008.[15] In contrast to these two datasets, the one from Michael Wahman, Teorell and Hadenius[16], which covers the period from 1972 to 2010, differs by determining regime types "not so much in terms of the characteristics or social origins of the elites in question, but instead on the institutions on which these elites rely in order to regulate the access and maintenance of public authority".[17] The former two also "cannot be used if the researcher believes that elections in general, and competitive elections in particular, are important institutions in authoritarian regimes".[18] The importance of elections in authoritarian regimes is revealed in recent literature about "electoral authoritarianism".[19] Authoritarian regimes modify the democratic institution of elections so it works with an authoritarian code and in most cases contributes to the stabilization of the regime.[20]

13 Geddes / Wright / Frantz: New Data on Autocratic Regimes.

14 José Antonio Cheibub / Jennifer Gandhi / James Raymond Vreeland: Democracy and Dictatorship Revisited. In: *Public Choice* 143,2–1 (2010), pp. 67–101.

15 Rose, in addition, combines data from Freedom House and Transparency International and distinguishes on that basis one democratic (accountable democracies) and three authoritarian types (constitutional oligarchies, unaccountable autocracies and plebiscitarian autocracies); see Richard Rose: Democratic and Undemocratic States. In: Christian W. Haerpfer / Patrick Bernhagen / Ronald F. Inglehart / Christian Welzel (eds): *Democratization*. Oxford: Oxford UP 2009, pp. 10–23, here pp. 16–17.

16 Michael Wahman / Jan Teorell / Axel Hadenius: Authoritarian Regime Types Revisited: Updated Data in Comparative Perspective. 2013. http://www.svet.lu.se/uploads/specialsidor/svet-mwaARD_dataset_2.pdf (accessed 29.05.2014).

17 Wahman / Teorell / Hadenius: Authoritarian Regime Types Revisited, p. 6.

18 Ibid., p. 29.

19 Schedler: *Electoral Authoritarianism*.

20 Petra Stykow: Wahlen in autoritären Regimen. Die postsowjetischen Länder im Vergleich. In: Steffen Kailitz / Patrick Köllner (eds): *Autokratien im Vergleich* (= *PVS Special Issue* 47). Baden-Baden: Nomos 2013, pp. 237–271.

Wahman et al.[21] differentiate three "modes of accessing and maintaining political power": hereditary succession, military force, and popular elections. These three modes represent three authoritarian regime types: monarchies, military regimes and electoral regimes. Monarchies are "those regimes in which a person of royal descent has inherited the position of head of state in accordance with accepted practice and/or the constitution".[22] In contrast, in military regimes military officers or armed forces control the politics of the state.[23] The "electoral regimes" category refers to the importance of elections in autocracies. This regime type is further discriminated in one-party regimes, multiparty regimes, and no-party regimes.[24] In no-party regimes elections are held, but no parties are allowed to participate,[25] while in one-party systems, only one legal party exists. Finally, the multiparty regimes refer to the category of electoral authoritarianism, in which more than one party competes in elections.[26]

To classify a regime as an autocracy, Wahman et al.[27] use the scores from the Polity and Freedom House (Civil Liberties and Political Rights) democracy indices, which they transform onto a 0–10 scale. All regimes with a score of seven or lower are classified as autocracies. But this method has several shortcomings, which can be seen by using the evaluation program by Gerardo L. Munck and Jay Verkuilen[28]: First, Wahman et al. argue that "democracy is an institutional quality that is principally a matter of degree"[29], but they don't define their concept of democracy or regime quality. This leads to a second problem, which is called conceptual stretching[30]: in their operationalization, they use the Civil Liberties scale by Freedom House, which doesn't

21 Wahman / Teorell / Hadenius: Authoritarian Regime Types Revisited, p. 4.

22 Ibid., p. 16.

23 Ibid., p. 15.

24 Ibid., pp. 19–21.

25 This means that only individual candidates compete in elections. However, no-party regimes are only represented by a few cases in the dataset of Wahman / Teorell / Hadenius: Authoritarian Regime Types Revisited, p. 19.

26 Still, these regimes are not democratic: "certain groups may be excluded, and the process may in various ways favor one side" (Hadenius / Teorell: Authoritarian Regimes, p. 7).

27 Wahman / Teorell / Hadenius: Authoritarian Regime Types Revisited, pp. 11–14.

28 Gerardo L. Munck / Jay Verkuilen: Conceptualizing and Measuring Democracy. In: *Comparative Political Studies* 35,1 (2002), pp. 5–34.

29 Wahman / Teorell / Hadenius: Authoritarian Regime Types Revisited, p. 7.

30 For the problem of 'conceptional stretching' see Giovanni Sartori: Concept Misformation in Comparative Politics. In: *American Political Science Review* 64 (1970), pp. 1033–1053.

necessarily measure the democratic quality of a regime (e.g. social rights).[31] Third, they don't take the rules of aggregation into account for their two indicators. Fourth, they can't differentiate between functioning and deficient democracies[32] because they don't have a concept of democracy. Finally, the category of multiparty regimes seems to have become a redundant category. Although they distinguished between dominant multiparty systems and traditionally multiparty systems during their first studies[33], they "refrained from imposing any qualitative threshold in [their] new dataset"[34].

To resolve these issues, we combined their dataset with the Combined Index of Democracy by Hans-Joachim Lauth.[35] The Combined Index of Democracy uses a three-dimensional concept of democratic quality, which was developed by abstracting from central arguments of democratic theory[36]: "Democratic participation in the political process finds its expression in the dimensions of freedom, equality and political and judicial control".[37] The Combined Index of Democracy uses data from Polity (DEMOC-Scale), Freedom House (Political Rights Scale), and the World Bank (Rule of Law and Political Stability) to calculate the quality of regimes between 1996 and 2012.[38] While selecting the indicators, attention was paid to only those which measure aspects of democracy. Thus, the Civil Liberty Scale is ignored. With the first two components representing the dimensions of freedom and equality, the control dimension will be captured using the Rule of Law Indicator of the World Bank. These components are aggregated by multiplication followed

31 Lauth: *Demokratie und Demokratiemessung.*

32 Hans-Joachim Lauth: The Matrix of Democracy. A Three-Dimensional Approach to Measuring. Paper prepared for the IPSA-Workshop: "Measuring Democracy", University of Frankfurt am Main, September 29 – October 1, 2013.

33 Hadenius / Teorell: Authoritarian Regimes; Hadenius / Teorell: Pathways from Authoritarianism.

34 Wahman / Teorell / Hadenius: Authoritarian Regime Types Revisited, p. 21.

35 Lauth / Kauff: Demokratiemessung.

36 Lauth: *Demokratie und Demokratiemessung.*

37 Lauth: The Matrix of Democracy, p. 5.

38 See for additional information about Polity: Monty G. Marshall / Ted R. Gurr / Keith Jaggers: Polity IV Project. Political Regime Characteristics and Transitions, 1800–2013. Dataset Users' Manual. Center for Systemic Peace 2014. http://www.systemicpeace.org/inscr/p4manualv2013.pdf (accessed 17.05.2014); about Freedom House: Freedom House: Freedom in the World 2014 Methodology. 2014. http://www.freedomhouse.org/sites/default/files/Methodology%20FIW%202014.pdf (accessed 17.05.2014); and about the Governance Indicators: Daniel Kaufmann / Aart Kraay / Massimo Mastruzzi: *The Worldwide Governance Indicators: Methodology and Analytical Issues. World Bank Policy Research Working Paper* 5430 (2010). All their datasets are free of charge and online accessible.

by taking the cube root, because a low value in one dimension shouldn't be offset by a high value in another (CID3D). The index also includes the factor 'stateness', as defined by the Political Stability Indicator. Failures in stateness reduce overall regime quality. Thus, the final Index (CID) is calculated by multiplying CID3D and Political Stability followed by extracting the root.[39] It distinguishes three types of regimes by placing thresholds on a zero to ten point scale: autocracies (CID3D: 0–6; CID: 0–5), deficient democracies (CID3D: 6–8; CID: 5–7), and functioning democracies (CID3D: 8–10; CID: 7–10).[40]

We merged the CID dataset with that from Wahman et al. to develop a new dataset. We used all the cases that the CID classifies as deficient democracies and functioning democracies. If the CID classified a regime as authoritarian, we used the data from Wahman et al. to differentiate between the authoritarian regime types. Instead of calling authoritarian regimes with elections "multiparty regimes", we call them "electoral autocracies". We prefer the term "electoral autocracy" as it emphasizes the difference from a democratic regime (because democracies are, by definition, multiparty systems). We think this procedure has certain advantages over the database from Wahman et al.: First, we use a theoretically rich approach to distinguish between democracy and autocracy. Second, we give reasons for the operationalization of this concept. This also means we don't use the Civil Liberties Scale of Freedom House to avoid the problem of conceptual stretching.[41] Finally, we can also distinguish between different types of democracies (deficient vs. functioning). Overall, we use a holistic approach that combines central findings of the research on autocracies and democracies.[42]

39 There are two special rules: a) if the value of the CID is higher than the value of the CID3D, the value of the CID3D is kept; b) the regime classification of the CID3D can only be abandoned if the CID classifies a regime as more autocratic, e. g. a regime can't become a functioning democracy by the CID if the CID3D classified it as a deficient democracy, but a regime can become a deficient democracy by the CID although it is categorized as a functioning democracy by the CID3D.

40 The CID also contains the category of "hybrid regimes", which are settled on the grey area between autocracies and democracies (see Lauth / Kauff: Demokratiemessung). These regimes are classified differently by the CID3D and CID because of their varying thresholds. In this study, these few cases will be counted as "authoritarian regimes" in accordance with the two special rules (see fn. 39).

41 Sartori: Concept Misformation.

42 Lauth / Kauff: Demokratiemessung, validate the CID by correlating it with the Corruption Perception Index by Transparency International. The idea behind this is that the higher the quality of democracy, the lower is the perceived corruption. The results show that the CID performs better than Freedom House or Polity alone.

But there are three problems as well: First, setting thresholds between regime types is rather arbitrary.[43] The CID tries to combine the thresholds of the three indices[44] to achieve meaningful thresholds. Second, whereas Wahman et al. analyze a time span of over 40 years, the time span of the CID is much shorter (14–16 years).[45] Finally, we also have fewer cases per year because – unlike the dataset of Wahman et al. – we haven't "imputed missing values [in the Polity dataset] by regressing the index on the FH scores, which have better country coverage than Polity"[46]. Nevertheless, this leads to an evolving risk of misjudging the Polity scores. Table 1 presents the main differences between the regime classifications of the merged dataset and that from Wahman et al. for cases in the period 1996–2010 for which both datasets have data available:

			Regime types from Wahman et al.	
			Multiparty	Democracy
Regime types from the merged dataset	Electoral autocracies	Count	348	**91**
		%	99.1 %	**14.5 %**
	Deficient Democracy	Count	3	**242**
		%	.9 %	**38.7 %**
	Functioning Democracy	Count	0	**293**
		%	.0 %	**46.8 %**
Total		Count	351	626
		%	100.0 %	100.0 %

Reading support: 14.5 % of the democracies in Wahman et al. are counted as electoral autocracies by the merged dataset.
Source: Own calculation based on Hans-Joachim Lauth: *Datensatz „Kombinierter Index der Demokratie (KID) 1996 2012".* Würzburg: Institut für Politikwissenschaft und Soziologie 2013. www.politikwissenschaft.uni-wuerzburg.de/lehrbereiche/vergleichende/forschung/kombinierter_index_der_demokratie_kid/ (accessed 21.04.2014); and Wahman / Teorell / Hadenius: Authoritarian Regime Types Revisited.

Table 1: Regime types from the merged dataset compared to the regime types from Wahman et al. (1996–2010).

43 Wahman / Teorell / Hadenius: Authoritarian Regime Types Revisited, p. 11.

44 Hans-Joachim Lauth: Die Qualität der Demokratie. Der NID als pragmatischer Vorschlag für die komparative Forschung. In: Kai-Uwe Schnapp / Nathalie Behnke / Joachim Behnke (eds): *Datenwelten. Datenerhebung und Datenbestände in der Politikwissenschaft.* Baden-Baden: Nomos 2008, pp. 373–390.

45 We couldn't compile the classifications and ratings for 2012 although the CID actually covers 2012. This is because the database of Wahman / Teorell / Hadenius: Authoritarian Regime Types Revisited, reaches only until 2010.

46 Hadenius / Teorell: Authoritarian Regimes, p. 25.

The main differences between the classifications in the merged dataset and those in Wahman et al. concern multiparty regimes and democracy types. The merged dataset classifies 15% of the democracies in Wahman et al. as electoral autocracies. It also classifies 39% of the democracies in Wahman et al. as deficient democracies and only 47% as functioning democracies. This means the merged dataset on the basis of the CID is more rigid in the distinction between autocracies and democracies, and Wahman et al., judged by these findings, overestimate the number of democracies. Overall, the new dataset provides a more reasonable differentiation.

Table 2 indicates that the majority of regime types in the period 1996–2010 for the merged dataset are electoral autocracies (36%) and democracies (Deficient Democracies: 20%; Functioning Democracies 23%). Hadenius and Teorell show that in "the 1970s and 1980s, military regimes and one-party states were the most common type of authoritarian government, [but since the 1990s] multiparty regimes [electoral autocracies] have been the most frequently found form of authoritarianism"[47]. Among authoritarian regime types, electoral autocracies have the highest democratic quality on average (3.19).[48] They also display the greatest range of CID values (0–5.9). While military regimes and monarchies also have high maximum CID values (4.46; 3.99)[49], the skewness of their values (2.47; 1.69; not shown) illustrates that these maximums are exceptions.

Regime Type in the merged dataset	Mean	Minimum	Maximum	% of Total N
Others	1.10	0.00	4.52	2.5%
Monarchy	0.41	0.00	3.99	6.3%
One-Party	0.00	0.00	.00	4.5%
Military	0.63	0.00	4.46	7.9%
Electoral Autocracy	3.19	**0.00**	**5.90**	35.5%
Deficient Democracy	6.50	4.96	7.89	19.8%
Functioning Democracy	8.91	7.05	10.00	23.4%
Source: Lauth: *Datensatz „Kombinierter Index der Demokratie (KID), 1996–2012"*; Wahman / Teorell / Hadenius: Authoritarian Regime Types Revisited.				

Table 2: Descriptive statistics for the regime types in the merged dataset (1996–2010).

47 Hadenius / Teorell: Authoritarian Regimes, p. 9.

48 Ibid.

49 The highest CID-values of the military regimes by far received Thailand (4.46; 2008) and Guinea-Bissau (4.41; 2010). The highest CID-values of the monarchies by far received Jordan (3.99; 1996) and Nepal (2.46; 2002).

Although the Wahman et al. classification is still valuable for a historical analysis, the empirical evidence presented here for 1996–2010 shows that we should distinguish between electoral autocracies to avoid them becoming a residual category, which isn't scientifically useful. In order to distinguish the electoral autocracies, it is reasonable to orientate ourselves on the CID-values. We argue that the institutions in electoral autocracies with low CID values work differently than those in electoral autocracies with higher CID values, because in contrast to monarchies or military regimes, the institutions in multiparty regimes are characterized by their closeness to the definition of democracy. In multiparty regimes, "elections take place where there is a degree of competition between candidates who either represent different parties or choose to act as individuals".[50] Thus, it is possible to differentiate the institutions of multiparty regimes according to their level of competition, which is represented by the CID value. The higher the level of competition inside the party system is, the higher the CID value.

We will try to verify this by using a linear regression (see Table 3). All regimes that have been multiparty systems for at least 10 years out of the 14 year period are included in the calculation to guarantee the impact of their institutions. The dependent variable is the mean CID value (1996–2010). As independent variables, we use the mean level of executive competition, which is measured by dividing the number of votes for the second favorite participant by that for the election winner.[51] We also control for the level of socio-economic development (mean of HDI for the years 2000, 2005 and 2010), ethnic fragmentation (1980–2000) and two economic indicators from the Fragile States Index (Uneven Economic Development, Poverty and Economic Decline for the years 2005 and 2010).[52] All in all, we tested 44 out of the 87 regimes which were classified as electoral autocracies at least once between 1996 and 2010.

50 Hadenius / Teorell: Authoritarian Regimes, p. 7.

51 The data for the elections was taken from the Adam Carr's Election Archive (http://psephos.adam-carr.net/). We have verified the source by comparing its election results with the article by Stykow: Wahlen in autoritären Regimen. All polity wide elections were taken, which took place in all the countries during the period of 1996 to 2010.

52 See for more information about the HDI: UNDP 2012, about the Fractionalization dataset: Alberto Alesina / Arnaud Devleeschauwer / William Easterly / Sergio Kurlat / Romain Wacziarg: Fractionalization. In: *Journal of Economic Growth* 8 (2003), pp. 155–194; about the Fragile States Index (former Failed States Index) and his indicators: The Fund For Peace: The Fragile States Index. The Methodology Behind the Index. 2014. http://ffp.statesindex.org/methodology (accessed 03.09.2014).

The effect of executive competition on CID values	
(Constant)	-4.561 (3.648)
Mean HDI	0.344 (2.580)
Mean Ethnic	0.041 (1.040)
Mean Economy (FSI)	0.036 (.237)
Mean Poverty (FSI)	0.330 (.260)
Mean Competition Executive	**0.595*** (.909)**
R-squared	**0.497*****
Adjusted R-squared	**0.431*****
Observations (n)	**44**
Note: Dependent variable: mean CID value; standard errors are reported in parentheses; standardized coefficients. *, **, *** indicates significance at the 90 %, 95 %, and 99 % level, respectively. Source: Own calculation based on Lauth: *Datensatz „Kombinierter Index der Demokratie (KID), 1996–2012"*; Wahman / Teorell / Hadenius: Authoritarian Regime Types Revisited; Adam Carr's Election Archive. http://psephos.adam-carr.net/ (accessed 21.04.2014); Alesina / Devleeschauwer / Easterly / Kurlat / Wacziarg: Fractionalization; The Fund For Peace: *Fragile States Index*; UNDP: *Human Development Index Trends, 1980–2012. A Statistical Update.* 2012. http://data.un.org/DocumentData.aspx?q=HDI&id=327 (accessed 17.05.2014).	

Table 3: Linear regression models.

Table 3 shows the results of the linear regression.[53] The main independent variable – executive competition – can explain 43 % of the CID values.[54] The competition variable has the strongest explanatory power (β = 0.595) and is also significant at the 99 % level. The result shows that competition in the executive increases with higher CID values. Thus, there is a huge difference between electoral autocracies, and CID values can be used as a rough proxy to classify between them.[55]

We claim that these new differences impact the key finding from Hadenius and Teorell, who argue that "multiparty regimes [electoral autocracies] are more prone to develop democratically (in a gradual way) than are other

53 We also test for the quality of the linear regression analyses. The standardized residuals are normally distributed (Kolmogorov-Smirnov Z: .902).

54 The constant of this model is not significant due to the inclusion of insignificant control variables. If we exclude them, the constant is significant at the 5 % level.

55 Results are similar when using the democracy measure (ifhpol) by Wahman et al. But it should also be clear that there are huge differences between these two democracy measures – be it the concept or the operationalization. This will affect the validity of the measure.

authoritarian regimes. This is not surprising since they hold elections offering at least a degree of openness and contestation and furnish at least some rudimentary political liberties".[56]

In Table 4, we reproduced their finding with the new merged dataset based on the CID. We compared the regime classification of the merged dataset from one measurement point to the next from 1996 to 2010. Electoral autocracies were shown to have a higher probability of democratizing than the other regime types, because all 28 transitions to democracies began in electoral autocracies. Nevertheless, we are able to show that these transformation probabilities do not directly lead to functioning democracies. Even electoral autocracy transition only led to a deficient democracy.

		Merged dataset: Regime type at the next measurement point					Total
		MOP	CEA	OEA	DD	FD	
Merged dataset	MOP	193	5	3	0	0	201
		96.0%	2.5%	1.5%	0%	0%	100.0%
	CEA	3	**124**	16	**1**	0	144
		2.1%	**86.1%**	11.1%	**0.7%**	0%	100.0%
	OEA	4	12	**189**	**27**	0	235
		1.7%	5.2%	**81.5%**	**11.6%**	0%	100.0%
	DD	2	0	19	184	8	213
		1.0%	0%	8.9%	86.4%	3.8%	100.0%

Reading support: 11.6% of the open electoral autocracies transformed into deficient democracies by the next measurement point.
Note: MOP = Monarchy, One-Party or Military Regime; CEA = Closed Electoral Autocracy; OEA = Open Electoral Autocracy; DD = Deficient Democracy; FD = Functioning Democracy.
Source: Own calculation based on Lauth: *Datensatz „Kombinierter Index der Demokratie (KID) 1996–2012"*; Wahman / Teorell / Hadenius: Authoritarian Regime Types Revisited.

Table 4: Transformation probabilities for the different regime types (1996–2010).

Furthermore, it seems not every electoral autocracy has the same chance to democratize. We classified electoral autocracies with a CID value of less than three as "closed electoral autocracies" and electoral autocracies with a CID value higher than three as "open electoral autocracies". Open electoral

56 Hadenius / Teorell: Authoritarian Regimes, pp. 23–24.

autocracies constitute 27 out of 28 transitions; we can find only one transition from a closed electoral autocracy to a deficient democracy (Croatia from 1998 to 2000) (see Table 4). This ties in with the findings of Hadenius and Teorell[57], who argue that dominant multiparty regimes[58] must transform into traditional multiparty systems before they can democratize. This is why we consider the new study by Wahman et al.[59], which lacks the differentiation of these two types of electoral autocracies, to be deficient. But the results should also be interpreted carefully: not all of these transitions were stable. Whereas the regimes in Albania (from 2006), Dominican Republic (from 1998), El Salvador (from 1998), Ghana (from 2002), Indonesia (from 2006), Macedonia (from 2006), Mali (from 2000), Mexico (from 2000), Senegal (from 2000), Serbia (from 2006), Suriname (from 2000), and Turkey (from 2004) remained democratic for a relatively long time[60], we can also find regimes like Moldova, Nicaragua, or Comoros, which fluctuate between authoritarianism and democracy. There are also regimes like Nepal, Sri Lanka, and Ukraine, which are predominantly electoral autocracies but transformed to a deficient democracy for a single measurement point. Finally, there are regimes which transformed to a deficient democracy before descending to a closed electoral autocracy (Madagascar from 2004). In the next chapter we can show that the amount of foreign aid flow differs both between authoritarian regime types and between these two types of multiparty regimes.

57 Ibid.; Hadenius / Teorell: Pathways from Authoritarianism.

58 Multiparty systems are dominant multiparty systems if the share of seats by the largest party is more than 66 % of the total seats. Traditional multiparty systems have a lower proportional share of seats. See Hadenius / Teorell: Authoritarian Regimes; Hadenius / Teorell: Pathways from Authoritarianism.

59 Wahman / Teorell / Hadenius: Authoritarian Regime Types Revisited.

60 For example, Mexico was characterized by a one-party hegemony (PRI: Partido Revolucionario Institucional) from 1929 to 2000 even though other parties like the Partido Acción Nacional (PAN) could also compete in the national elections. Through small electoral reforms in the time between 1977 and the mid-1990s (e. g. establishing the Instituto Federal Electoral in 1991, which observed the elections), the leaders of the PRI tried to compensate for the loss in legitimacy. In the end, the PRI lost their majority in the parliament in 1998 and also the presidential elections in 2000. From 2000 on, Mexico transformed from an open electoral autocracy to a deficient democracy (see for Mexico and other examples Wolfgang Merkel: *Systemtransformation*. 2th ed. Wiesbaden: VS Verlag für Sozialwissenschaften 2010).

Who Gets What? Foreign Aid Flows to Different Types of Autocracies

In this chapter, we want to test the new merged dataset's classification by analyzing foreign aid flows to different types of autocracies in the semi-periphery and periphery. The concept of the periphery seems old-fashioned to most contemporary political scientists, because it is a term rooted in the discussions of Dependency Theories and World-Systems Analysis from the 1970s and 1980s. But the debate on globalization has rekindled interest in these ideas, as several publications show.[61]

World-Systems Theory distinguishes three "zones" for countries within the world economy: the center (or the "core countries") (C), the semi-periphery (SP), and the periphery (P).[62] Rob Clark defines these zones as follows:

> Core states refer to the set of wealthy and powerful countries that feature dense economic ties with other nations. Peripheral states, by contrast, refer to a larger collection of poor and isolated nations, whose exchange relations are concentrated with the core. Semi-peripheral states […] occupy an intermediate position.[63]

These countries are, therefore, defined not geographically, but economically. Clark shows that during the period 1972 to 2008, some countries moved from the periphery to the semi-periphery and some moved from the semi-periphery to the core areas.[64] So there is obviously a kind of a global dynamic in the world economic system, best illustrated by the development and importance of the rising BRICS-states (Brazil, Russia, India, China and South Africa).

When we look at Figure 1, we can see the different patterns of regime types in the core, semi-peripheral and peripheral countries. Therefore, we used Clark's classification of countries for 1990 to 2008, because our data covers nearly the same period (1996–2010).[65] In contrast to the semi-periphery and especially the core, there are only a few functional democracies in the periphery (Cape Verde, Mauritius, Trinidad and Tobago, Estonia). Military regimes are naturally dominant in the periphery, whereas monarchies and one-party regimes are more common in the semi-periphery. Both types of electoral autocracies can be found in the semi-periphery and the periphery,

61 See fn. 12.

62 Clark: World-System Position and Democracy, p. 371.

63 Ibid., pp. 371–372.

64 P to SP: Bahrain, Costa Rica, Cuba, Ecuador, Ghana, Guatemala, Jordan, Lebanon, Malta, North Korea, Syria, Tanzania, Vietnam; SP to C: Chile, Israel, United Arabic Emirates; P to C: South Africa; C to SP: Morocco; SP to P: Iraq. See ibid., p. 394.

65 Ibid.

but electoral autocracies are more highly represented in the latter. We can conclude that the semi-periphery is heterogeneous rather than homogenous.[66] These findings about regime types are in line with Andreas Boeck, who states that there is not *a* periphery but *many* peripheries.[67] But Figure 1 also shows that the core is inhomogeneous, too.

The next step is to look at foreign aid flows and use them as a proxy variable in the relationship between the core and peripheral countries. In general, foreign aid is aid "that people in one country give to another".[68] It can take different forms (money, food, technical assistance, or military weapons) and have different types of donors (national governments, intergovernmental organizations, or private donors).[69] As Kenneth Bollen states, "a core country is more likely to give than to receive foreign aid."[70]
There are studies that prove the institutional designs of aid-receiving countries make a difference to the effect of foreign aid for those countries. Bruce Bueno de Mesquita and Alastair Smith show that, in large coalition systems, this aid is "most likely to improve the welfare of citizens" because "the majority of the additional resources are allocated to public goods, and the

66 A distribution of the regime types based on the regional classification by the merged dataset produces the following picture for the period 1996–2010: In North America, West-, North- and South Europe, we can see that functioning democracies are the regular regime types. The other world regions (Central- and Eastern Europe, Latin America, Asia and Pacific, the Middle East and North Africa, Sub-Saharan Africa) are interesting in three ways: First, they are distinguishable from the "western" countries because we can see more measurements of deficient democracies and authoritarian regime types. Second, it is obvious that these other regions are quite heterogeneous by themselves: a) by the amount of functioning and deficient democracies, b) by the different types of authoritarian regimes and c) by the different amounts of closed and open multi-party systems that exist in each peripheral region. Finally, multi-party systems are the most dominant authoritarian regime types in at least all but one (the Middle East and North Africa) of the non-western regions (see Fig. A1 in the Appendix).

67 Besides, the globalized world also shows in economic and political perspectives, that there is a global dynamic that challenges this old hierarchy of core and peripheral countries rising countries of the core (e.g. the BRICS-states) and perhaps also the decline of one or another old industrial country. See Andreas Boeck: Vergleichende Analyse peripherer Gesellschaften, oder: Die Auflösung der Peripherie. In: Dirk Berg-Schlosser / Ferdinand Müller-Rommel (eds): *Vergleichende Politikwissenschaft. Ein einführendes Studienhandbuch.* 4th ed. Wiesbaden: VS 2006, pp. 277–295, here pp. 278–279.

68 William Roberts Clark / Matt Golder / Sona Nadenichek Golder: *Principles of Comparative Politics.* 2nd ed. Los Angeles: CQ Press / Sage 2013, p. 200.

69 Ibid.

70 Kenneth Bollen: World System Position, Dependency, and Democracy: The Cross-National Evidence. In: *American Sociological Review* 48 (1983), pp. 468–479, here p. 474.

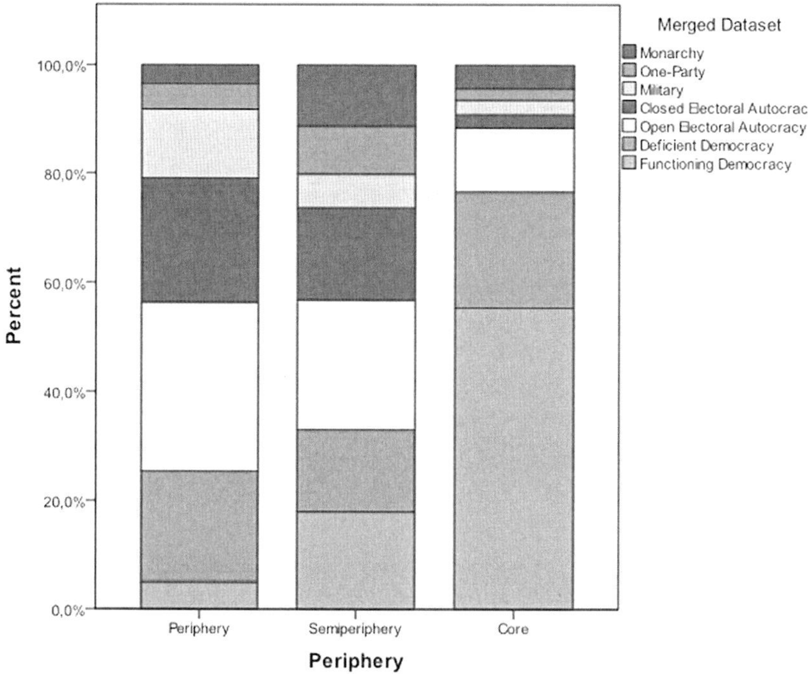

Fig. 1: Classification of countries from the merged dataset for the core, semi-periphery, and periphery (1996–2010).
Source: Lauth: *Datensatz „Kombinierter Index der Demokratie (KID), 1996–2012"*; Wahman / Teorell / Hadenius: Authoritarian Regime Types Revisited; Clark: World-System Position and Democracy.

leader can retain only limited resources for her own discretionary projects."[71] Joseph Wright points out that in countries with less personalist institutions, foreign aid can increase economic growth.[72] In another study, Wright shows that authoritarian rulers with large distributional coalitions are more likely to respond to aid by democratizing than rulers with small coalitions, because the former have a higher chance of remaining in power after fair elections.[73] We

71 Bruce Bueno de Mesquita / Alastair Smith: Foreign Aid and Policy Concessions. In: *Journal of Conflict Resolution* 51,2 (2007), pp. 251–284, here p. 280.

72 Joseph Wright: Aid Effectiveness and the Politics of Personalism. In: *Comparative Political Studies* 43,6 (2010), pp. 735–762.

73 Joseph Wright: How Foreign Aid Can Foster Democratization in Authoritarian Regimes. In: *American Journal of Political Science* 53,3 (2009), pp. 552–571.

want to test whether the different institutional designs in authoritarian regime types affect the amount of foreign aid flows received.

To measure foreign aid for peripheral and semi-peripheral countries, we use data from the World Bank for the period 1996 to 2010, which collects information on Official Development Assistance (ODA) flows. These net ODA flows

> [consist] of disbursements of loans made on concessional terms (net of repayments of principal) and grants by official agencies of the members of the Development Assistance Committee (DAC), by multilateral institutions, and by non-DAC countries to promote economic development and welfare in countries and territories in the DAC list of ODA recipients. It includes loans with a grant element of at least 25 percent (calculated at a rate of discount of 10 percent).[74]

These ODA flows have been adjusted using the GNI for each measurement point to improve the comparability between peripheral and semi-peripheral states by accounting for their different levels of economic development.

Table 5 shows that open electoral autocracies receive more foreign aid than monarchies, one-party systems, closed electoral autocracies, and deficient and functioning democracies.[75] It is clear that foreign aid flows differ between the institutional settings of the authoritarian regime types. The different amount of foreign aid flows to open and closed electoral autocracies again shows the value of making this distinction. It could be that, for donors, open electoral autocracies are more similar to democracies than any other autocratic regime type because of their institutional design and their more or less frequent elections.[76] In the case of open electoral autocracies – which, as already shown, have a higher chance of democratizing – it should also be easier for donor governments to justify their foreign aid donations to their voters.[77]

74 See World Bank: Net ODA received (% of GNI). http://data.worldbank.org/indicator/DT.ODA.ODAT.GN.ZS/countries (accessed 17.05.2014).

75 The ANOVA-test is significant (p = .000) between groups (sum of squares = 6273,447; df = 6; mean square = 1045,574; F = 8,096), but not within groups.

76 Peter Meyns: Demokratische Transition, hybride Regime und Wahlen in Afrika. Das Beispiel Sambia. In: Claudia Derichs / Thomas Heberer (eds): *Wahlsystem und Wahltypen. Politische Systeme und regionale Kontexte im Vergleich.* Wiesbaden: VS Verlag für Sozialwissenschaften 2006, pp. 278–301, here pp. 298–299.

77 But the role of foreign aid in democratization processes is quite disputed in the research literature. Bollen: World System Position, p. 476, fn. 13, who argues from a World-Systems Analysis-Perspective, says that foreign aid could be seen as a continuous dependency measure. The higher the amount of foreign aid a country receives, the greater the dependence on the interests of the donor(s). But in his empirical analysis, he doesn't find any evidence for that hypothesis.

(I) Regime Type CID with Wahman et al.	(J) Regime Type CID with Wahman et al.	Mean Difference ODA (I-J)	Std. Error
Closed Electoral Autocracy	Monarchy	4.30784	2.26918
	One-Party	2.90410	2.01814
	Military	-1.61666	1.66486
	Open Electoral Autocracy	**-4.83835*****	1.19744
	Deficient Democracy	1.13381	1.34460
	Functioning Democracy	3.43872	1.99854
Open Electoral Autocracy	**Monarchy**	**9.14618*****	2.21241
	One-Party	**7.74245*****	1.95410
	Military	3.22169	1.58662
	Closed Electoral Autocracy	**4.83835*****	1.19744
	Deficient Democracy	**5.97216*****	1.24641
	Functioning Democracy	**8.27707*****	1.93385

*, **, *** indicates significance at the 90 %, 95 %, and 99 % level, respectively.
Method: Tukey HSD
Source: Lauth: *Datensatz „Kombinierter Index der Demokratie (KID), 1996–2012“*; Wahman / Teorell / Hadenius: Authoritarian Regime Types Revisited; World Bank: *Net ODA Received.*

Table 5: Comparisons of electoral autocracies in terms of received foreign aid (ODA).

Clark et al. argue that foreign aid could potentially reduce the dependence of a state on its citizens because it is "reducing the incentive of the state to produce good economic performance, thereby making the life of the average citizen more miserable and making future donations of foreign aid more necessary." (Clark / Golder / Golder: *Principles of Comparative Politics*, p. 200.) So in the long run, it could be seen more problematic than not giving aid.
In the context of authoritarian regimes, where we can see less responsiveness of the political elites on the demands of their citizens, foreign aid could be working as a stabilizer of authoritarian rule in two ways: First, it could improve or at least stabilize the performance of the system and therefore increase or stabilize the legitimacy of the regime. This is in contrast to Lipsets Modernization Theory-argument that the chances of democratization rise if the country becomes wealthier. But the reality shows that countries can be rich and autocratic at the same time for a long period (e. g. China). See Seymour M. Lipset: Some Social Requisites of Democracy: Economic Development and Political Legitimacy. In: *American Political Science Review* 53,1 (1959), pp. 69–105. Second, getting aid by functioning democracies could help the ruling elites to justify their rule by showing their "good relations with democratic leaders" to their people. Clark et al. show that there are several empirical studies that prove that foreign aid towards authoritarian regimes could have negative effects on the welfare of the citizens in these countries and stabilizes the rule of those elites through corruption and exploitation; see Clark / Golder / Golder: *Principles of Comparative Politics*, p. 200; Deborah A. Bräutigam / Stephen Knack: Foreign Aid, Institutions, and Governance in Sub-Saharan Africa. In: *Economic Development and Cultural Change* 52 (2004), pp. 255–285; Simeon Djankov / Jose

Looking again at Table 5, we can see that only the money flows directed to military regimes collapse. These regimes don't receive significantly different levels of foreign aid than open electoral autocracies. Table 6 gives an overview of the military regimes in the periphery or semi-periphery which received ODA. We counted all the political systems that had been categorized as a military regime at least three times. The table shows that, of the top five receiving countries – which are all located in Sub-Saharan Africa – two countries had been counted as a military regime seven times in the period 1996 to 2010 (Rwanda, Uganda). The DR Congo[78], the Central African Republic, and Burundi also received a high amount of ODA, but they had each only been counted as military regimes three or four times. Also, while Algeria and Sudan were described as military regimes seven or eight times, they received much less ODA during that period.[79]

The reasons for this variation in the amount of ODA flows to military regimes are unclear. First, most of the military regimes are based in the periphery, and they also receive more foreign aid as percentage of their GNI than the four military regimes in the semi-periphery (Morocco, Syria, Nigeria and Algeria). One explanation could be that semi-peripheral military regimes have a higher socio-economic development level and thus receive less ODA as a percentage of their GNI. Second, we assume that the degree of political stability could be an indicator for the difference in aid flows, because all the top recipients saw different degrees of violence during 1996 to 2010. For example, the DR Congo "entered a long period of 'wars within wars'"[80] after the overthrow of Mobutu and the leadership of Laurent Kabila in 1996–1997, which included

G. Montalvo / Marta Reynal-Querol: Does Foreign Aid Help? In: *Cato Journal* 26,1 (2006), pp. 1–28; Simeon Djankov / Jose G. Montalvo / Marta Reynal-Querol: *The Curse of Aid*. Washington, DC: World Bank 2005. Kunihiko Imais findings can only partly show that there is a positive effect of foreign aid to democratization. He states that "the impact of closer ties with major powers upon democratization is limited by the conditions under which they are applied" (Kunihiko Imai: Internal versus External Requisites of Democracy. In: *International Journal on World Peace* 27,3 (2010), pp. 49–87, here p. 77).

78 In the CID Dataset the 'Democratic Republic of the Congo' (DR Congo) is named 'Congo (Kinshasa)', whereas the 'Republic of Congo' (Congo) is named 'Congo (Brazzaville)'. In this paper we use the labels 'DR Congo' and 'Congo'.

79 Probably, one would miss, for example, the case of Egypt in this table. In the dataset of Wahman et al., Egypt is being classified as a multiparty regime. We, therefore, used this classification, too. If we would change this classification, we have to look at the fit of all other countries, too.

80 Bertelsmann Stiftung: *BTI 2014 – Democratic Republic of the Congo Country Report*. Gütersloh: Bertelsmann Stiftung 2014, p. 4. http://www.bti-project.de/fileadmin/Inhalte/reports/2014/pdf/BTI%202014%20Congo%20DR.pdf (accessed 21.05.2014).

a regional war with Rwanda and Uganda, two other top ODA recipients and military regimes. Looking at the correlation between the amount of money and the degree of political stability, we can only see a slight trend that military regimes with a lower degree of political stability receive more foreign aid than more stable ones. So there have to be other causes for this variation, which should be looked at in future research.

Country	ODA (Mean) as % of GNI	MRs counted (1996–2010)	PS (Mean)	P/SP
DR Congo	23.9546	3	1.49	P
Rwanda	22.2469	7	3.49	P
Uganda	13.0090	7	3.55	P
Central African Republic	11.0414	4	2.92	P
Burundi	10.4044	3	1.59	P
Mauritania	9.9469	3	5.7	P
Togo	6.2892	5	5.60	P
Congo	6.2859	5	4.15	P
Sudan	3.5501	8	1.48	P
Fiji	1.8627	3	6.56	P
Syria	0.7137	6	5.43	SP
Algeria	0.4455	7	2.75	SP
Mean	*7.7049*	*3.86*	*4.08*	

Reading support: Nearly 24% of the GNI of the DR Congo consists of foreign aid.
Note: The amount of foreign aid and the mean of political stability are calculated based on the number of counted military regimes in each country during 1996 to 2010. MR = Military Regime; ODA = Official Development Assistance; PS = Political Stability; P=Periphery; SP= Semi-Periphery.
Source: Lauth: *Datensatz „Kombinierter Index der Demokratie (KID), 1996–2012"*; Wahman / Teorell / Hadenius: Authoritarian Regime Types Revisited; World Bank: *Net ODA Received.*

Table 6: Military regimes, foreign aid, and political stability, 1996–2010.

Conclusion

This paper presents several key findings. First, the CID is based on a theoretical approach which proves superior to the democracy measure used by Wahman et al.[81]. Therefore, the CID, combined with the authoritarian regime classifications by Wahman et al., produces more valid regime classifications. Second, the CID values can be used as a rough proxy for classifying electoral autocracies into closed and open ones. Third, we can show that open electoral autocracies are more likely to democratize than closed ones. Fourth, the flows of foreign aid from the center to the periphery are aligned to the different regime types, i. e. open electoral autocracies receive significantly more foreign aid than the other regime types. The only exceptions are military regimes, which also receive a high amount of foreign aid.

But our analysis also identifies several research gaps which should be investigated. Although it is fruitful to distinguish between open and closed electoral autocracies, the criteria for classifying those systems should be further elaborated, preventing them from becoming a residual category. This is an important task because electoral authoritarian regimes are the most dominant regime type in the semi-periphery and the periphery.

An additional task concerns the foreign aid flows to military regimes. What causes the highest levels of these aid flows, e. g. political stability, level of economic development, or their global placement in the three zones? Also, research should focus on the contribution of foreign aid to enhancing the democratization processes in open electoral autocracies. It would be useful here to look not only at the ODA, but also at foreign aid flows that are conditioned to special democracy assistance programs.[82]

81 Wahman / Teorell / Hadenius: Authoritarian Regime Types Revisited.

82 There is a database that differs between economic and democracy assistance, but it only includes the foreign aid flows of the US and only for the period 1970–2004. See Steven E. Finkel / Aníbal Pérez-Liñán / Mitchell A. Seligson / C. Neal Tate: Democracy Assistance Project. Phase II (2006–2007). http://www.pitt.edu/~politics/democracy/democracy.html (accessed 21.04.2014).

Appendix

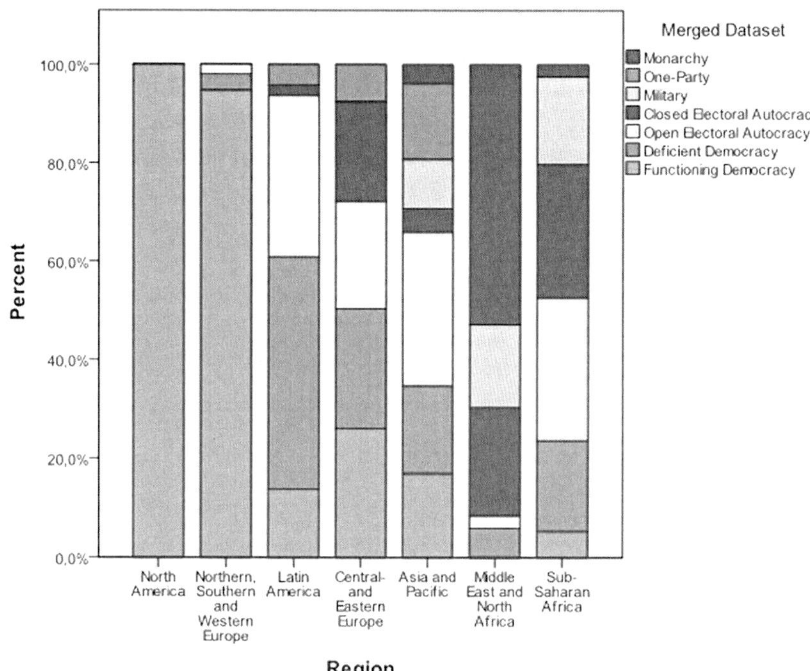

Fig. A1: Classification of countries from the merged dataset per region (1996–2010).
Source: Own presentation on the basis of Lauth: *Datensatz „Kombinierter Index der Demokratie (KID), 1996–2012"*; Wahman / Teorell / Hadenius: Authoritarian Regime Types Revisited.

Centers, Peripheries and Technical Progress

Evangelidis Vasileios

Prolonged Productive Continuities versus Militaristic Ruptures

A notorious controversy among historians refers to the issue of 'technological determinism' and the categories related to theoretical aspects of modernization. The ambivalence between instrumental, contextual and social approaches is obvious in these disputes.[1] A justified answer to these problems may be that the mediators of technology are not simply channeling technology, but neither are the users passive consumers. Societies resist and eventually incorporate the new into the old, and their citizens selectively modify and use technologies to create new cultures and new forms of modernization. There is an interactive social construction which modifies technologies and creates new forms of artificial life.

Technology has been defined as the 'tool-making' ability, which characterizes humans and intelligent apes.[2] Moreover: "When each process has been reduced to the use of some simple tool, the union of all these tools, actuated by one moving power, constitutes a machine".[3] From prehistoric times, technical skills were used mainly for collective work. But if agrarian and urban communities were the organizations facilitating the productive activities of their members, wars destroyed this cycle. Regardless of the differences in access to technology between peace and wartime, the latter was particularly rare in southeastern ancient populations, which were well-acquainted with Asiatic despotism,[4] rural and urban civil war.

In pre-capitalistic societies, the primal distinctive marks of the exercise of power were the division between *worker* and *warrior,* the significance of dispersed copper and tin ores and ingots, the importance of long distance trade

1 Keith Grint / Steve Woolgar: *The Machine at Work: Technology, Work and Organisation.* Cambridge: Polity 1997 (Chapter 1 – Theories of Technology, especially on social shaping and technological determinism); Ronald Kline: *Consumers in the Country, Technology and Social Change in Rural America.* Baltimore / London: John Hopkins UP 2000.

2 David E. Nye: *Technology Matters, Questions to Live With.* Cambridge, MA: The MIT Press 2006.

3 Charles Babbage: *On the Economy of Machinery and Manufactures.* Cambridge: Cambridge UP 2009 [first published 1832], p. 136.

4 John Milios: Asiatic Mode of Production. In: Phillip Anthony O'Hara (ed.): *Encyclopedia of Political Economy.* London: Routledge 1999, pp. 18–20.

and 'organized robbery', the introduction of taxes, rents and administrative systems for military victuals.[5]

Just as agrarian communities failed to innovate production, so state formation did not always merge commercial and military spirit. Critical improvements, such as the spoked wheel, chariots and wheelwrights, archery and bow-making, facilitated the barbarian conquests between 1800 and 1500 B.C. Chariot warrior élites formed aristocratic, slaveholding societies, which remained stable until the introduction of iron, around 1200 B.C. Not only iron weaponry but also iron plowshares, made the widespread diffusion of cheap metal applications a possibility.

The formation of markets, states, and cities such as Troy were critical frameworks for the interaction between technologies and communities. Crossroads and gateways, especially Dunhuang, were also important sites for connecting peripheries. Cities and countries between China and Syria were joined by the old Silk Roads.[6] Cultural, artistic and religious monuments, such as the *Diamond Sutra*,[7] verify this significant instrumentality:

> Dunhuang is only one of many Buddhist cave complexes along the Silk Road. Others of almost equal importance are the complexes at Bezeklik, northeast of the Taklamakan Desert, and Kizil in western Xinjiang. In 1906, the German explorer Albert von Le Coq removed many of the most important of Bezeklik and Kizil's murals, which he then deposited in Berlin. A significant number of them were destroyed in the bombings of World War II; the survivors are today in Berlin's Museum of Asian Art. Fragments of the murals also made their way to Japan, Korea, Russia, and the United States.[8]

The economic policies of the Song (960–1276), Yuan (1271–1368), and Ming (1368–1644) dynasties had influenced global trade, as shown by the historic travels of Zheng He (1371–1433), who voyaged around Africa and up to Portugal before Henry the Navigator's expeditions.[9]

Meanwhile, after the dissemination of stirrups, feudal reorganization was introduced in the West, with Charles Martel's new style of cavalry, in A.D. 732;

5 William H. McNeill: *The Pursuit of Power. Technology, Armed Force, and Society since A.D. 1000*. Chicago: Chicago UP 1982.

6 Alfred J. Andrea: The Silk Road in World History: A Review Essay. In: *Asian Review of World Histories* 2,1 (2014), pp. 105–127.

7 Frances Wood / Mark Barnard: *The Diamond Sutra: The Story of the World's Earliest Dated Printed Book*. London: British Library 2010.

8 Andrea: The Silk Road, p. 110.

9 Tansen Sen / Victor H. Mair: *Traditional China in Asian and World History*. Ann Arbor: Association for Asian Studies 2012; Paul Kennedy: *The Rise and Fall of the Great Powers: Economic Change and Military Conflict from 1500 to 2000*. New York: Random House 1987.

this occurred in the Byzantine East only after A.D. 900. In parallel, the rise of Islam, according to William H. McNeill,[10] proves the influential impetus of ideas, with their preference toward urban, mercantile, and bureaucratic principles rather than feudal ones.

Technological Invention and Slaveholding Centers

A prominent theme of the debates surrounding ancient history is the relationship between slavery and technological innovation. According to Benjamin Farrington,[11] the ancient Greek and Roman societies' lack of technological inventions was because slavery rendered cheap labor overabundant, and the philosophy of Plato and other Greek scholars focused on mathematics and astronomy rather than labor-saving technology.

This argument was rejected by Aage G. Drachmann,[12] who claimed that slavery cannot provide sufficient explanation for the technological delay until 1759, since unlike in antiquity slaves increased competition between large companies, especially in technological matters, with a wide range of applications and machinery production.

Drachmann argued that technology in antiquity (i.e. between 900 B.C. and 500 A.D.) had reached the stage of replacing slave labor with animal and water power. Simultaneously, technological applications were disseminated in the uses of fire; agriculture; taming domestic animals; building houses with wood, clay tiles and stones; spinning and weaving; the wheel; shipping; pottery; the extraction and processing of metals, especially iron; and writing.

In the peripatetic *Problemata Mechanica*, we read about the simple tools known in ancient times, i.e. the lever, pulley, balance, wedge, screw, and wheel and axle.[13] The development from the ancient to classic and modern culture was incredibly gradual, from the Pythagorean belief that things are numbers, to the corpuscular theories, the invention of the concept of energy, the contributions of Latin and Islamic Science, etc. There were frequent transfers between centers and peripheries:

> When, in the year 529, the last school of ancient philosophy in Athens was closed by the Emperor Justinian and Alexandria, at about the same time, lost its importance as a cultural

10 McNeill: *The Pursuit of Power.*

11 Benjamin Farrington: *Greek Science. Its Meaning for Us.* Nottingham: Spokesman 2000.

12 Aage G. Drachmann: *Große Griechische Erfinder.* Zürich: Artemis 1967.

13 Eduard J. Dijksterhuis: Die Mechanisierung des Weltbildes. In: *Physikalische Blätter* 11 (1956), pp. 481–494.

> centre, the ancient sources for the light of science became in fact extinguished, but this light itself by no means disappeared; it had already reached, long ago, other centres, which should emit it once again from the beginning.[14]

Byzantium, of course, became a center for centuries, while other centers such as Chartres, Antioch, Baghdad, Damascus, Cordova, Toledo and Salerno were also famous. An insightful, retrospective view of the power-antagonisms from antiquity and the Middle Ages until the eve of the modern industrial era is helpful to understand the historical roots of our topic, and the great transformation achieved.

From Archimedes' to Leonardo da Vinci's Peripheries

The argument that we want to support insists that the establishment of world centers – in other words, the systematic concentration of knowledge and power – was based on three main sources of scientific and technological advance: measurement, experiment and construction, more recently incorporated into global business systems.

Construction, in scientists such as Menelaus, was critical for the discovery and representation of the intuitive, synthetic and analytical methods leading to proof.[15] Heron and Philon's works are excellent examples of the constructivist transformation of space. Archimedes' experiments are certainly the most representative instances of this new innovative science. Measurement by construction, experiment and observation became exact only after Archimedes and Heron's approaches that facilitated a physical science fully justified, because it measured, for the first time, liquids, air and gases.[16]

However, these contributions required very broad exchanges between cultures. Babylon, Egypt, and Greece, at least in ancient times, were centers in the continuous quest for practical and theoretical discoveries. The benchmarks of this concentration of knowledge were mainly advances in mechanics, navigation, geography, astronomy, and geometry.

Colonization was an important factor of this creative movement. The communities' plans for survival, their trading activities, their wondering about the unknown were natural attitudes, always accompanying scientific practice.

14 Eduard J. Dijksterhuis: *Die Mechanisierung des Weltbildes.* Berlin / Heidelberg / New York: Springer 1983, p. 121.

15 Stephen W. Hawking: *On the Shoulders of Giants. The Great Works of Physics and Astronomy.* London: Penguin 2003.

16 Thomas Heath: *A History of Greek Mathematics.* Oxford: Clarendon 1921.

Confidence in the infinitude of space was increased by maritime commerce and colonization. Optimistic beliefs were related with various theoretical and empirical conceptions of space, for instance, with the early establishment of geometry and geography, as expressed in the worldviews of the Egyptians, during their practical achievements after the 18th dynasty.[17]

Further historical fields of argumentation emerged in antiquity, many concerning novel sciences and technologies, e. g. metallurgy, medicine, linguistics, numismatics etc., while the interaction between knowledge, production, centers, and peripheries was always dynamic.

Apart from the political and social circumstances, the aforementioned instrumental aspect of the scientific exploration of space is very important. The ancient scientists used various instruments, such as sundials, heavenly spheres, the diopter, the *astrolabon organon*, the parallactic instrument and the mural quadrant.

The conscience of this progress appears again, as *Homo Universalis* in Leonardo's mechanics and in Galileo's kinetics. At the same time, the founders of the Enlightenment movement supported a European and global international cooperation; for example, Gottfried Wilhelm Leibniz had correspondents ranging from London to Beijing.[18]

Capital Accumulation in the "Real Home of Capitalism"

After the so-called Dark Ages, during the fourteenth and fifteenth centuries, the development of mining and industry in Europe increased the demand for gold, silver, iron, copper, and other materials. From 1771, the Industrial Revolution, the age of steam and railways, the introduction of steel, electricity, and heavy engineering in England, USA, Germany, and so on, built a global market and a world system, which was further diversified in the age of oil, automobiles, and mass production.

Along with modernity, the foundation of public electric and telecommunications utilities, the introduction of new technology and machinery, accelerated the division of labor as never before, while formulating internal markets and promoting commercialization. Industrialization appeared as a revolutionary force, with the introduction of electricity, the internal combustion engine, pumps, roller mills, cement, steel constructions, transportation, land reclamation, chemical industry, etc. Thus, technology radically transformed

17 John Chang'ach: *History of Science. Students' Handbook*. Saarbrücken: Lambert 2012.

18 Reinhard Finster / Gerd van der Heuvel: *Gottfried Wilhelm Leibniz*. Reinbek: Rowohlt 1990.

community life, by repeatedly introducing and transferring multifaceted innovations.

Competition, interaction, peripherization, subsidiarity, decentralization, border regions, financialization, "disengagement from and integration into the world market" are characteristic aspects of the modern age.[19] In parallel, imperialism had been a continuous process from antiquity up to the industrial epoch, although decolonization processes were accelerated after 1945.[20]

Around 1880, Ethiopia, Liberia, Japan, China, and Thailand were the only sovereign states in Asia and Africa, while Japan was also imperialistic. Uprisings for territorial liberation were widely disseminated with increasing frequency, from Cuba, to West and East Africa, up to The Philippines.

From this perspective, Africa, Asia, Latin America, Russia, and the Middle East may constitute significant case studies of center-periphery historical and geopolitical issues, in correlation with the maritime exchanges, the agrarian nexus to mechanization and industrialization (e.g. mechanical engineering), the transformation in energy production, and the presumed transition from closed or semi-closed economies to the shaping of an international global market.

The relevant historical explanations must analyze the framework of the transition from city-centered economies to the emergence of neo-colonialism, i.e. the interstate competition for mobile capital; because the global sequence of leading capitalist states consists of units of increasing size, resources, and global power.[21]

Non Complementary Development in the Peripheries

The specific difference between center and periphery is expressed as a contradiction between capital-intensive production in highly industrialized countries and labor-intensive production in the periphery; in terms of redistribution between center and periphery, the developed countries import raw materials and cheap labor, acquire profits from direct capital investments, gain the periphery's markets for exports, etc.[22] This uneven redistribution and

19 Martin Heintel: *Einmal Peripherie – immer Peripherie? Szenarien regionaler Entwicklung anhand ausgewählter Fallbeispiele. Abhandlungen zur Geographie und Regionalforschung*, vol. 5. Wien: Institut für Geographie der Universität 1998.

20 Michael Collins: Decolonisation and the 'Federal Moment'. In: *Diplomacy & Statecraft* 24,1 (2013), pp. 21–40.

21 Max Weber: *General Economic History*. New York: Collier 1961.

22 Immanuel Wallerstein: *The Modern World System II: Mercantilism and the Consolidation of the European World-Economy, 1600–1750*. New York: Academic Press 1980.

inequality is caused by the demand for endless accumulation of capital, which requires high profits through monopolized commodity chains.[23]

When a region supports "free trade and freedom of movement for the labor force and enterprises"[24] and distributes a high per capita income, it is called an industrial core region. However, the core regions were developed only when "direct producers were losing their direct access to the means of subsistence and therefore becoming dependent upon markets for their access to subsistence goods".[25]

Therefore, the analysis of internal markets should not presuppose the peasantry's unwillingness to trade, but look to the other side, stressing the inherent tendency of commercial capital to move abroad, to prefer liquidity and financial expansion.[26] For instance, the role of London and Manhattan maritime companies is crucial today, as their leaders – most of them Greek shipping owners – are among the most mature in the global naval sector.

Rising shifts in global trade are compatible with capital-intensive production in highly industrialized countries and with labor-intensive production in peripheral countries. The center obtains access to a large quantity of minerals, e.g. African gold,[27] skilled professional labor through migration etc., facilitating its own technological superiority. From the other side, the periphery has no choice but to increase imports from developed countries, but not from other periphery countries, because dependent industrial enterprises are not complementary to each other. The same is true for agriculture. Almost all other productive sectors, apart from international trading, remain non-complementary in peripheries.

In developing countries, the so-called capitalist globalization has not surpassed the fragmented industrialization, causing a growing trend for vital industrial imports (raw industrial materials; intermediate products; mechanical equipment; industrial consumer products, etc.) as a result of urbanization.

23 Terence K. Hopkins / Immanuel Wallerstein (eds): *The Age of Transition.* London: Zed Books 1996.

24 Konrad Lammers: *Die Osterweiterung aus raumwirtschaftlicher Perspektive. Prognosen regionalökonomischer Theorien und Erfahrungen aus der bisherigen Integration in Europa* (= HWWA Discussion Paper 195). Hamburg: Hamburgisches Weltwirtschaftsarchiv 2002, p. 3.

25 Michael Andrew Žmolek: *Rethinking the Industrial Revolution. Five Centuries of Transition from Agrarian to Industrial Capitalism in England.* Leiden: Brill 2013, p. 3.

26 Giovanni Arrighi: *The Long Twentieth Century. Money, Power, and the Origins of Our Times.* London / New York: Verso 1994, p. 14.

27 Marian Malowist: Quelques observations sur le commerce de l'or dans le Soudan occidental au moyen âge. In: *Annales. Économies, Sociétés, Civilisations* 25,6 (1970), pp. 1630–1636.

The following is an example of the non-complementarity of the periphery's industrial infrastructure. During the second half of the 20th century, Greek industrial production included some basic metal industries: mainly aluminum, ferronickel, to some extent, and steel. However, the entirety of this nickel production and 85% of the aluminum was exported. The aluminum industries which were settled in Greece only processed the bauxite for the first two stages. The aluminum was then exported abroad, e.g. to France, for further processing.

This happens because, in the context of globalization, the penetration of capital is based on the comparative advantages of each country, and does not take into account the needs of the country hosting the investments. The forms of control employed by capital include direct equity participation, assigning labels and similar agreements, and subcontracting, e.g. clothing, footwear, and textiles. For instance, multinational firms outsource clothing production to periphery countries with low wages for the final stages of processing, which are labor-intensive. Thus, in 1983, 43% of total Greek exports in clothing and shoes were subcontracted products. Immigrant laborers from Asia, Middle East, Africa, and the Balkans worked in these jobs. At the same time, "unpaid subsistence and domestic work, underpaid work in informal and precarious conditions, shadow work, slave- and other forced labor" coexisted.[28]

However, throughout the period 1950–1980, this export orientation and increasing imports led the Greek economy to face international competition. The result was that capital-intensive techniques (investment in buildings, structures, and machines) ultimately prevailed, and employment growth was curbed.[29]

Global powers are economically diversified, highly industrialized, specialized in information, finance and high-technology, possess considerable military power, and so on. That is to say, the core countries dominate in the fields of production, trade and finance. Under these criteria, Greece, Africa, or the Middle East cannot be considered as belonging to the center. What is more, the periphery countries lack diversified social-political organization, while the

28 Andrea Komlosy: Arbeit und Werttransfer im Kapitalismus. Vielfalt der Erscheinungsformen und Operationalisierung. In: *Sozial.Geschichte Online* 9 (2012), pp. 36–62.

29 Sofia Antonopoulou: *The After War Economy and the Housing Phenomenon* (Special Lessons of City Planning I, 7th Semester). Department of Architecture Engineering, Sector: City and Social Practices. Athens: National Technical University 1989.

leading capitalist states develop "political structures endowed with ever-more extensive and complex organizational capabilities".[30]

Maritime Trade and Global Repositioning

Additional starting points of research might include the related problems of technology transfer and global transition e.g. from sail to steamships, gas, railway, electricity, oil, automobiles, informatics, and biotechnology. Until recently, the main feature of Greece and its broader region was investments in transportation and steamships (during the second half of the 19th century) and particularly seagoing ships (in the second half of the 20th century). Since 1950, the transport and communications sector has seen a remarkable increase in overall investment activity, both public and private, soaring from 2.62 billion drachmas in 1958 to 22.97 billion drachmas in 1974. The transport and communications sector saw larger public than private gross investments only because seagoing ships were not included in the data.[31]

With regards the proportion of shipping in private investments, we must consider the upgrading of the role of the Greek entrepreneurs in Anglo-American commercial antagonism, rising from being region-dependent (e.g. Greek communities in Egypt) to the status of asset teammate (e.g. Greek ship-owners). This was the result of: i) the high technological advances that accelerated the internationalization of markets; b) the war reparations that reached to 500% of the value of the entire commercial fleet; and c) the 100 Liberty ships endowed by the U.S. to Greek ship-owners in 1947. These Liberties tripled the capacity of the fleet. Thus, the ship-owner Laimos[32] argued that the value of the ships in the Greek commercial navy was $5.5 billion in 1967, while the country's national wealth without shipping amounted to $10.5 billion.[33] Clearly, in this particular place and time, territorialism was not a factor:

> In the territorialist strategy control over territory and population is the objective, and control over mobile capital the means, of state- and war-making. In the capitalist strategy, the relationship between ends and means is turned upside down: control over mobile capital is the objective, and control over territory and population the means.[34]

30 Arrighi: *The Long Twentieth Century*, p. 15.

31 Hellenic Republic: *National Accounts of Greece, 1958–1975*. Athens: Ministry of Coordination, General Administration of National Accounts 1976, Table 17.

32 Andreas Laimos: *The Navy of the Greek Nation*, 2 vol. Athens: Tsikopoulos 1969.

33 Nikos Psyroukis: *History of Modern Greece*. Athens: Epikairotita 1975.

34 Arrighi: *The Long Twentieth Century*, p. 35.

But the fact remains that neither global cities nor territorial self-maintenance offer a sufficient strategy against monocentric misdistribution, as seen in the enormous differences in profits and GDP.[35]

Hegemony or Polycentrism?

During the second half of the 20th century, the transatlantic contribution to European economic and scientific development was similar and decisive in many countries, by promoting and monitoring international advancements in science and technology,[36] while posing critical questions about hegemony, e.g. the Rockefeller Foundation.[37]

The corresponding challenge today, however, is the redefinition of intellectual and moral leadership[38]: international cooperation in the fields of information technology and communications, eased by unlimited and free bandwidth, processing, speech technology, videoconferencing etc.[39]

Regardless of the disputes over historicists' arguments, it is clear that innovative transformations are possible only at the level of global cooperation, which emerged after the birth and expansion of global trade.[40] However, this transition cannot be fruitful without substantial progress in democratic and economic reforms, rather than categorizing entire regions and productive sectors as 'problematic'.

Therefore, such a repositioning should be both regionally and globally questioned, without exceptions e.g. placements in shipping, which comprise 80% of global transportation, benefited from the internationalization of markets, rather than the development of local economies. The reformers should stress the common experiences, repeated in various times and places, such as the

35 Christine Schmid / Christine Unrau: Territoriale Zentren und Peripherien. In: Dorothee Koch / Arbeitsgruppe "Zentrum und Peripherie in soziologischen Differenzierungstheorien" (eds): *Mythos Mitte. Wirkmächtigkeit, Potenzial und Grenzen der Unterscheidung 'Zentrum/Peripherie'.* Wiesbaden: VS 2011.

36 Henry Gilman: Some General Observations Related to Organometallic Chemistry in the U.S.S.R.. In: *Transactions of the New York Academy of Sciences* 26,5 (1962), pp. 585–589.

37 Jean-Paul Gaudillière: The U.S. in the Rebuilding of European Science. In: *Science* 317 (2007), pp. 1173–1174.

38 Stephen Gill (ed.): *Gramsci, Historical Materialism and International Relations.* Cambridge: Cambridge UP 1993.

39 Robert Lucky: The Quickening of Science Communication. In: *Science* 289 (2000), pp. 259–264.

40 Lincoln P. Paine: Maritime History. In: *Berkshire Encyclopedia of World History*, vol. 3, ed. by W. H. McNeill et al. Massachusetts: Great Barrington 2005, pp. 1188–1195.

historical examples of printing, the cotton industry, the rotary kiln, 'railroadization', and electrification, which managed to unify scattered populations and bridge gaps in development.

The solution to the current threat of unequal development, visible from Greece to Africa, the Middle East, Russia, and Asia, is possible only through an "integration to the extent of combining mining, rail-roads, docks, and fleets," with an information revolution and international, transatlantic cooperation.[41]

41 Joseph A. Schumpeter: *Business Cycles. A Theoretical, Historical and Statistical Analysis of the Capitalist Process*. New York: McGraw-Hill 1939.

Self-Transcendence in Thomas Merton, Reza Arasteh, and Daisetz Suzuki

Jeffrey M. Shaw

Throughout history, religious and philosophical thinkers have often focused on identifying the "true self." Whether through philosophical speculation, religious devotion, or mysticism and contemplation, various traditions have emerged which have sought to achieve a type of "self-transcendence" which can either allow for a closer union with the creator, or for a more complete understanding of one's true nature. This desire is not unique to only one culture, as it has appeared in one form or another across cultures. Three twentieth-century figures who have sought to evaluate the importance of self-transcendence are the American Catholic monk Thomas Merton, the Iranian psychoanalyst A. Reza Arasteh, and the Japanese Buddhist monk Daisetz T. Suzuki. Their thinking on the subject often overlaps, and they represent a unique convergence of thought which crosses cultural boundaries and has had a lasting impact on contemporary thinking in the realm of contemplative thought. In addition, examining the interaction between Merton and Arasteh on the one hand, and Merton and Suzuki on the other, offers an interesting approach to the study of cross-cultural dialogue in the humanities. Merton, a Westerner, borrows from and synthesizes the ideas of two thinkers from the East, and in doing so he contributed immeasurably to interfaith and cross-cultural dialogue. This article examines Thomas Merton primarily as a Western thinker who benefited from his reading of both Arasteh and Suzuki. The concept of self-transcendence and some background on its importance will be followed by a brief sketch of Merton and the value that he placed in his correspondence with both Arasteh and Suzuki. Following the section on Merton, a similar section on Arasteh and then one on Suzuki will round out the discussion, with the focus being specifically on Merton's engagement with their ideas.

Self-Transcendence

The idea that one must transcend the common conception of "self" is inherent in numerous religious traditions. Thomas Merton, Reza Arasteh, and D.T. Suzuki all acknowledged this fundamental idea. The self is often associated with worldly, immanent concerns, while transcending the ordinary conception of the self can lead to a state of mind and of awareness that is a central concept in most mystical and contemplative traditions. Christianity has seen an element of self-transcendence as an integral concept in the thinking of St. John of the Cross and Theresa of Avila. While self-transcendence is not necessarily a central tenet of Christian doctrine or dogma, it figures prominently in certain areas of Christian thought. In the Islamic faith, it is primarily within the Sufi tradition that self-transcendence is stressed as a fundamental tenet. And within Buddhism, the Zen tradition adheres most strongly to a position of self-transcendence as prerequisite for attaining enlightenment.

Thomas Merton elaborated upon the idea of self-transcendence in much of his work. As a contemplative Trappist monk, he was a firm believer in the notion that true communion with God was to be found only once the false self was overcome. In *New Seeds of Contemplation*, his one work that can be considered a systematic treatment of theology, he stated that "the true inner self must be drawn up like a jewel from the bottom of the sea, rescued from confusion, from in-distinction, from immersion in the common, the nondescript, the trivial, the evanescent."[1] Further elaborating on this idea, he stated, "the creative and mysterious inner self must be delivered from the wasteful, hedonistic and destructive ego that seeks only to cover itself with disguises."[2] However, the notion of self-transcendence runs much deeper than merely escaping the trappings of contemporary society. For Merton, the very understanding of who we are as human beings created in God's image rests on discovering the true self. He wrote, "To say I was born in sin is to say I came into the world with a false self. I was born in a mask [...] thus I came into existence and non-existence at the same time because from the very start I was something that I am not."[3] He also stated that, "to be 'lost' is to be left to the arbitrariness and pretenses of the contingent ego, the smoke-self that must inevitably vanish. To be 'saved' is to return to one's inviolate and eternal reality and to live in God."[4] Clearly for Merton, transcending the ordinary self was a key aspect of his theological worldview.

Ironically, it is through dialogue that the concept of "self" emerges. In his dialogue with Arasteh and Suzuki, Merton is able to identify an element of "selfness," and at the same time identify some of the means to transcend it.

1 Thomas Merton: *New Seeds of Contemplation*. New York: New Directions 1961, p. 38.

2 Ibid.

3 Ibid., pp. 33–34.

4 Ibid., p. 38.

It is in fact one of the more interesting aspects of Thomas Merton's life that "he has no sooner achieved his hard-won sense of self than he is willing to abandon it."[5] A look at Thomas Merton's life and work will indicate that he sought out those thinkers with whom he shared an affinity for the most penetrating and sophisticated thoughts on the idea of self-transcendence. Among these thinkers were Reza Arasteh and Daisetz T. Suzuki.

Thomas Merton

> I am myself of course living the monastic life, and also very much interested in contemplative disciplines of other than Christian traditions, especially Zen and Sufism.[6]

One of the prevailing themes in Merton's works is the struggle for self-transcendence through continual self-transformation. His is a quest for the true self, for the "person" as opposed to the mere "individual," and this quest is simultaneously a quest for ultimate reality.[7] Along the way, Merton's correspondence with Arasteh and Suzuki would help him clarify his own thinking on this topic which inspired so much of his thought and his writing. He was born in Prades (France) on January 31, 1915, and of his birth, he later wrote "I came into the world [...] Free by nature, in the image of God; I was nevertheless the prisoner of my own violence and my own selfishness, in the image of the world into which I was born."[8] He believed that from the beginning of his life, he was free, yet the world conspired to prevent him from realizing his freedom, or in other words, from identifying the true nature of his own humanity. He would spend his life searching for a way to find it – in a sense, searching for a way to discover his true self. It is not possible in this short paper to elaborate on Merton's fascinating life story, which he recounts in his autobiography *The Seven Storey Mountain.* His extensive journals have also been posthumously published. However, one facet of his quest for understanding the human condition involved his thinking on the matter of self-transcendence. This topic is our concern, and the manner in which Merton examined

5 John S. Porter: Thomas Merton's Late Metaphors of the Self. In: *Merton Annual* 7 (1994), pp. 58–67, here p. 59.

6 Thomas Merton: Letter to Linda (Parsons) Sabbath, April 25, 1965. In: Thomas Merton: *The Hidden Ground of Love. Letters*, ed. by William Shannon. New York: Farrar, Strauss and Giroux 1985, pp. 516–533, here p. 517.

7 Joseph Quinn Raab: *Openness and Fidelity: Thomas Merton's Dialogue with D. T. Suzuki, and Self-Transcendence.* PhD, University of Saint Michael's College, Toronto 2000, p. 52.

8 Thomas Merton: The *Seven Storey Mountain.* New York: Harcourt, Brace & Co. 1948, p. 3.

this important concept, and the correspondence that he shared with Reza Arasteh and D.T. Suzuki is the focus of this paper.

Thomas Merton referred to the "false self" as opposed to the "true self." He wrote, "The word of God calls man back out of this delusion to his true self."[9] He also referred to his own past and considered the false self as the entity that was born into the world upon his birth. Merton indicated in this passage that he was born free, yet a false self-imprisoned him even at an early age. In order to transcend the false self, Merton's entrance into the monastery can be seen as "a kind of instinctual flinch at the culture of modernity, a life-preserving, involuntary recoil from civilization"[10]. The monastery was where Merton would seek to cast away his false self. On December 10, 1941, Thomas Merton entered the Gethsemani monastery in Kentucky and became a cloistered monk, while ironically also becoming one of the most celebrated literary figures in America during the mid-twentieth century. While Merton had written a few literary pieces prior to entering the monastery, he would not achieve any fame or recognition until after taking his vow of silence. However, even before his days as a monk, Merton was a voracious reader. Merton's close friend Ed Rice recounts that Merton's reading of Aldous Huxley's *Ends and Means* (1937) led him to delve deeper into mysticism and into Zen Buddhism in particular.[11] Rice also attributes two main themes to Merton's later life; the first being peace, whether through an adherence to non-violence or racial justice, and the second being the pursuit of the interior life through contemplation.[12] This interior life was the holy grail of Merton's thinking on self-transcendence. Identifying and coming to terms with the true self that could only be discovered through contemplative thought occupied much of Merton's writing and of his correspondence as well.

Merton would also read Aldous Huxley's *The Perennial Philosophy* (1944), an anthology of the salient ideas that feature in all of the world's major religions. However, it would be "D.T. Suzuki who stimulated Merton's deep interest in Zen Buddhism."[13] Following the *way* of Zen Buddhism, Merton stressed that Western adherents to Buddhism, such as himself, were seeking an antidote

9 Thomas Merton: *Mystics and Zen Masters*. New York: Noonday 1961, p. 272.

10 Robert Inchausti: *Thomas Merton's American Prophecy*. New York: State University of New York Press 1998, p. 41.

11 Edward Rice: *The Man in the Sycamore Tree*. New York: Doubleday / Image 1972, p. 13.

12 Ibid., p. 12.

13 Bonnie Bowman Thurston: Unfolding of a New World: Thomas Merton & Buddhism. In: Id. (ed.): *Merton and Buddhism*. Louisville, KY: Fons Vitae 2007, pp. 15–30, p. 17.

to the "widespread dissatisfaction with the spiritual sterility of mass society, dominated by technology and propaganda, in which there is no room left for personal spontaneity."[14] In following this path, Merton uncovered deep-seated truths about himself, and about the nature of the "true self" writ large. In a visit to Sri Lanka in 1968 – a visit which is chronicled in numerous books by and about Merton, and a visit which also took place only weeks before his untimely death in Bangkok on December 10, 1968, Merton visited the great Buddha statue at Polonnaruwa. He recorded:

> Looking at these figures I was suddenly, almost forcibly, jerked clean out of the habitual, half-tied vision of things, and an inner clearness, clarity, as if exploding from the rocks themselves, became evident and obvious.[15]

The great statues at Polonnaruwa had led to Merton's transcendent experience; an example of his willingness to consider the value and meaning of ideas and symbols from faith traditions other than his own. This experience was consistent with the journey upon which he had begun after entering the monastery, about which he stated:

> what I abandoned when I "left the world" and entered the monastery was the understanding of myself that I had developed in the context of civil society—my identification with what appeared to me to be its aims. Certainly, in the concrete, "the world" did not mean for me either riches (I was poor) or a life of luxury [...] But it did mean a set of servitudes that I could no longer accept. [...] Many of these were trivial, some of them were erroneous, all are closely related [...] The image of a society that is happy because it drinks Coca-Cola, or Seagram's, or both and is protected by the bomb. The society that is imaged in the mass media and in advertising, in the movies, in TV [...] in all the pompous and trifling masks with which it hides callousness, sensuality, hypocrisy, cruelty, and fear.[16]

Part of the act of self-transcendence involved putting behind those things that contemporary society deemed important, which for Merton were merely distractions that were placed in front of those who sought greater freedom to explore the inner realms of contemplative thought.[17]

Demonstrating that one must make a distinction between the self that we present to others and the true self, Merton stated:

14 Rice: *The Man in the Sycamore Tree*, p. 13.

15 Naomi Burton (ed.): *The Asian Journal of Thomas Merton*. New York: New Directions 1973, p. 233.

16 Thomas Merton: *Conjectures of a Guilty Bystander*. Garden City, NY: Doubleday 1966, p. 41.

17 For more on this idea, see Jeffrey M. Shaw: *Thomas Merton and Jacques Ellul on Technology and the Human Condition*. Eugene, OR: Wipf and Stock 2014.

> We must be saved from immersion in the sea of lies and passions which is called "the world." And we must be saved above all from that abyss of confusion and absurdity which is our own worldly self. The person must be rescued from the individual.[18]

Having set out to discover some elements of Asian religion that might be compatible with Christian contemplation and meditation, Merton had found himself before the great statue of a reclining Buddha. His comments at this time reflect a degree of understanding and relief in having finally come face-to-face with the reality of the true nature of the self. His initial introduction to Zen Buddhism through D.T. Suzuki's writing had come full circle, as had, ironically, his very productive life. He further elaborated upon his observation of the statue:

> I don't know when in my life I have ever had such a sense of beauty and spiritual validity running together in one aesthetic illumination. Surely, with […] Polonnaruwa my Asian pilgrimage has come clear and purified itself. I mean, I know I have seen what I was obscurely looking for. I don't know what else remains but I have now seen and have pierced through the surface and have got beyond the shadow and the disguise.[19]

No matter how impressed he was by the statues of the Buddha in Sri Lanka, Merton was not seeking to explain his opinions about the statues to interested readers or to present some well-thought-out description of the statues. It was genuine experience which he sought, and "for all of Merton's intellectual acumen, it is abundantly clear from everything he wrote prior to and during his Asian journey that he had come to that continent to learn from the *experience* of those who, like himself, were dedicated pilgrims on the contemplative path."[20] Merton did not rely on intellectual formulations, on any kind of doctrine or on dogma in order to uncover the true nature of the self. Instead, he turned to mystical contemplation and the insights offered by direct, lived experience. He was always more concerned with experience rather than knowledge. He was not conscious of any particular idea or thing, but rather was conscious of consciousness itself. He believed that "for the West, consciousness is always 'consciousness *of*.' In the East, this is not necessarily so: it can be simply 'consciousness.'"[21] Merton's reading of both Arasteh and Suzuki would help clarify his own thinking on the nature of consciousness.

18 Merton: *New Seeds of Contemplation*, p. 38.

19 Burton (ed.): *The Asian Journal of Thomas Merton*, p. 236.

20 James Wiseman: Thomas Merton and Theravada Buddhism. In: Bowman Thurston (ed.): *Thomas Merton and Buddhism*, pp. 31–50, here p. 35.

21 Merton: *Mystics and Zen Masters*, p. 238.

Describing Zen Buddhism in *Mystics and Zen Masters*, Merton wrote,

> The practice of Zen aims at the deepening, purification, and transformation of the consciousness. But it does not rest satisfied with any 'deepening' or a superficial 'purification.' It seeks the most radical transformation: it works on depths that would seem to go beyond even depth psychology. It has, in other words, a metaphysical and spiritual dimension.[22]

Merton understood the fundamental tenets of Buddhist thought, and had corresponded with Suzuki and Arasteh on topics such as self-transcendence and the true meaning of reality. His engagement with both and other intellectuals, "widely broaden[ed] his conception of a spiritual integrity, seeing now a complementarity between psychological, spiritual integrity and a Christian notion of supernatural holiness in union with God in Christ."[23] Merton explained that pride and desire centers around the false self, and that "God Himself works to purify us of this inner 'self' that tends to resist Him and to assert itself against Him."[24] Merton identified many of the great intellectual traditions as means that one can employ in order to rise above the false self:

> The great question, not only for Marxism, but for liberal democracy, for Christianity, and for Zen, is how, in practice, such freedom can be the possession of any but the rare few who have undergone the trouble, discipline, and sacrifice necessary to attain it."[25]

These "rare few" are those who have turned away from the false self. One should not conclude that Merton ever succeeded in transcending his own "false self," even insofar as he emphasized the importance of doing so. While the rare few have achieved some degree of self-transcendence, even those who realize the necessity to grapple with this difficult task could be considered part of the rare few as well.

Merton, though a cloistered monk, occasionally chafed at the stultifying conditions under which he and his fellow monks found themselves. He was not convinced that the cenobitic tradition was the one true path to self-transcendence and to union with God. He wrote that he and his fellow monks were living in a system which "urges us to go forward and forbids us to move."[26] He also added that, "Sometimes it may be very useful to discover new and

22 Ibid.

23 Raab: *Openness and Fidelity*, p. 44.

24 Merton: *The Hidden Ground of Love*, p. 53.

25 Merton: *Mystics and Zen Masters*, p. 283.

26 Thomas Merton: *Contemplation in a World of Action*. New York: Image 1973, p. 219.

unfamiliar ways in which the human task of maturation and self-discovery is defined. The book of a Persian psychoanalyst, Dr. Reza Arasteh, who practices and teaches in America, might prove very valuable on this subject."[27] Merton's dialogue with Arasteh was an important element in his own understanding of some of the ways in which one can begin to transcend the false self and discover the hidden truth of one's own existence.

Reza Arasteh

Merton wrote to Reza Arasteh frequently in the mid-1960s. On December 27, 1965, he wrote, "I am interested in your book [*Final Integration in the Adult Personality*], which I am sure will fill a great need in this country."[28] Reza Arasteh was born in Shiraz (Iran) in September 1927. He earned his bachelor's and master's degrees there, and a doctorate from Louisiana State University in 1953. He wrote *Final Integration* in 1965, although he was somewhat disappointed with the final version, claiming that it did not go far enough in reconciling psychoanalysis and spirituality. He stated, "Despite the book's value in introducing new notions or reinterpreting old ones and bringing together common features of the self in transformation, it fails in its avowed aim to fill the gap between psychoanalytic writings, and the great variety of spiritual, philosophical and literary endeavors."[29] However, Merton found Arasteh's book to be an important addition to his thinking on self-transcendence, and noted that "this excellent and suggestive study which establishes that the full integration of the human personality is to be found not merely in 'sublimation' and adjustment to society, but at the end of an arduous and sacrificial path of spiritual seeking."[30] Much of what Merton had observed regarding an individual's relationship to society was reflected in *Final Integration.* "The act of separation from culture, coupled with anxiety, produces a sort of shedding of the old self in order to make way for a new reality."[31] Clearly, Reza Arasteh's writing influenced Merton as he formulated his views on the meaning of the true self.

27 Merton: *Contemplation in a World of Action*, p. 222.

28 Merton: *The Hidden Ground of Love*, p. 41.

29 Reza Arasteh: *Final Integration*. Leiden: Brill 1965, p. 31.

30 Patricia A. Burton: Final Integration of a Bibliographic Puzzle. In: *The Merton Seasonal* 35 (2010), pp. 30–36, here p. 30.

31 Joshua L. Knabb / Robert K. Welch: Reconsidering A. Reza Arasteh: Sufism and Psychotherapy. In: *The Journal of Transpersonal Psychology* 41 (2009), pp. 44–60, here p. 55.

Arasteh, like Merton, read widely and incorporated a number of different metaphysical views into his work. He observed that

> in Eastern thought the problem of final integration in adult personality is symbolized by Buddha; in the West by Socrates. The collective voice of society, however, ignored for a long time Socrates' dictims [sic]: 'know thyself' and 'life which is not re-examined is not worth living.' These concepts did not gain prominence until the Renaissance, an age of greater awareness which required a new sense of identity and a greater transcendental self.[32]

The years in which Arasteh wrote *Final Integration* correspond with the years in which Merton was formulating his mature worldview, and coming to a greater awareness of the transcendental self and the relationship between the individual and society. Arasteh's book opened new avenues of inquiry for Merton, and helped him to integrate various ideas into a coherent whole. For example, he observed that "in Sufism and Zen the spiritual master is as essential as the analyst in psychoanalysis."[33] Merton also observed that Arasteh's observations of Western psychoanalysis leveled a harsh indictment of the practice, noting that "psychoanalysis has become a technique for making people conform to a society that prevents them from growing and developing as they should."[34] Although by no means a psychoanalyst himself, Merton went on to note that "one of the points made by Dr. Arasteh's book [is] the importance of existential anxiety seen not as a symptom of something wrong, but as a summons to growth and painful development."[35] Like Merton, Arasteh was critical of certain facets of Western society. For example, he criticized the Western idea that when an individual has successfully passed through adolescence he emerges as a fully mature person, proposing instead that "man's final task is to *transcend* his social self and his cultural 'filters' and to become 'a universal self.'"[36] This idea aligns perfectly with Merton's proposal that one must transcend the false self in order to become a fully human person. Citing a list of faith traditions, Arasteh's ideas on final integration and self-transcendence were described as "the high mystical experience of the world's religions [...] known as 'no-knowledge' in Taoism, enlightenment or 'satori' in Zen

32 Arasteh: *Final Integration*, p. 85.

33 Merton: *Contemplation in a World of Action*, p. 221.

34 Ibid., p. 222.

35 Ibid., p. 223.

36 Joseph Havens: Review of Final Integration. In: *Journal for the Scientific Study of Religion* 6 (1967), pp. 300–304, here p. 301.

Buddhism, 'individuality in non-individuality' in Islamic Sufism."[37] By integrating Arasteh's general premise that final integration can lead to a renewed sense of self, and an overthrow of the false self, Merton had tapped into a deep ecumenical tradition.

One of the reasons that Merton was attracted to *Final* Integration was "because it aimed not merely at adjustment to prevailing social norms but at an inner transformation of consciousness, a psychological and spiritual 'rebirth' that is also the ultimate goal of authentic monasticism."[38] Merton's appreciation for a cross-cultural approach to the idea of self-transcendence can be seen in his statement that "the state of insight which is final integration implies an openness, an 'emptiness,' a 'poverty' similar to those described in such detail not only by the Rhenish mystics, by St. John of the Cross, by the early Franciscans, but also by the Sufis, the early Taoist masters, and Zen Buddhists."[39] Alluding to Western philosophy throughout *Final Integration,* Arasteh noted that Plato, in "*Phaedrus* and *The Republic* [...] compares the two lower levels of the soul with two wild horses which can be handled by the rational soul."[40] Likewise, the Buddhist "Ox Herding Parable" uses a similar analogy, an analogy which had also been applied to Merton, of whom "one can say that he was both a Christian monk and a Zen man. Anyone familiar with his fascinating life can see in it a fine example of how the inner 'Boy' and the 'Ox' merged within him"[41]. This interesting application of the metaphor of a wild animal to the false self was noted by Arasteh, is prevalent in Buddhism, and has been applied to Merton.

Thomas Merton wrote extensively on Zen. He was not hoping to incorporate any elements of Buddhist metaphysics or doctrine into the Christian faith, or to implement some crude syncretism by cherry picking the two faith traditions for the most worthwhile attributes. Instead, he sought to identify practices within each tradition that might help strengthen each other. He noted that,

37 Havens: Review of Final Integration, p. 301.

38 Patrick O'Connell: Introduction to Thomas Merton: Final integration: Toward a "Monastic Therapy". In: Thomas Merton: *Selected Essays.* Maryknoll, NY: Orbis 2013, pp. 452–462, here p. 452.

39 Merton: *Contemplation in a World of Action*, p. 225.

40 Arasteh: *Final Integration*, p. 74.

41 Addison Hodges Hart: *The Ox Herder and the Good Shepherd.* Grand Rapids: Eerdmans 2013, p. 89.

> Anyone who has any familiarity with Zen will immediately admit that this is the only way to talk about it. To approach the subject with an intellectual or theological chip on the shoulder would only end in confusion [...] Buddhism does not seek primarily to understand or to 'believe in' the enlightenment of Buddha as the solution to all human problems, but seeks an existential and empirical participation in that enlightenment experience.[42]

Merton's primary source for knowledge of the Zen tradition was the Japanese monk Daisetz T. Suzuki.

Daisetz T. Suzuki

Most Westerners are familiar with Zen Buddhism thanks to Daisetz T. Suzuki. Zen is a difficult concept to grasp, and as such it presents "a surface so bizarre and irrational, yet so colorful and striking, that some Westerners who approach it for the first time fail to make sense of it, while others, attracted by this surface, take it up in a purely frivolous and superficial spirit."[43] While Suzuki wrote extensively on Zen and its meaning, our concern is only with his correspondence with Thomas Merton, and on his observations of self-transcendence.

Situating Suzuki within the panoply of twentieth-century religious and philosophical figures is important. Although born in Japan in 1870, his life "took a turn in the early 1890s when he became acquainted with the writings of Paul Carus (1852–1919), an offbeat German philosopher and writer who had immigrated to the United States and was working as a writer for Open Court Press in LaSalle, Illinois."[44] Carus's interests included monism, and his "evolutionary approach to religion, and his attempt to reconcile religion and science are all in evidence in Suzuki's later writings on Buddhism."[45] The irony here is that an American Catholic monk – Thomas Merton – came to learn about Zen Buddhism from a Japanese monk living in the US, who patterned his thinking on the essential nature of Buddhism based on the ideas professed by a German monist also living in the US. Be that as it may, Suzuki helped Merton to realize that Buddhism contained ideas which could help Christians see their own faith in a new light, and in the process to perhaps discover something of the nature of their own true selves. Suzuki himself wrote that "the story of the prodigal son in the *Saddharmapundarika*, in the

42 Thomas Merton: A Christian Looks at Zen. In: Id.: *Selected Essays*, pp. 342–360, here p. 343.

43 William Barrett: Introduction. In: D. T. Suzuki: *Zen Buddhism: Selected Writings*. New York: Doubleday 1956, pp. vii–xxiii, here p. vii.

44 Lindsay Gale: *Encyclopedia of Religion*. New York: MacMillan 2005, p. 8885.

45 Ibid.

Vajra-samadhi, and also in the New Testament points to the same feeling one has at the moment of satori experience."[46] It was these examples of looking beyond his own life experience and worldview that attracted Merton to Suzuki. Rather than simply adopt Buddhist ideas directly, Merton reflected deeply on Buddhism and used his readings of Suzuki's work to come to a fuller understanding of various ideas with which he had been grappling for some time. For example, Merton stated that "very often, on the Christian side, we identify 'personality' with the illusory and exterior ego-self, which is certainly not the true Christian 'person.' On the Buddhist side there seems to be no positive idea of personality at all."[47] Suzuki's writing helped Merton reach this conclusion.

In another example of cross-cultural exchange, Suzuki was influenced by the American psychologist William James (1842–1910), author of *The Varieties of Religious Experience* (1902). This book "was also responsible for Suzuki's later emphasis on Zen as a form of religious mysticism predicated on 'Pure Experience.'"[48] Suzuki was integrating ideas from outside of his own religious tradition in order to come to a fuller understanding of that tradition, just as Merton was doing in order to come to a fuller understanding of Christianity. So while it was not Merton's intent to select random elements from the various religious traditions and incorporate them ad hoc into his own, by taking from Suzuki's interpretation of Buddhism, perhaps Merton unwittingly ended up engaging in the syncretism that he had hoped to avoid.[49] However, Merton was becoming more aware of transcendental elements of religious beliefs from outside of the Christian faith. From Suzuki, he would have been able to grapple with ideas such as, "Zen in its essence is the art of seeing into the nature of one's own being, and it points the way from bondage to freedom."[50] This type of freedom is expressed though the practice of self-transcendence, and is an idea similar to that proposed by Arasteh in his thoughts on final integration. Self-transcendence, contemplation, and introspection are the practices which Merton, Arasteh, and Suzuki would recommend in order to

46 Suzuki: *Zen Buddhism*, p. 123.

47 Thomas Merton: *Zen and the Birds of Appetite*. New York: New Directions 1968, p. 118.

48 Gale: *Encyclopedia of Religion*, p. 8885.

49 Merton's grasp of Buddhist fundamentals is the subject of much of Bowman Thurston (ed.): *Thomas Merton and Buddhism*. Ruben L. F. Habito's "Hearing the Cries of the World: Thomas Merton's Zen Experience" (in: ibid., pp. 91–117) deals specifically with Merton's exposure to Suzuki and how this helped, or possibly hindered, Merton's true understanding of Buddhism, and Zen Buddhism in particular.

50 Suzuki: *Zen Buddhism*, p. 3.

discover the true self. They would all agree that "No amount of worldly explanations will ever lead us into the nature of our own selves. The more you explain, the further it runs away from you."[51]

Perhaps the most fitting testimony to Merton's legacy, and to his persistent efforts to integrate an Asian understanding of contemplation into his world-view, can be found in the words of his fellow monk Father Jean LeClercq. In 1973, five years after Merton's untimely death at age 53 in Bangkok, LeClercq wrote that in order to carry on Merton's ecumenical work and to continue with his exploration of Asian spirituality:

> Representatives of monasticism from five Asian countries will remember Merton and his presence among them and try to find ways of becoming at the same time more truly Christian, more completely monks, more wholly Asiatic.[52]

This tribute to Merton and his vision of integrating an Asian perspective into his contemplative world view is testimony to the correspondence that he maintained with two great philosophical and religious figures – A. Reza Arasteh and D. T. Suzuki. Merton was, along with these two, one who sought to uncover the true nature of reality by shedding the false self. One Christian, one Muslim, and one Buddhist, they present contemporary thinkers on a cross-cultural quest for understanding. They represent an interesting approach to the study of the center and the periphery in the humanities at large. Thomas Merton, the only Western figure of the three, grew in his own appraisal of the meaning of self-transcendence through his consideration of Arasteh's and Suzuki's words and ideas. The periphery and the center merged into one, and these three luminaries transcended the paradigm inherent in the idea of Western as opposed to Eastern mindsets. Respectful of each other's cultures and beliefs, the interaction between these men demonstrates that some forms of cross-cultural communication are of a high benefit for all parties involved. While it is true that all too often, prejudices and pre-determined values can become a barrier between effective communications or cultural groups, the interaction between these individuals provides a case study in meaningful and valuable sharing of ideas. Each of these individuals approached an idea through not only their own intellectual and spiritual paradigms, but through the best elements of each other's tradition as well.

51 Ibid., p. 13.

52 Jean LeClerq: Introduction. In: Thomas Merton: *Contemplation in a World of Action.* New York: Image 1973, pp. 7–20, here pp. 8–9.

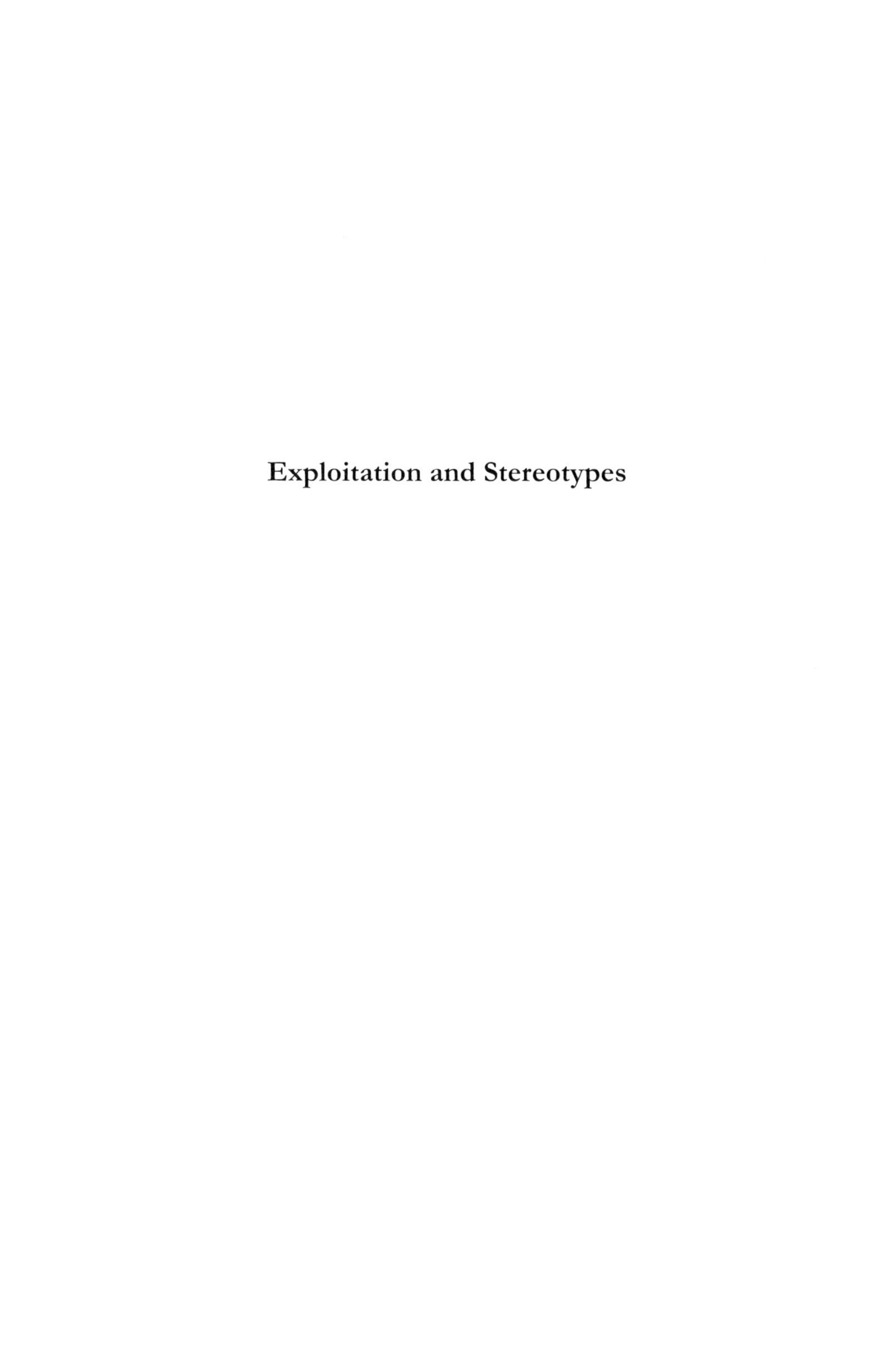

Exploitation and Stereotypes

Labor-Relations and the Periphery

The Example of *trabalho escravo* in Pará (Brazil)[1]

Julia Harnoncourt

The relation between centers and peripheries, as I use it here, is defined as an unequal power relationship in the capitalist system, most crucially an economic one. The center builds its power, wealth, and access to resources by abusing the weaker position of the periphery, which at the same time enables the continuation of this power relation as well as the functioning of capitalism. This relation enables the redistribution of wealth toward companies and facilitates relatively high wages in the centers through the extremely low wages in the peripheral regions and by the different products produced: the peripheries produce and sell unfinished primary products and the centers sell manufactured goods. This imperialist relationship is introduced and propagated by military, political, and economic powers, thereby reproducing itself and giving the periphery a considerably smaller range of margins.[2]

Beyond the economic realm, the center-periphery framework can also be used to describe social, cultural, or other political power relationships, which are also intertwined with economics and function in a similar manner, reproducing through the accumulation of capital, [3] in the sense used by Pierre Bourdieu.[4]

One important indicator of the center periphery model is the labor market, which is also the focus of this study. The system constructs a divided global

1 *Trabalho escravo* is a Brazilian synonym for forced labor; it mostly takes place in Pará. This article puts *trabalho escravo* into the scheme of peripheral labor relations, and tries to find out how much they coincide, and whether this kind of forced labor is typical or atypical in the peripheral regions, and how Brazil and Pará fit into the center-periphery model. On forced labor see: Lisa Carstensen: Trabalho Forçado e Tráfico de Pessoas. Uma Análise do Discurso em Instituições e Organizações Internacionais e Brasileiras. In: *Brasiliana – Journal of Brazilian Studies* 2,2 (2013), pp. 3–31, here p. 10.

2 Stefan Schmalz: Weltsystemtheorie. In: Joscha Wullweber / Antonia Behrens / Maria Graf (eds): *Theorien der Internationalen Politischen Ökonomie*. Wiesbaden: Springer 2014, pp. 101–116; *Oxford Dictionary of Sociology*, ed. by John Scott / Gordon Marshall. 3rd ed. New York: Oxford UP 2009, p. 71; *Sociology Dictionary*, ed. by Rajana Subberwal. New Delhi: Tata McGraw Hill 2009, p. 5.

3 *Sociology Dictionary*, p. 5.

4 Cultural, social, and symbolic. For more see e.g. David Schwartz: *Culture & Power. The Sociology of Pierre Bourdieu*. London: University of Chicago Press 1997, Chapter 4.

labor market, aimed at the accumulation of wealth and made possible by outsourcing processes or subcontracting local companies in the periphery to create commodity chains.[5] The outsourcing of labor exploitation not only provides cheap labor but also ensures the purchasing power in the centers through incomes, enabling its workers to participate in the local economies as customers. Thus the price of commodities can be minimized through the low wages paid in the peripheries, while the purchasing power of the workers in the centers stays relatively stable.[6]

The difference between the peripheries and the centers is not only seen in income, education, and skills disparities, but also in different labors regimes, modes of production, and the treatment and concrete rights of laborers.[7] In general wage labor is the more frequent mode of employment in centers, while in the peripheries, informal labor is the norm[8] and unfree or forced labor relationships are no different. Some social scientists claim that non-wage, or even unfree labor, is the worldwide standard and that workers in the periphery are the ones responsible for the majority of capital accumulation.[9]

Finally, the centers do have forms of forced labor. However, the majority of laborers in this specific form of exploitation comes from the same parts of the world:

> Thus Third World people are at the same time reassembled as the global workforce of multinational capital in the 'world' cities of the west and exploited in situ in their own

5 Jennifer Bair: Globaler Kapitalismus und Güterketten. Rückblick und Ausblick. In: Karin Fischer / Christian Reiner / Cornelia Staritz (eds): *Globale Güterketten. Weltweite Arbeitsteilung und ungleiche Entwicklung.* Vienna: Promedia / Südwind 2009; Andrea Komlosy: *Globalgeschichte. Methoden und Theorien.* Vienna: Böhlau 2011, pp. 24–42; *Oxford Dictionary of Sociology*, p. 71.

6 Tom Brass: Introduction. Free and Unfree Labour. The Debate Continues. In: Id. / Marcel van der Linden (eds.): *Free and Unfree Labour. The Debate Continues.* Bern / Wien: Peter Lang 1997, pp. 11–42, here p. 29.

7 Robert Brenner: Das Weltsystem. Theoretische und historische Perspektiven. In: Jochen Blaschke (ed.): *Perspektiven des Weltsystems. Materialien zu Immanuel Wallerstein, "Das moderne Weltsystem".* Frankfurt am Main / New York: Campus 1983, pp. 80–111; Schmalz: Weltsystemtheorie, p. 105.

8 Informal labor is also increasing in the centers.

9 Franz Delapina: Die Erschließung der Peripherie. Zur Geschichte informeller Arbeitsverhältnisse in der außereuropäischen Welt. In: Andrea Komlosy / Christof Parnreiter / Irene Stacher / Susan Zimmermann (eds): *Ungeregelt und unbezahlt. Der informelle Sektor in der Weltwirtschaft.* Frankfurt am Main: Südwind 1997, pp. 29–44, here p. 43; International Labour Office (ed.): *Decent Work and the Informal Economy. Sixth Item on the Agenda.* Geneva, International Labour Conference, 90th session, Report VI, 2002, p. 2; Peter Worsley: Drei Welten oder eine? Eine Kritik der Weltsystemtheorie. In: Blaschke (ed.): *Perspektiven des Weltsystems*, pp. 32–79, here p. 68; Jan Lucassen: Free and Unfree Labour Before the Twentieth Century. A Brief Overview. In: Brass / van der Linden (eds): *Free and Unfree Labour*, pp. 45–56, here p. 45.

> countries, as the workers, sectors and regions of an earlier round of accumulation are rejected.[10]

The important role of women as unpaid workers in reproduction must be mentioned to emphasize how the actual labor regime reinforces not only geographical power positions, but also class and gender inequalities, as well as those based on skin color (institutional racism).[11]

The interconnection between racist enterprises, the exploitation of labor, and the international labor division is not new. Today's international labor division, with its similar geographic regions and a continuous history of exploitation, begins with the Atlantic slave trade, which can also be seen as an extremely brutish process of proletarianization.[12] This history starts with the triangular trade, buying slaves from Africa, producing primary products in the Americas and manufactured goods in Europe, and selling them back to the "southern"[13] countries. With the colonization of Africa, labor exploitation occurred directly in the birthplaces of the exploited laborers, the new colonies.[14] The beginning of the so-called "new international labor division" is more or less determined by the decolonization process of Africa. At this time, industries were also established in the imperialized countries, and industrial labor exploitation was provided outside the markets of the centers.[15] *Trabalho escravo* in Pará fits directly with this concept.

In Brazilian literature, *trabalho escravo* is defined as labor,

> where employers or representatives resort to physical or moral coercion and deprivation of the liberty of the employee. Common measures are the retention of documents and practices of servitude based in depths incurred by the consumption on the job, like for alimentation, clothing, tools, accommodation and transport, resulting in depth slavery.[16]

10 Linda McDowell: Life without Father and Ford: The New Gender Order of Post-Fordism. In: *Transactions of the Institute of British Geographers, New Series* 16,4 (1991), pp. 400–419, here p. 417.

11 David L. Levy: Political Contestation in Global Production Networks. In: *The Academy of Management Review* 33,4 (2008), pp. 943–963, here p. 945; Karl Heinz Roth / Marcel van der Linden: Ergebnisse und Perspektiven. In: Iid. (eds): *Über Marx hinaus. Arbeitsgeschichte und Arbeitsbegriff in der Konfrontation mit den globalen Arbeitsverhältnissen des 21. Jahrhunderts.* 2nd ed. Berlin: Assoziation A 2011, pp. 557–600, here p. 571.

12 Roth / van der Linden: Ergebnisse und Perspektiven, p. 561

13 Meant in the sense in which "global south" is used nowadays.

14 Martin Staniland: The Rhetoric of Centre-Periphery Relations. In: *The Journal of Modern African Studies* 8,4 (1970), pp. 617–636, here p. 623.

15 Jörg Flecker: Bewegliche Ziele. Aufstieg in globalen Wertschöpfungsketten und die Qualität der Arbeit. In: Fischer / Reiner / Staritz (eds): *Globale Güterketten*, pp. 43–57, here p. 46.

16 Translated by the author from Portuguese; original: "[…] em que empregadores ou

Another definition, used to justify the use of the term slavery[17] for today's forced labor relations, is that following the League of Nations' 1926 slavery convention, which states that anyone over whom titles of possession are exercised is to be defined as a slave.[18]

The number of laborers working in *trabalho escravo* in Brazil is estimated very differently. While the official estimate assumes that 25,000 people are trapped in these kinds of labor,[19] scholars like José Souza de Martins estimate the number to be between 250,000 and half a million.[20] This wide range of appraisals makes it clear how difficult it is to work with numbers when they interplay with illegal conditions, and therefore, intentional invisibility. The *lista suja*[21], on the other hand, contains all the companies and farms sentenced by the courts in the last two years for using *trabalho escravo* and the number of persons legally recognized as having been in this situation. It shows approximately 12,000 people in Brazil in around 600 companies recognized as being in the position of *trabalho escravo*. About a quarter of both of these are in Pará. Most of the work is done in the agricultural sector, thus it will receive special focus.[22]

prepostos recorrem à coação física ou moral e privação da liberdade do empregado, sendo comum a retenção de documentos e práticas de servidão baseadas em dívidas contraídas para o consumo, no próprio trabalho, de alimentos, roupas, ferramentas, alojamento e transporte, configurando-se na escravidão por dívida." (Cintia de Rodrigues Olivera / Valdir Machado Valadão Júnior / Rodrigo Miranda: Culpada ou Inocente? Comentários de Internautas Sobre Crimes Corporativos. In: *RAE – Revista de Administração de Empresas* 53, 6 (2013), pp. 617–628, here pp. 619–620.)

17 Using "slavery" in the international discourse is highly controversial. This is also true in Brazil, but since 1995 the term has been officially used by the government. Maranhão Costa / Patricía Trindade: *Fighting Forced Labour: The Example of Brazil. International Labour Organization*. Geneva: Special Action Programme to Combat Forced Labour 2009, p. 7.

18 Rebecca J. Scott: O Trabalho Escravo Contemporâneo e os Usos da História. In: *Public Law and Legal Theory Research Paper Series* 333 (2013), pp. 1–16, here p. 2.

19 Leonardo Sakamoto (ed.): *Trabalho escravo no Brasil do século XXI*. Brasilia: OIT 2007,. p. 18.

20 The estimate for forced labor worldwide are 20.9 million people. Carstensen: Trabalho Forçado e Tráfico, p. 3; José Souza de Martins: The Reappearance of Slavery and the Reproduction of Capital on the Brazilian Frontier. In: Brass / van der Linden (eds): *Free and Unfree Labour*, pp. 281–302, here p. 285.

21 A list, made by the government as one of its strategies to fight *trabalho escravo*, which contains all legally sentenced companies, their location, their owners, and how many people were working in this condition for two years. If they comply with labor laws for two years, their name is deleted from the list.

22 Reporter Brasil (ed.): *Lista Suja*. http://reporterbrasil.org.br/listasuja/resultado.php (accessed 17.05.2014).

To explain the situation of workers captive in *trabalho escravo* (the *cativos*[23], as they call themselves), it is important to understand the process of their "capture". Normally, so-called *gatos*, "contractors who arrange slave labour for the farms"[24], come to villages enticing potential workers with false promises or by seemingly helping them with existing money problems. Individuals passing through and migrants, especially from Bolivia, are also frequently used for this kind of work.

After a long trip – a strategy to disconnect the workers from their social bonds – they are held by debts, artificially created through the trip, food, and tools among other things. Their legal documents are also withdrawn, and normally the farms, where the *cativos* now work and live, are very large and isolated. To complete the coercion, armed overseers – who are more than willing to use their weapons – prevent the workers from fleeing.[25]

The working and living conditions on the farms are very precarious. There is insufficient food and drink, and what there is fails to meet minimal hygiene standards. Workers often have to work with hazardous tools (like pesticides), but their work gear is mostly insufficient and there is no medical care. Disobedience is punished by the armed guards. Generally the work does not require much skill, but it is highly physically demanding.[26] Thus relatively young men are the main targets of the *gatos*, even though globally there are more women than men in forced labor.[27] The workdays are very long and the *cativos* are paid very little, if at all. Some of them even leave their employment with debts.[28]

Similar to the concept of informal labor – even though *trabalho escravo* occurs outside the official labor market – the types of products are the same as those produced under legal working conditions.[29] Most commodities made by *cativos* are produced in the agricultural sector, such as cattle, timber and arable land (through deforestation)[30], cotton, corn, rice, beans, coffee, rubber

23 Costa / Trindade: *Fighting Forced Labour*, p. 55.

24 Martins: The Reappearance of Slavery, p. 284.

25 Costa / Trindade: *Fighting Forced Labour*; Carstensen: Trabalho Forçado e Tráfico, p. 19.

26 José Souza de Martins: A Reprodução do Capital na Frente Pioneira e o Renascimento da Escravidão no Brasil. In: *Tempo Social* 6 (1995), pp. 1–25; Costa / Trindade: *Fighting Forced Labour*.

27 Carstensen: Trabalho Forçado e Tráfico, p. 21; Costa / Trindade: *Fighting Forced Labour*, p. 63

28 Martins: A Reprodução do Capital; Costa / Trindade: *Fighting Forced Labour*.

29 Susan Zimmermann: Der informelle Sektor: Konzepte, Widersprüche und Debatten. In: Komlosy / Parnreiter / Stacher / Zimmermann (eds): *Ungeregelt und unbezahlt*, pp. 9–28.

30 *Trabalho escravo* is most used in beef production and deforestation. They are often linked, as deforestation is often done to produce pasture for the cattle to graze. See Martins: The Reappearance of Slavery, p. 291.

(latex), sugar cane (mostly for bio fuels and alcohol), soy, fruits, and oil. However, *trabalho escravo* is also involved in the production of metals (like iron ore and steel), chemical products and clothes, work in the service sector, and in construction.[31] The main aim of these labor relations is the accumulation of capital, so large parts of these companies, even though they work in agriculture, are mechanized.[32]

Finally, all these products are sold on the international market and are manufactured for both local and international companies.[33] Brazil is the world's number one exporter of beef, poultry, oranges and sugar cane. It is also a major producer of natural gas, cotton, linen, soy, and pig iron, which is known for its very high quality.[34] Many of these products are clearly also involved with *trabalho escravo*, and as the products are mostly raw materials[35], it can be assumed that the *trabalho escravo* occupies a low position in the production chains. Even though liabilities often seem to be clear[36], companies at the higher end of the production chain do not take responsibility for the actions of the enterprises they depend on in the peripheries.[37]

Brazil, being a strong economic power[38], cannot be seen as a periphery. While its main global exports are raw materials, in Latin America, Brazil is one of the major exporters of finished products. Following Immanuel Wallerstein, categorizing Brazil as a semi-periphery might be accurate:

> This is in what I call the semiperiphery, that is all those states who play an intermediate role in the world-economy: large along at least one crucial dimension (population, skilled manpower, total industrial output, per capita income), tending to produce manufactured

31 Carstensen: Trabalho Forçado e Tráfico, p. 10; Ricardo Rezende Figueira: A Persistência da Escravidão Ilegal no Brasil. In: Brion Maybury-Lewis / Sonia Ranincheski (eds): *Desafios aos Direitos Humanos no Brasil Contemporâneo*. Brasilia: Verbena 2011, pp. 49–64, here pp. 58–59; Costa / Trindade: *Fighting Forced Labour* ; Martins: A Reprodução do Capital, p. 8.

32 Martins: A Reprodução do Capital.

33 Martins: The Reappearance of Slavery, p. 286.

34 Costa / Trindade: *Fighting Forced Labour*; Daniel C. Nepstad / Claudia M. Stickler / Oriana T. Almeida: Globalization of the Amazon Soy and Beef Industries: Opportunities for Conservation. In: *Conservation Biology* 20,6 (2006), pp. 1595–1603.

35 This means exportation of raw materials for the international market. In a strictly Latin-American context, the export of clothes (particularly shoes) is very important.

36 See for example the case of Zara: Conexão Sindical: *Informe Zara é Responsabilizada na Justiça por Escravidão de Trabalhadores*, 2014. http://www.observatoriosocial.org.br/conexaosindical/node/8486#.U1exUqLxGAI (accessed 24.05.2014).

37 Costa / Trindade: *Fighting Forced Labour.*

38 Brazil is one of the ten biggest economies in the world. Alexandre Ardichvili / Elena Zavyalova / Vera Minina: Human Capital Development: Comparative Analysis of BRICS. In: *European Journal of Training and Development* 36,2–3 (2012), pp. 213–233, here p. 216.

> goods for an internal market and weaker neighbours but still an exporter of primary products, playing the role of peripheral partners to core countries and core partners to some peripheral countries.[39]

Pará, on the other hand, is definitely a periphery, both in a global context and in Brazil, as the north and northeast are the poorest regions of the country.[40] In some regards, Pará's peripheral position clearly facilitates working conditions like *trabalho escravo*. The existence of *trabalho escravo* depends on people being poor and struggling for their subsistence. Also, its geographical position supports the invisibility of these enterprises, as well as providing an area with wide expanses of land, irregular infrastructure and thus farms which are inherently clandestine and isolated.[41]

An oft-mentioned project, *ocupação econômica da Amazônia* (economic occupation of the Amazon), was implemented by the military regime (1964–1985) and reinforces the center-periphery gap inside Brazil. Its official goal was to bring modernity and governmental control into the region, which includes Pará and other states. This program offered economic incentives to big businesses to build up their companies in this area and fill spaces seen as vacant. As small farmers and indigenous groups already inhabited these spaces, this was a classical form of land grabbing. The former inhabitants were not only stripped of their land but also lost their means of subsistence and their territory. This is another form of proletarianization, as Tom Brass defines it, as these actions also provided an available workforce:

> labouring subjects ('direct producers') are 'freed' from access to the means of production that secure their reproduction, and consequently they are (and must be) free to exchange their labour power with capital for wages with which to purchase subsistence.[42]

This provides another advantage for big businesses, as this workforce was much needed for the labor-intensive agricultural processes, established at the laborer's own expense.[43]

39 Immanuel Wallerstein: *The Capitalist World-Economy*. Cambridge: Cambridge UP 1979, pp. 246–247.

40 Robert M. Levine / John J. Crocitti: Introduction. In: Iid. (eds): *The Brazil Reader*. Durham: Duke UP 1999, pp. 1–9; Howard Winant: Rethinking Race in Brazil. In: *Journal of Latin American Studies* 24,1 (1992), pp. 173–192, here p. 178.

41 Costa / Trindade: *Fighting Forced Labour*.

42 Tom Brass: Some Observations on Unfree Labour, Capitalist Restructuring, and Deproletarization. In: Brass / van der Linden (eds): *Free and Unfree Labour*, pp. 57–75, here p. 59.

43 Martins: A Reprodução do Capital.

The influence of this political strategy on power relations in Pará and the whole Amazon region continues today. Not only is the enforcement of land titles for small farmers and indigenous groups still very weak, and thus land grabbing still relatively easy, but major landowners still have a lot of power in these regions, as they are often involved with local politics.[44] Viewing the position of these landowners in a center-periphery model, their power margin turns out to be ambiguous; while they dominate on a local basis, they have nearly no power on an international scale, which, following Andreas Novy, is typical for the ruling class in the peripheries and enforces specific strategies:

> This double role of being powerful/powerless is rooted in a doubled spatiality: He [the landowner] acts locally, but is also integrated into a bigger – national and global – spatial structure, where he does not count.
> The ruling class at the periphery builds up their strategies of power based on their local position of authority, knowing about their powerlessness on the international scale. They are managing an always unstable social position on-site and, in this manner, avoid radical upheavals of the consisting.[45]

Even though these landowners are not as powerful on the national level, the Brazilian government, according to some authors, still seems to struggle with their power positions when trying to enforce and strengthen labor laws surrounding *trabalho escravo.*[46] Brazil's economic position was remarkably strengthened by this imperialist, national project of *ocupação*, so much so that "the 'Brazilian miracle' was not so much cattle breeding but rather [...] the 'production of farms'"[47]. Therefore, the state had economic incentives to marginalize some parts of the country, and may still do. Regardless, labor relations like *trabalho escravo* certainly contributed to the economic rise of Brazil.
The existence of hidden agendas from some powerful groups in Brazil is an interesting question which unfortunately cannot be answered here.

44 Figueira: A Persistência da Escravidão Ilegal, p. 63.

45 Translated by the author from German; original: "Diese Doppelrolle von mächtig/ohnmächtig wurzelt in einer doppelten Räumlichkeit: Er agiert vor Ort und ist in eine größere – nationale und globale – Raumstruktur eingebunden, in der er nichts zu reden hat.
Die Herrschenden an der Peripherie bauen ihre Machtstrategien auf ihrer Macht vor Ort auf; wissend um ihre Machtlosigkeit auf der internationalen Ebene. Sie managen eine immer labile soziale Lage vor Ort und vermeiden so, daß es zu radikalen Umbrüchen des Bestehenden kommt." (Andreas Novy: *Die Unordnung der Peripherie. Von der Sklavenhaltergesellschaft zur Diktatur des Geldes*. Wien: Promedia 2001, p. 14.)

46 See for example Figueira: A Persistência da Escravidão Ilegal.

47 Brass: Introduction, p. 15.

Although the focus has been on *trabalho escravo* in the countryside of Pará, a peripheral region, it is important to note that there also are existing cases of this kind of labor exploitation in Brazilian centers. Thus I will now briefly focus on the marginalization of people instead of geographical regions.

Trabalho escravo is not confined to the countryside or to the Amazon region.[48] These labor situations seem to coincide with the theoretical descriptions of forced labor in the centers as an "importation into metropolitan capitalism of a work regime historically associated with the colonial periphery"[49]. Since in both cities and the countryside, the vast majority of persons in *trabalho escravo* are categorized as people of color,[50] the connection to the colony seems to be confirmed. The notion of also institutionalized racism springs to mind.

Institutional racism is racism that does not rely on interpersonal relations but constitutes an important, intrinsic and highly integral part of a society, which at the same time does not openly present itself. "On these accounts, institutional racism is to be camouflaged to the point where its specific causes are virtually undetectable, but its effects are visible in its results".[51] The most visible effects of institutional racism in Brazil are the high inequality rates, which are to an extremely large extent based on skin color, making so-called people of color the less fortunate.[52] Nevertheless, this inequality problem is not just one of money or income; there are also considerable numbers of people, who do not have the same access to their civil or even human rights.[53]

Finally, even in the cities and centers of Brazil, there are people who are marginalized, disenfranchised and made invisible, and are therefore targets for *trabalho escravo*. So, it can be stated that *trabalho escravo* not only establishes itself in geographical peripheries but also uses "peripherized people." Through it, marginalization, invisibility, and the lack of possibilities to enforce legal rights or statuses are exploited and reproduced.

48 Figueira: A Persistência da Escravidão Ilegal, pp. 58–59.

49 Brass: Introduction, p. 36.

50 Costa / Trindade: *Fighting Forced Labour.*

51 *Encyclopedia of Race and Ethnic Studies*, ed. by Ellis Cashmore. London: Routledge 2004, p. 204.

52 Lucila Bandeira Beato: Inequality and Human Rights of African Descendants in Brazil. In: *Journal of Black Studies* 34,6 (2004), pp. 766–786; Maria Mercedes Jeria Caceres: More Training, Less Security? Training and the Quality of Life at Work in Argentina, Brazil and Chile. In: *International Labour Review* 141,4 (2002), pp. 359–383, here p. 366.

53 Figueira: A Persistência da Escravidão Ilegal, pp. 58–59.

Finally, *trabalho escravo* must be seen as a structural, not an individual, problem.[54] The peripheral positions of people and regions are not only used to build up labor relations like *trabalho escravo* but are also created to make these kinds of labor possible, so the highest capital accumulation can be extracted from the laborers.[55]

For comparative purposes, the center-periphery model can easily be superimposed on the concept of power relations between people, where an unequal power distribution is based on economics but is not only effective in that sphere. Additionally, the reproduction of power or powerlessness is also influenced by concepts of race, gender, and class, and their labor relations reproduce social statuses, which in a dialectic manner, are abused again to exploit laborers in degrading labor positions.

It is surely uncontentious to state that "capitalism is not only compatible with unfree labour but in certain situations actually prefers this to a free workforce"[56], and agricultural labor in the countryside of Pará is one of them. Therefore, forced labor, and thus also *trabalho escravo*, cannot be categorized as an atypical labor relation in the capitalist system as we have it today. This is even more true for the peripheries, as unfree labor is often located there.

54 Carstensen: Trabalho Forçado e Tráfico, pp. 19–20.

55 See for example the often-mentioned theory that racism is also part of an unconscious strategy to enable lower labor conditions. See for example Dik van Arkel: Why Are Historical Labour-market Studies Relevant to the Understanding of Racism? In: Marcel van der Linden / Jan Lucassen (eds): *Racism and the Labour Market. Historical Studies.* Bern: Peter Lang 1995, pp. 22–53.

56 Brass: Some Observations on Unfree Labour, p. 57.

Can German Nationalism after WWII Be Characterized by the Concept of 'Economic Securitization'?

Case Study: Securitization of the Roma Minority

Liony Bauer

Introduction

In order to understand why a person, a community or a state acts in a certain way, it is essential to examine the impact that a globalizing world is having on individual, social and national identities. It would be naive to assume that increasing global interconnectedness through the exchange of goods, human beings and ideas only creates benefits. This article will focus on the causal relationship between the changing nature of German national identity after 1945 and the socio-economic inequalities experienced by the Roma minority in Germany.

Difference is a concept that plays an important role in the construction of identities. As with other group identity categories such as religion or ethnicity, nationalism requires the distinction between an 'In-Group' and an 'Out-Group'. The classification of human beings into citizens of different nation states has resulted in the development of shared narratives; history, culture and society have been assigned a national character, and 'communities of fate' have been created. Matti Jutila believes that the concept of nationalism produces a hierarchy of identities and argues that it "is understood as a drama in which the nation is the key actor".[1] As a consequence, difference is propagated: the 'outsider' does not belong to the group. In many cases throughout the world, minorities or migrants have historically been denied equal rights; nation states are still not willing to (or claim that they are not able to) fully integrate all human beings who are located in their sovereign geographical territory.

After 1945, Germany had to rebuild its economy and remodel its national identity. After the atrocities committed and the social and economic breakdown after defeat in World War II, German identity had to be significantly altered; the fascist and supremacist social order propagated and implemented by the Nazi-Regime had defined a radical nationalism as the instrument

1 Matti Jutila: Desecuritizing Minority Rights: Against Determinism. In: *Security Dialogue* 37,2 (2006), pp. 167–185, here p. 177.

through which the German race would prevail in a world understood within the frame of Social Darwinism. 'Non-Aryans', especially Jews, but also Roma were excluded from the circle of 'proper' Germans. Discrimination and persecution leading to millionfold genocide have since then been part of the national identity; German nationalism has evolved from determining race and ancestry as the defining characteristics of the 'In-Group' and has recently developed a new category: economic utility. Rather than between races, a large part of the public now distinguishes between useful ('good') and inconvenient ('bad') migrants and minorities, based on whether they are contributing to the German economy.

Discrimination and racism are both illegal in Germany. However, the Roma minority, which is a target of discrimination in many European countries, is still excluded from the 'In-Group'. I have chosen to focus on the Roma because this minority is an example of how German society treats human beings that are not considered to be beneficial to the economy. In contrast to other minorities, the Roma do not have their own state (like the persecuted European Jews before the State of Israel was established in 1948); they are not perceived as the 'In-Group' in any country. The lack of statehood has resulted in discrimination and marginalization without any option of returning to a homeland that considers the Roma to be native citizens.[2]

The first part of the article will focus on the development and, to a certain degree, progress of the character of German national identity after World War II. I will outline not only how German nationalism has changed under the pressure of the international community, but also how the German '*Wirtschaftswunder*' ('economic miracle') and Germany's better management of the 2008 financial and monetary crisis (compared to other European states) have led to a new form of exclusion rationale: the 'Economic Securitization' of minorities and migrants.

The second part of the present article will examine the consequences of 'Economic Securitization' for a minority that has suffered from persecution in European history: namely the Roma who still face extraordinary discrimination. However, instead of openly justifying the refusal to integrate the Roma with traditional nationalist arguments, German politics and society present 'rational' economic reasons; the majority accuses the Roma of being unwilling

2 Istvan Pogány: Pariah Peoples: Roma and the Multiple Failures of Law in Central and Eastern Europe. In: *Social & Legal Studies* 21,3 (2012), pp. 375–393.

to work and of deliberately and mischievously exploiting the generous '*Sozialstaat*' (national welfare system).
The main argument of this article will be that German nationalism has changed and that it may be characterized by the concept of 'Economic Securitization' because the celebration of economic accomplishments after World War II has led to the construction of 'Out-Groups' that are mainly identified by a propagated economic inutility and a threat to the social welfare system. In comparison to other minorities in Germany, the Roma are a unique example of how nationalism still plays an important role in the shaping of political and individual narratives in an era of European integration. To conclude, I will try to evaluate whether there is a viable chance for de-securitization for the case of the Roma living in post-1945 Germany.

German Nationalism in the 20th and 21st Centuries: From Institutionalized Scientific Racism to 'Economic Securitization'

The character of German nationalism from 1933 to 1945 and the devastating impacts fascism, anti-Semitism and Social Darwinism have had on the people in Germany and other European nations are issues that Germans are still constantly confronted with today. The belief in a supreme race and the consequent conviction that this supremacy must prevail over inferior peoples, was the driving force behind an inhumane system that led to some of the most dreadful crimes committed by a state in modern history. However, oppression, persecution and mass murder were not only justified by 'scientifically derived' racist propaganda of the inferiority of certain people(s) but also by the extreme securitization of these groups.
The concept of minority securitization describes that by 'speaking security', social or political actors create widespread anxiety that certain groups of people present existential threats to the society's short- and long-term well-being. Securitization leads to the justification and acceptance of extraordinary means that would otherwise be considered illegitimate or illegal. A state of emergency is created in order to legitimize instruments of surveillance, confinement and penalization targeted at certain (groups of) people.[3]

3 Jef Huysmans: Migrants as a Security Problem: Dangers of 'Securitizing' Societal Issues. In: Robert Miles / Dietrich Thranhardt (eds): *Migration and European Integration: The Dynamics of Inclusion and Exclusion*. London: Pinter 1995, pp. 53–72; Ole Wæver: Securitization and Desecuritization. In: Ronnie D. Lipschutz (ed.): *On Security*. New York: Columbia UP 1995, pp. 46–86; Barry Buzan / Ole Wæver / Jaap de Wilde: *Security: A New Framework for Analysis*. London: Lynne Reinner 1998; Michael C. Williams: Words, Images, Enemies: Securitization

The German National Socialist Party (NSDAP) and its leader Adolf Hitler strategically used securitization as political instrument; the party owed its success to a large degree to an effective propaganda machine that persuaded the German people of a threat due to 'infiltration' by 'inferior' people such as the Jews or, to a lesser extent, the Roma into the 'Aryan race'. Provoking Social Darwinism was a major part of Nazi Propaganda; demanding the prevalence of the fittest over the invading menace led to the establishment of a system, which severely punished individuals for the alleged threat of their extraneousness. The identification of the German people with the regime was essential for the construction of an 'In-Group'; the Nuremberg laws provided a clear definition of who was excluded.[4]

When the Third Reich was defeated, occupied Germany was soon split up into two nation states: the Federal Republic of Germany ('West Germany') and the German Democratic Republic ('East Germany'). After 1949, German territory and identity were divided again, having only been unified since 1871. Although the denazification campaign was seen as an important part of rebuilding the shattered German social and political system, the Allied forces in the Federal Republic of Germany saw economic reconstruction as the best method to rebuild a functioning state and to make sure that there would be no strong resentments that might lead to a return to a securitized fascist system or an approach to the communist Soviet enemy. The 'European Recovery Program' ('Marshall Plan') was installed in order to prevent a chaotic breakdown by stimulating the German economy and promoting an image of a rebuilt state: economically, socially and politically.

The subsequent decades were characterized by stable conditions, economic growth and political cooperation. The Federal Republic of Germany benefited from the creation of the EU as a system of supranational economic and political institutions and developed the largest GDP of all member states. Increased labor productivity, effective measures against inflation, lower tax

and International Politics. In: *International Studies Quarterly* 47,4 (2003), pp. 511–531; Paul Roe: Securitization and Minority Rights: Conditions of Desecuritization. In: *Security Dialogue* 35,3 (2004), pp. 279–294; Jutila: Desecuritizing Minority Rights; Rens van Munster: *Securitizing Immigration. The Politics of Risks in the EU*. Basingstoke: Palgrave Macmillan 2009; Jef Huysmans: What's in an Act? On Security Speech Acts and Little Security Nothings. In: *Security Dialogue* 42,4–5 (2011), pp. 371–383; Ole Wæver: Politics, Security, Theory. In: *Security Dialogue* 42,4–5 (2011), pp. 465–480.

4 Sybil Milton: Sinti and Roma in Twentieth-Century Austria and Germany. In: *German Studies Review* 23,2 (2000), pp. 317–331.

rates and a more liberal market economy, that still provided for those in need, led to low unemployment rates and economic growth.[5]

In the 1960s, the German economy grew too quickly; the domestic labor supply could not satisfy the increasing demand. The strategy was to invite foreigners to Germany as '*Gastarbeiter*' ('guest workers'). Most of these workers came from Italy, Greece, Spain, Yugoslavia, Portugal and Turkey. The German Democratic Republic maintained similar programs with countries from the Communist bloc, mainly Vietnam. The *Gastarbeiter* in East Germany worked under harsh conditions and, in contrast to those in West Germany, were generally not allowed to stay and become permanent residents or citizens. One effect of the '*Gastarbeiter*-agreements' was the increasing share of non-Germans living in West Germany.

Similar to other countries, Germany's economic success in the 1950s and 1960s led to an increased birth rate. These highly productive 'baby boomers' will mostly retire in the next 5 to 15 years. In addition, according to the most recent census of 2011, the overall population of Germany has shrunk from 81.8 to 80.3 million,[6] with the birth rate being extremely low and the number of childless women increasing. The result is a further shrinking population[7] and thus a decreasing supply of workers and tax-payers. The German government has understood that the demand for a skilled workforce will not decrease. Therefore, social and economic policies have to find ways of attracting laborers and of saving on unemployment and pension spending. (Re)integrating mothers into the workforce through a better provision of childcare facilities, postponing the retirement age and imposing stricter conditions for the allocation of unemployment benefits are part of the German strategy to cope with the consequences of demographic change.

However, the political elites are realizing that Germany will not be able to compensate for the decline in the native labor force. Therefore, the state has to attract immigrants and promote an image of a German society that

5 Henry C. Wallich: *Mainsprings of the German Revival.* New Haven: Yale UP 1955; Brad Delong: Post WWII Western Europe Exceptionalism: The Economic Dimension. 1997. http://econ161.berkeley.edu/econ_articles/ucla/ucla_marshall2.html (accessed 20.05.2014); David R. Henderson: *German Economic Miracle. The Concise Encyclopedia of Economics.* Library of Economics and Liberty 2008. http://www.econlib.org/library/Enc/GermanEconomicMiracle.html (accessed 20.05.2014).

6 Federal Statistical Office of Germany: *Statistical Yearbook Germany.* 2012, Chapter 2: Population, Families, Living Arrangements. https://www.destatis.de/EN/Publica tions/Specialized/Population/StatYearbook_Chapter2_5011001129004.html (accessed 20.05.2014).

7 Ibid., p. 14.

considers itself an '*Einwanderungsland*' ('immigration country'). Creating an inclusive national identity in a globalizing world has to be an important part of any effective immigration policy. Nevertheless, although many German citizens understand that their workforce is shrinking, there is still a large number of people who openly or secretly admit that they are afraid that migrants from poorer countries will only immigrate to Germany with the intention of benefiting from the social welfare system.

The 2005 '*Hartz IV Reform*' (reform of citizens' entitlements to unemployment benefits) has further divided German society and has led to a growing societal condemnation of people in need. Populist forces like the extreme right-wing National Democratic Party of Germany (NPD) have exploited these feelings by propagating the image of an existential threat to the German socio-economic well-being. While their racist terminology only appeals to a small number and is rejected by most citizens, the ideas that the employment of immigrants causes unemployment among Germans and that non-citizens should not be entitled to social welfare are quite popular. According to a 2012 study, almost half of the German population agrees that the natural law of the survival of the fittest should be applied to society; 60% are convinced that Germans are superior to other peoples and almost half of the participants agreed with the statements that foreigners "only immigrate to take advantage of the welfare system" and "should be sent home when jobs are scarce".[8]

The study shows how widespread xenophobic attitudes still are in German society. Although it seems that many citizens do not even desire highly-skilled immigrants whose hard work contributes to the German economic success story, the idea of immigrants who are unwilling to work seems to be the main reason why people are suspicious or even hostile towards a more open and inviting immigration policy. As mentioned before, large parts of the German society divide migrants into two categories: the good and the bad ones. The public perception of the (Eastern) enlargement of the European Union serves as a good example of how the 'In-Group/Out-Group'-distinction based on traditional xenophobic stereotypes is 'modernized' to discriminate and exclude those who are not seen as equally ambitious. With the EU accession of Bulgaria and Romania in 2007, the cultural rejection of the Roma minority has been converted into a supposedly rationally justified

8 Oliver Decker / Johannes Kiess / Elmar Brähler: *Die Mitte im Umbruch. Rechtsextreme Einstellungen in Deutschland 2012*. Friedrich-Ebert-Foundation. Bonn: Dietz 2012, pp. 29–30.

discrimination based on the prejudice that the Roma are unwilling to work and to adapt to the local culture. Hence, all Roma migrating to Germany are accused of having the intention to exploit the welfare system.

The 'Economic Securitization' of the Roma as a European Minority: The Vicious Cycle of Stereotypes and Socio-Economic Inequality

Since 2007, immigration numbers to Germany from the new EU members Romania and Bulgaria have significantly increased, and nationals from these two countries now belong to the 'TOP 3-group' of new immigrants.[9] However, there is no data on how many of them belong to the Roma minority. In addition, the authorities do not know how many Roma are already living in Germany. The estimated number by the '*Zentralrat Deutscher Sinti und Roma*' ('Central Council of German Sinti and Roma') and the German Federal Ministry of the Interior is 70,000.[10]

After the collapse of the Third Reich, the German state stopped collecting data on ethnicity. As a result, the lack of information has facilitated ignorance related to minorities. Consequently it is difficult to examine whether the Roma face more severe discrimination than other minorities in Germany. In the UK, a recent report has shown that 5 % of prisoners are Roma, while they only make up 0.1 % of the general population.[11] This kind of data cannot be collected when a government is unaware of its citizens' ethnicities. In addition, many Roma are aware of stereotypes and therefore conceal their identity.[12] These circumstances lead to a distortion of 'facts'; a university student or employee might not tell anyone that they belong to the Roma minority.

9 Federal Statistical Office of Germany: *Statistical Yearbook Germany*. 2012, Chapter 2; Lisa Caspari: Verarmte Roma, überforderte Kommunen. In: *Zeit Online*, 19.02.2013. http://www.zeit.de/gesellschaft/zeitgeschehen/2013-02/roma-grossstaedte-bulgarien-rumaenien-staedtetag-strategie (accessed 20.05.2014).

10 German Federal Ministry of the Interior: *Report from the Federal Republic of Germany to the European Commission. An EU Framework for National Roma Integration Strategies up to 2020 – Integrated Packages of Measures to Promote the Integration and Participation of Sinti and Roma in Germany*. 2011. http://ec.europa.eu/justice/discrimination/files/roma_germany_strategy_en.pdf (accessed 20.05.2014).

11 HM Inspectorate of Prisons: *People in Prison: Gypsies, Romany and Travellers*. 2014. www.justice.gov.uk/downloads/publications/inspectorate-reports/hmiprobation/joint-thematic/gypsies-romany-travellers-findings.pdf (accessed 20.05.2014).

12 Claude Cahn: The Unseen Powers: Perception, Stigma, and Roma Rights. European Roma Rights Centre 2007. http://www.errc.org/article/the-unseen-powers-perception-stigma-and-roma-rights/2870 (accessed 20.05.2014); Galina Kostadinova: Minority Rights as a Normative Framework for Addressing the Situation of Roma in Europe. In: *Oxford Development Studies* 39,2 (2011), pp. 163–183.

The accession of Romania and Bulgaria to the European Union was highly economically securitized by the German media. In 2014, the German government (along with other EU member states) lifted a ban on Romanian and Bulgarian citizens' right to work in Germany[13] and the European Commission soon demanded that all European citizens residing in Germany should have equal access to welfare benefits.[14] The German media reported heavily on the feared consequences of an assumed invasion of unemployed Roma asking for 'Kindergeld', 'Arbeitslosengeld' and 'Rente' (state-financed child allowance, unemployment benefits and pensions). TV stations and newspapers play an essential role in perpetuating the stereotypes about the Roma minority[15]; in fact, their role cannot be stressed enough. Headlines like

> Verfallene Häuser, riesige Müllberge, Uringestank – Roma-Nachbarin zeigt die schlimmsten Ecken [Deteriorated houses, enormous piles of garbage, stench of urine – neighbor of Roma shows the worst spots][16]
>
> "Klau-Kid" Elisabeta (14) wieder vor Gericht [Stealing child in court again][17]
>
> Asylum Crisis: How Many Refugees Can Germany Handle?[18]

13 BBC News: Q&A: Bulgarian and Romanian immigration. http://www.bbc.co.uk/news/uk-politics-21523319 (accessed 20.05.2014).

14 Welfare for Immigrants: EU Wants Fortress Germany to Open Up. In: *Spiegel Online*, 14.01.2014. http://www.spiegel.de/international/germany/brussels-may-force-germany-to-loosen-access-to-social-benefits-a-943224.html (accessed 20.05.2014).

15 Irina Bohn / Wolfgang Feuerhelm / Franz Hamburger: Die Erzeugung von Plausibilität als Konstruktion von Wirklichkeit. Eine Fallrekonstruktion zur Berichterstattung über Sinti und Roma. In: Klaus Kraimer (ed.): *Die Fallrekonstruktion. Sinnverstehen in der Sozialwissenschaftlichen Forschung*. Frankfurt am Main: Suhrkamp 2000, pp. 532–560; Margaret Brearley: The Persecution of Gypsies in Europe. In: *American Behavioral Scientist* 45,4 (2001), pp. 588–599; Arun Kundnani: The Media War against Migrants: A New Front. Comment. 21.01.2004. http://www.irr.org.uk/news/the-media-war-against-migrants-a-new-front/ (accessed 20.05.2014); OSCE: *Conference on Anti-Semitism and on Other Forms of Intolerance: Report on Anti-Gypsy-ism in European Media*. 2005. http://www.osce.org/cio/15491 (accessed 20.05.2014); Marius Dragomir: Media as Scare-mongering. Open Society Institute 2009. http://www.opensocietyfoundations.org/briefing-papers/media-scare-mongering (accessed 20.05.2014).

16 Verfallene Häuser, riesige Müllberge, Uringestank. Roma-Nachbarin zeigt die schlimmsten Ecken. In: *Bild*, 18.01.2013. http://www.bild.de/bild-plus/politik/inland/roma/duisburger-roma-nachbarin-zeigt-schlimmste-ecken-34294118,view=conversionToLogin.bild.html (accessed 20.05.2014).

17 'Klau-Kid' Elisabeta (14) wieder vor Gericht. In: *Bild*, 24.04.2014. http://www.bild.de/regional/ruhrgebiet/trick-betrug/klau-kid-elisabeta-wieder-vor-gericht35679926.bild.html (accessed 20.05.2014).

18 Jürgen Dahlkamp / Maximilian Popp: Asylum Crisis: How Many Refugees Can Germany Handle? In: *Spiegel Online*, 14.10.2013. http://www.spiegel.de/international/germany/lampedusa-prompts-broader-reexamination-of-eu-asylum-policy-a-927684.html (accessed 20.05.2014).

The Plight of the Roma: Europe's Unwanted People[19]

Entführungsverdacht: Erneut Mädchen aus Roma-Familie genommen [Suspected abduction: Yet another girl removed from Roma family][20]

do create strong feelings and reinforce the common perception of the inconsolable differences between the 'hard-working and tidy' German citizen and the 'idle and dirty' Roma migrant. In contrast, the media also reiterates a romanticized view of the travelling 'gypsies' (a term dating back to the 16th century, mostly used in derogatory fashion by non-Roma; some Roma and Roma groups themselves have adopted the term though).[21] The beautiful dancer, Esmeralda, in Victor Hugo's 1831 and Disney's 1996 'The Hunchback of Notre Dame' gives an idea of this mystical image. In movies, novels and musicals, Roma are often presented as "freedom loving, easy going, and carefree nomads, wearing colorful clothes and lots of golden jewelry. They are passionate dancers, gifted artisans, and great musicians. Their women are beautiful and seductive".[22]

The systematic discrimination of the Roma is closely connected to the schizophrenic image that is constructed and perpetuated through the media. Despite the romanticized idea of the 'travelling people', an entire ethnic group is vilified. Roma are constantly discriminated against; they are devalued as criminal, unhygienic, uneducated and unwilling to integrate. In other words, Roma are not considered to be modern and civilized people. This is not a new phenomenon: in the Middle Ages, this minority was already classified as an 'Out-Group' and accused of causing societal dilapidation and bringing illnesses. By focusing on stories about bag-snatching, burglary and ghettoization and ignoring stories of successful socio-economic integration, the media is playing into the hands of xenophobic political parties.

19 The Plight of the Roma: Europe's Unwanted People. In: *Spiegel Online*, 07.01.2014. http://www.spiegel.de/international/europe/europe-failing-to-protect-romafromdiscrimination-poverty-a-942057.html (accessed 20.05.2014).

20 Entführungsverdacht: Erneut Mädchen aus Roma-Familie genommen. In: *Süddeutsche Zeitung*, 13.11.2013. http://www.sueddeutsche.de/panorama/entfuehrungsverdacht-erneut-kleines-maedchen-aus-roma-familie-genommen-1.1817233 (accessed 20.05.2014).

21 Nicolae Gheorghe: The Social Construction of Romani Identity. In: Thomas Acton (ed.): *Gypsy Politics and Traveller Identity*. Hatfield: University of Hertfordshire Press 1997, pp. 153–171; Milton: Sinti and Roma in Twentieth-Century Austria and Germany.

22 Council of Europe: Dosta Campaign. Is this a Stereotype? A Tool for Fighting Stereotypes towards Roma. 2006. http://www.coe.int/t/dg3/romatravellers/dosta_en.asp (accessed 20.05.2014).

One may assume that xenophobia and the refusal to tolerate different cultures should decrease in a globalizing world. People travel all over the planet, encounter different customs and multinational companies benefit from global market sales and lower production prices. However, nation states are still the main actors in the international arena; instead of decreasing nationalism, globalization is maybe even invigorating the fact that many people still identify themselves through their nationality. In the EU, national identification is still much stronger for many citizens than a European identity,[23] and inner-European migrants are primarily considered to be citizens of their native state. The Roma are affected by this attitude to a special degree[24] because they do not have their own nation state. Wherever they live, – whether it is in Romania or Germany – they are not considered to be part of the 'In-Group' and are considered to be migrants even when they are native or naturalized citizens.
Recently, the crisis of the Eurozone and the general decrease in public approval of political and economic decisions of the European institutions have been leading to an increasing rejection of the European idea and a comeback of nationalist forces that attract many voters, also in Germany. Citizens of the richer member states are persuaded to believe that they are paying for economic integration and that (Eastern) Enlargement will force them to subsidize more countries without benefiting from them. The Roma are part of the xenophobic propaganda because "Western countries [...] perceive them as perfect illustrations of the poverty and deregulation with which the enlargement of the EU threatens its old members. [...] [T]hey are rejected and seen as Oriental rather than properly European".[25]
Officially, discrimination based on ethnicity is illegal in the European Union. However, the everyday reality of minorities is often different. Many members of minority groups encounter difficulties when they are looking for employment, housing or social assistance. Social policy, even when it is created and implemented through a supranational organization, is not independent of national practices. If the Roma minority is securitized in all member states, it will also be securitized in the EU. The European Union may thus even be

23 Jos de Beus: Quasi-National European Identity and European Democracy. In: *Law and Philosophy* 20,3 (2011), pp. 283–311.

24 Aidan McGarry: The Dilemma of the European Union's Roma Policy. In: *Critical Social Policy* 32,1 (2012), pp. 126–136.

25 Étienne Balibar: Foreword. In: Nando Sigona / Nidhi Trehan (eds): *Romani Politics in Contemporary Europe. Poverty, Ethnic Mobilization, and the Neo-liberal Order.* Basingstoke: Palgrave Macmillan 2010, pp. viii–xiii.

responsible for perpetuating the discrimination and non-integration of the Roma in its individual member states because it does not fulfill its assigned purpose of dealing with this transnational issue.

The "European minority"[26] of the Roma is neither accepted[27] nor integrated. Prevailing stereotypes prevent de-securitization and the improvement of the Roma minority's situation. Therefore, their case resembles a vicious circle: members of the national majority are doubtful or afraid and try not to make contact with Roma. The result is that people are ignorant and easily accept the image conveyed by the media. Eventually, landlords do not want to rent their apartments to Roma (with the excuse that they only accept people with a proper income) and employers do not hire them (with the convenient excuse that they only accept people with proper housing). Correspondingly, generated 'Roma settlements' lead to a separation of peoples living in the same country: German children go to different schools and usually do not play with Roma children.[28] When growing up, Germans learn about this specific minority from the media and will eventually have a negative image without having had any (negative or positive) encounters. One generation later, their own children will be socialized in the same manner.

It is a common effect that constant exclusion from mainstream society may lead to higher crime rates. A long-term lack of equal education and employment opportunities as well as societal aversion for Roma culture and identity, have led to the creation of a sub-culture which (in parts) does engage in criminal activity. The situation of the Roma is a self-fulfilling prophecy: the German society will hear about crimes in the media and see their prejudices confirmed, and the vicious cycle of stereotypes and marginalization continues.[29]

26 Huub van Baar: Commentary. Europe's Romaphobia: Problematization, Securitization, Nomadization. In: *Environment and Planning D: Society and Space* 29,2 (2011), pp. 203–212.

27 *PewResearch Global Attitudes Forum.* 2009, Chapter 6: Opinions of Ethnic and Religious Minorities. http://www.pewglobal.org/2009/11/02/chapter-6-opinions-of-ethnic-and-religious-minorities/ (accessed 20.05.2014).

28 Pogány: Pariah Peoples.

29 Nicolae Gheorghe: Roma-Gypsy Ethnicity in Eastern Europe. In: *Social Research* 58,4 (1991), pp. 829–844; Zoltan Barany: Living on the Edge: The East European Roma in Postcommunist Politics and Societies. In: *Slavic Review* 53,2 (1994), pp. 321–344; Brearley: The Persecution of Gypsies in Europe; Kostadinova: Minority Rights as a Normative Framework; Horia Barbulescu: Constructing the Roma People as a Societal Threat: The Roma Expulsions from France. In: *European Journal of Science and Theology* 8,1 (2012), pp. 279–289; McGarry: The Dilemma of the European Union's Roma Policy.

The situation is dire: the unemployment rate among Roma living in the European Union is estimated to be between 50 % and 80 %.[30] On paper, integrating the Roma into the labor market is considered to be an important aim.[31] But with many EU member states facing high unemployment rates among their citizens, Germany will have to find solutions on its own and should not wait for European answers to all national minority issues. Roma advocacy groups hope that Germany will not follow the highly securitized example of France where deportation is seen as the most adequate instrument of (literally) "getting rid of the problem".[32]

Although the living conditions of the Roma may be better in German cities than in rural areas of Romania or Bulgaria, the socio-economic inequality between the majority and the minority groups is particularly striking in Europe's largest economy. In addition to substandard housing conditions, Roma face a lack of health care, high infant mortality rates and other problems connected to poverty and social exclusion.[33] The economic crisis and the perceived impotence of European institutions and national governments have led to an increased occurrence of scapegoating: almost 70 % of Italians stated in a 2008 survey that they are in favor of deporting the Roma, even those that are Italian citizens.[34]

In all of Europe, the Roma are highly securitized. The public debate in France or Italy is more cultural than in Germany,[35] where the same resentments may only be shared in secret because of the feeling that 'due to German history, certain things may not be said in public'. However, the comparative strength of the German economy and the demanded economic utility is used as a rational and value-neutral measurement to highlight that the 'In-Group' is, in

30 European Commission Directorate-General for Employment and Social Affairs: *The Situation of Roma in an Enlarged European Union*. 2004. http://ec.europa.eu/social/BlobServlet?docId=99&langId=en (accessed 20.05.2014); McGarry: The Dilemma of the European Union's Roma Policy.

31 Will Guy: EU Initiatives on Roma: Limitations and Ways Forward. In: Sigona / Trehan (eds): *Romani Politics in Contemporary Europe*, pp. 23–59.

32 McGarry: The Dilemma of the European Union's Roma Policy; Alexandra Nacu: From Silent Marginality to Spotlight Scapegoating? A Brief Case Study of France's Policy towards the Roma. In: *Journal of Ethnic and Migration Studies* 38,8 (2012), pp. 1323–1328; Owen Parker: Roma and the Politics of EU Citizenship in France: Everyday Security and Resistance. In: *Journal of Common Market Studies* 50,3 (2012), pp. 475–491.

33 Kostadinova: Minority Rights as a Normative Framework.

34 Tom Kington: 68 % of Italians Want Roma Expelled – Poll. In: *The Guardian Online*, 17.05.2008. http://www.guardian.co.uk/world/2008/may/17/italy (accessed 20.05.2014).

35 Parker: Roma and the Politics of EU Citizenship in France.

fact, more valuable than the Roma minority. Furthermore, this 'Out-Group' is believed to be not only not contributing to but even harming the hard-earned success that relies on the German virtues of order and ambition.
In order to de-securitize the Roma minority, the approach has to be tailored to German culture. It does not make any sense to try and develop a 'one size fits all' policy for all European states. Local issues of segregated minorities should rather be tackled more often through community projects by local or regional governments instead of delegating the responsibilities to national, supranational or transnational bodies.[36] In addition, although I agree with the statement that "the various types of injustice faced by the Roma in terms of agency and socio-economic conditions are interdependent", I do not believe that they "need to be tackled in a single normative framework".[37] Such a proposed framework carries the risk of being too general and thus not being able to de-securitize and to improve concrete grievances.
A better approach would include several policy strategies to combat existing inequalities in the areas of employment, housing and education. Social policies should address these issues as problems involving the entire society and not single out a minority as a major problem. Unemployment and social exclusion are not only faced by the Roma but also by many members of the majority population. Therefore, it is essential to focus on integrating all people into the German labor market, education system and society. On paper, the German government has already realized that the societal integration of minorities is essential and that it "does not just improve the day-to-day situation of the Roma, but also means economic benefits for the Member States of the EU. Higher levels of employment and productivity have stabilizing effects on budgets and health and welfare systems. In turn, economic integration reinforces social cohesion".[38] The German government is aware of the issue of minority discrimination and cooperates with NGOs and the European Commission.[39] However, German and European advocacy networks have to be strengthened in order to give more agencies to the Roma people.[40]

36 Andrew Ryder: Snakes and Ladders: Inclusive Community Development and Gypsies and Travellers. In: *Community Development Journal* 49,1 (2014), pp. 21–36.

37 Kostadinova: Minority Rights as a Normative Framework, p. 163.

38 German Federal Ministry of the Interior: *Report from the Federal Republic of Germany to the European Commission. An EU Framework for National Roma Integration Strategies up to 2020*, p. 9.

39 Ibid.

40 Melanie H. Ram: Interests, Norms, and Advocacy: Explaining the Emergence of the Roma onto the EU's Agenda. In: *Ethnopolitics* 9,2 (2010), pp. 197–217; McGarry: The Dilemma of the European Union's Roma Policy; Ryder: Snakes and Ladders.

Another important step to de-securitize the Roma is to provide more information to the public. 'The Roma' is a name for a heterogeneous group of more than 30 groupings, including the Romanian Kalderaš and the German Sinti.[41] Although there is a common language ('Romani'), the Roma communities "have different traditions, cultures, [...], religions, as well as divergent levels of education and socio-economic status".[42] Many people are not aware that although some Roma subgroups may practice "self-segregation", most try to integrate.[43] Stereotypes may not easily be eliminated, but they can be reduced by transparently dealing with the issue. Discussing the situation of minorities and raising awareness of the socio-economic conditions of the Roma should not be claimed by the ultra-right wing parties but be a part of mainstream politics and public debate.

There are some signs of a positive outlook. The attitudes of German citizens towards the Roma seem to be improving. Since 1989, the number of people who admit that they have an unfavorable view of the Roma has halved to 30% in 2009.[44] Furthermore, most Germans are aware of the discrimination that this minority is facing.[45] However, 30% of Germans still believe that citizens would feel "totally uncomfortable" if their children had Roma classmates. Although empirical data disproves the public theory of rising unemployment rates, – they did not increase in Germany after the free movement of workers was granted to Romanian and Bulgarian citizens in 2014[46] – the fear is still widespread.

This still present rejection is used e.g. by the extreme right-wing NPD in order to win voters with a campaign slogan that demands that social welfare spending should be reserved to Germans, particularly denouncing the Roma.[47] A German court ruled that these posters were permissible. Just

41 Rombase: Didactically Edited Information on Roma. History and Politics: Current Situation. http://romani.uni-graz.at/rombase/ (accessed 20.05.2014).

42 McGarry: The Dilemma of the European Union's Roma Policy, p. 127.

43 Pogány: Pariah Peoples.

44 *PewResearch Global Attitudes Forum.* Chapter 6. http://www.pewglobal.org/2009/11/02/chapter-6-opinions-of-ethnic-and-religious-minorities/ (accessed 20.05.2014).

45 European Commission: *Eurobarometer. Discrimination in the EU in 2012.* 5: Perceptions of the Roma Situation in Society. 2012. http://ec.europa.eu/public_opinion/archives/eb_special_399_380_en.htm (accessed 20.05.2014).

46 Federal Statistical Office of Germany: *Short-term Indicators: Unemployment.* 2014. https://www.destatis.de/EN/FactsFigures/Indicators/ShortTermIndicators/ShortTermIndicators.html (accessed 20.05.2014).

47 David Crossland: City Made to Re-Hang Far-Right Campaign Posters. In: *Spiegel Online*,

recently, the Christian Democratic Union (CDU, the party of the current German chancellor Angela Merkel) has exploited the dire situation of the Roma in the city of Duisburg as a negative example for 'social democratic policies' on their local election campaign posters.[48] Minority exclusion is part of mainstream German society. Even though discrimination based on ethnicity is illegal, it does occur.

Conclusion

The main argument of this article has been that German nationalism has changed after the abominable crimes of the Third Reich; minorities are not openly discriminated against based on their origin or religion but based on whether they are beneficial to the German economy. 'Economic Securitization' is therefore an adequate label for the systematic exclusion of societal 'Out-Groups'. The Roma minority in Germany is particularly affected by this economically motivated concept of nationalism because stereotypes are exceptionally persistent and constantly reinforced through the mainstream media and the political elites.

The situation of the German Roma confirms the claim that German nationalism after World War II can be characterized by the concept of 'Economic Securitization' because the effect of the growing number of Roma in the European Union is publicly exaggerated and presented as an existential threat to the German economy and the preservation of the social welfare system. Skepticism towards the EU's concept of "harmonization, [...] ensuring that the mobility of capital, goods and persons within the EU is unimpeded by national economic, political or social constraints" is growing[49] because it is regarded as an obstacle to the successful development of the German economy. Apparently, the introduction of a European citizenship has not replaced national identities.

Nationalist identity construction cannot function without the 'othering' of minorities. It may be worthwhile to consider the apparently resilient character of nationalism in a globalizing world (and a Europeanizing continent) when examining the situation of a stateless minority.[50] Between 1933 and

10.09.2013. http://www.spiegel.de/international/germany/a-921440.html (accessed 20.05.2014).

48 Partei wirbt mit "Problemhaus". CDU-Chef aus Duisburg verteidigt das Wahlplakat. In: *Rheinische Post Online*, 26.04.2014. http://www.rp-online.de/nrw/staedte/duisburg/cdu-chef-aus-duisburg-verteidigt-das-wahlplakat-aid-1.4198548 (accessed 20.05.2014).

49 Van Munster: *Securitizing Immigration*, p. 9.

50 Pogány: Pariah Peoples.

1945, German nationalism was based on the racist concept of superior ethnicity; in 2014, it is economic superiority. To conclude, this article has shown that German politics and media are 'speaking economic security': discrimination and societal exclusion of the Roma is initiated by projecting citizens' fears of economic disadvantages, and decreasing national sovereignty in the context of the EU onto the established scapegoat of the Roma minority. The securitization of the Roma minority is "a socially manufactured problem"; the aim of de-securitization is "to unmake the fabrication of migration as an existential threat to a particular community".[51] Unfortunately, there have been no effective campaigns or policies so far that were able to de-securitize the Roma minority in Germany. I dare to predict that this will not change in the close future.

51 Jef Huysmans: The Question of the Limit: Desecuritisation and the Aesthetics of Horror in Political Realism. In: *Millennium – Journal of International Studies* 27 (1998), pp. 569–589, here pp. 569, 572.

Defiance, Rhetoric and Ideologies of Order, and the Rewriting of Colonial Historiography

An Exploration of Cultural Nationalism in Colonial and Post-Colonial Ghana

De-Valera N. Y. M. Botchway

Introduction: A Brief Contextualised View of African Cultural Nationalism in the Colonial Milieu

The extension and consolidation of the imperialistic and colonisation enterprise of European nation states in Africa that started around the 15th century invited confrontational African nationalism(s). In the African context, this multifaceted phenomenon included the consciousness of belonging to a particular African ethnic and by extension an imagined African family of parallel ethnics, and the attitude of opposition to alien control, and pride in the cultural constructs, traditions, institutions and achievements of indigenous Africa.[1] This ethnic awareness and cultural contentment, like the responsibility to protect African indigenous cultures, traditions, institutions, and achievements form the phenomenon of *African Cultural Nationalism* in the milieu of this study.

The Intrusion of European Cultural Imperialism in Gold Coast: An Examination

The sustained contact between European imperial powers and Africa from the 15th century, according to Mojola Agbebi, formerly D. B. Vincent, introduced "the usages and institutions of European life into the African social system […] a disordering and a dislocation of the latter"[2] and yielded colonialism but more importantly a complex cultural interaction, which Andrew D. Roberts describes as "transformations", i. e. "transformations in social identities,

1 Further insights into nationalism in the African context are found in James S. Coleman: Nationalism in Tropical Africa. In: *American Political Science Review* 48,2 (1954), pp. 404–426; James S. Coleman: *Nigeria: Background to Nationalism*. Berkeley: University of California Press 1958; Thomas L. Hodgkin: *Nationalism in Colonial Africa*. London: Frederick Muller 1956, p. 23.

2 Pastor Mojola Agbebi: On the West African Problem. From: *Papers on Inter-Racial Problems Communicated to the First Universal Races Congress*, ed. by Gustav Spiller, 1911, pp. 343–348. In: Henry S. Wilson (ed.): *Origins of West African Nationalism*. London / New York: Macmillan / St. Martin's 1969, p. 304.

cognitive systems and means of communication"[3]. Roger S. Gocking believes that much absorption and adaptation featured in that transformative process.[4] However, the extension and consolidation of European missionary influence, education, and political control, particularly from the mid-nineteenth century, swayed the pendulum and hegemonized European (Western) culture. This cultural ascendancy unleashed "the complete and deliberate break-down of cultural patterns among the suppressed peoples".[5] For example, Great Britain's Anglicization component of its colonial interaction with Gold Coast, from the mid-19th century, weakened indigenous religious, artistic, political, judicial, and linguistic constructs. The expansionist Western cultural constructs, which Britain sustained when she became the sole political mistress of the colony, threatened prevailing autochthonous economic and socio-political systems, "of self-government as perfect and as efficient as the most forward nations of the earth today can possibly conceive"[6]. The British Colony, which became the independent country of Ghana on March 6, 1957, was created on January 1, 1902. Between 1902 and 1957, the Gold Coast was demarcated into three regions, i. e. Gold Coast, Asante and the Northern Territories. Britain's control, obtained through martial might in combination with brute force, and Eurocentric Christianity and formal schooling, yielded Anglicised systems, which "led indirectly to a Western-modelled restructuring (Westernisation) of the society as a whole."[7] This influence strongly evolved particularly in the urban communities of Gold Coast littoral societies, over which Britain illegally exercised and gradually developed control from the beginning of the 19th century to the proclamation of the Crown Colony in 1874. Hence, by the late nineteenth and twentieth century, those areas had become what Raymond Jenkins describes as "Euro-African Societies".[8]

3 Andrew D. Roberts (ed.): *The Colonial Moment in Africa: Essays in the Movement of Minds and Materials, 1900–1940*. Cambridge: Cambridge UP 1990, p. 1.

4 Roger S. Gocking: *Facing Two Ways: Ghana's Coastal Communities under Colonial Rule*. Lanham, MD / New York / Oxford: University Press of America 1999, p. 3.

5 William E. B. Du Bois: *The World and Africa*. New York: International Publishers 1965, p. 35.

6 Joseph E. Casely Hayford: *Gold Coast Native Institutions*. London: Frank Cass 1903 (reprinted in 1971), p. 128.

7 Bjorn M. Edsman: *Lawyers in Gold Coast Politics, c. 1900–1945: From Mensah Sarbah to J. B. Danquah*. Uppsala: Acta Universitatis Upsaliensa 1979, p. 214.

8 Raymond Jenkins: *Gold Coast Historians and Their Pursuit of the Gold Coast Pasts: 1882–1917*. Ph.D. Dissertation, University of Birmingham 1985, pp. 43–50. See also Raymond Jenkins: Gold Coasters Overseas, 1880–1919: With Specific Reference to their Activities in Britain. In: *Immigrants and Minorities* 4,3 (1985), pp. 5–52.

School curricula, largely centred on Western epistemic and cosmological ethos, marginalised and peripheralized indigenous values, norms and epistemic traditions. It Europeanized many of its aborigine students and alienated them from their local customs. However, it also produced a corps of Western educated Gold Coasters whose acquisition of literary skills did not only confer on them the title of "enlightened" elites but gave them sufficient prospects for leadership position in the rising "modern" and complex societies of the colony, for which many would have been unqualified for in their indigenous societies. Many became appendages (the "periphery") to the colonial administration (the "core") and for years served as consultants, advisors, diplomats, teacher-catechists,[9] and useful mediators for the establishment's bureaucracy and the public, and between the hinterland aborigines and coastal Europeans. This relatively small homogenised yet influential nouveaux riches corpus of Europeanized Africans or Black English, and Anglo-Fantis[10] (as one critic described them in the Euro-African society of Cape Coast) wherever they were, considered themselves the natural inheritors of colonial rule in the colony. Many of the grassroots aspired to join this group.
Eurocentric indoctrination from pulpits and schools demeaned most indigenous beliefs, institutions and practices and practitioners as heathen and promised the wrath of a Christian God and torments of hellfire on them. In the name of "civilising and pacifying" so-called "barbarous and fierce" people, wars of aggression were commonly unleashed on indigenous societies. Joseph E. Casely Hayford opined that such wars sought to seize the independence and eliminate the institutions, customs, laws and rights, which such people had created.[11] Coercion and out of place imposition of intimidating colonial laws, acts and ordinances, animated by European legal philosophies, enhanced and anchored European cultural infringement in the territory. From 1874, and particularly after 1900, the colonisation endeavours of Britain antagonised most indigenous efforts to defend the sanctity of time-honoured cultures and sovereignty. For example, it took about four major wars – 1824, 1826, 1874, 1900/1901, for the British to finally subjugate the Asante. The Crown deliberately humiliated Prempe, the Asantehene (Paramount chief of

9 Adu Boahen: *Ghana, Evolution and Change in the Nineteenth and Twentieth Centuries*. London: Longman 1975.

10 Kobina Sekyi: *The Blinkards*. London: Rex Collings 1974. Originally written in c. 1915. An original typescript can be found in Public Records and Archives Administration Department (PRAAD), Cape Coast, 644/64.

11 Casely Hayford: *Gold Coast Native Institutions*, p. 258.

Asante), whose person and office symbolized the custodianship and sanctity of Asante culture. The Asantehene, who culture required to not submit in public, was coerced to perform a public act of submission aimed to breach the sacredness of Asante culture before the British governor. The monarch Prempe and his mother Yaa Kyiaa, the Queen of Asante, were threatened and forced to prostrate before a mere officer of the British monarch.[12] They embraced his feet and those of Sir Francis Scott and Colonel Kempster.[13] This humiliating rite, for now, suffices as one of the cases where the foundation of an indigenous culture was assaulted by British force.

"Raw" Defiance as Resistance: Indigenous Rulers and Cultural Nationalism

The character of resistance emerged among endogenous elements who, upon becoming conscious of that adverse cultural onslaught (Westernization and Anglicization), adopted different methods to restrain it and protect the foundation of local cultures. A continuum of initiatives and acts of defiance fertilised and sustained this tradition of nationalism until independence in 1957. Incidentally, Western educated Gold Coasters were part of those who took up arms against the system that produced them. They were primarily incited by two worries: (i) Eurocentric colonial historiography excised and/or belittled the role of indigenous ancestors and their deep thought and culture to the development of the histories of the territory, and (ii) claiming it as its "colony" Britain increasingly positioned itself as the suzerain of Gold Coast. But what kind of colony was it? The Western educated people, who were living in the colony, wanted to define whether or not it was a colony by settlement or cession or conquest in order to be able to define the actual nature of the relationship that should exist between the local territory and Britain. Their reaction, which Philip D. Curtin labelled as "intellectual responses to European culture"[14] manifested in the form of writings – books and newspaper articles, and argumentative speeches, and establishment of study groups, like *Mfantse Amanbuhu Fekuw* (Fante Nationalist Society) in Cape Coast,[15] about local aboriginal history, culture, society, law and government. The Fante

12 Francis K. Buah: *A History of Ghana.* London: Macmillan 1989, p. 96.

13 Du Bois: *The World*, p. 36.

14 Philip D. Curtin (ed.): *Africa and the West: Intellectual Responses to European Culture.* Madison: University of Wisconsin Press 1972.

15 David Kimble: *A Political History of Ghana.* Oxford: Clarendon 1963, p. 150.

Nationalist Society, a pioneer of well-organised cultural nationalist groups in the colonial territory, eventually birthed the Aborigines Rights Protection Society, in the 1890s, to take opposition to and halt the advancement of the infamous Crown Lands Bill of 1894–1897, which was one of the ill-judged British judicial interference with the indigenous system of land holding in the colonial territory.

The Gold Coast, which Henry S. Wilson, in *Origins of West African Nationalism*, deemed as "fertile in men [and women] who could give sustained thought to these matters"[16] had both some un-Westernized ethnic chieftains like Prempe and Yaa Asantewaa, the Queen of Ejisu, and Western educated middle-class African elites like Reverends J. B. Anaman, C. C. Reindorf, Attoh Ahuma alias S. R. B. Solomon, and lawyers J. M. Sarbah, J. E. Casely Hayford and Kobina Sekyi alias William Essuman Gwira Sekyi, nourishing its cultural nationalism to protect and promote cultural basics like music, language, names, dressing, cuisine, ways of eating, dancing, religion, rites, chieftaincy institution, egalitarianism and communalism. These actors worked to protect their societies from unreasonable and political culture corroding colonial legislation, like the Native Jurisdiction Ordinance of 1878.[17] Open defiance, engendered by a cultural nationalist cause, played out from some indigenous rulers and ordinary citizens. For example the "Natural Rulers" of Asante, suspicious of cultural ramifications of missionary and colonial supported formal schooling and Christianity, fiercely proscribed them from entering Asante. Hence, the first Basel evangelist to visit Asante disappointedly felt that proselytising efforts into Asante "had to wait for better hints from the Lord".[18] The Wesleyans reporting on their missionary work wrote:

> The state of the work of God in Asante is rather discouraging at present, from the circumstance of the people being afraid to expose themselves to the ire of the king, whose frown is indeed death for the people becoming Christians [...] They always do what their king sanctions, whether good or bad, so that, the king himself being a pagan still, they all remain pagans still.[19]

16 Henry S. Wilson: *Origins of West African Nationalism*. London / New York: Macmillan / St. Martin's 1969, p. 265.

17 Buah: *History of Ghana*, p. 106.

18 Extract from a letter, Reverend F. Ramseyer to Freeling, 18th December 1877, mentioning the journey to Kumasi in 1839 by Reverend A. Riis; CO/96/122, as mentioned in Kimble: *Political History*, p. 152.

19 Report of Reverend T. Laing as quoted by Carl C. Reindorf : *History of the Gold Coast and Asante*. Basel: Basel Mission 1895, pp. 242–243, as mentioned in Kimble: *Political History*, p. 153.

Missionary work in Asante became effective only after Britain militarily defeated Asante in 1874 and later in 1896 banished the Asante overlord Prempe.[20] Furthermore, the unveiled defiance and refusal of the rulers of Asante to satisfy Governor Sir Frederick Hodgson's demand for Sikadwa Kofi, which is the legendary Golden Stool, a sacred relic symbolising the totality of Asante political and cultural unity, spawned the Yaa Asantewaa War, which Asante lost to Britain. It was a war which Asante, inspired by Queen Yaa Asantewaa, engaged in to protect the sacredness of its culture. Even though its capital Kumasi was scorched and Asante was finally defeated in 1901,[21] the relic was protected.

On the other hand, the "educated elites" preferred intellectual resistance, with what Casely Hayford defined as "appeal to the logic of facts",[22] because the lethal nature of the new potent military technology of Europe taught them that belligerent rebellion was hopelessly doomed. Their writings and speeches aimed to question European interventions and sensitise readers, particularly Africans, about the truths and imperativeness of African history, and the need to salvage aboriginal cultures. Their satires ridiculed the shortcomings of the colonial agenda, and absurdities in the lifestyle of the "Black Victorians", whom the nationalist sage Kobina Sekyi lampooned as Mr/Mrs. Brofusem.[23] The concepts of cultural revitalisation, what the local sage Attoh Ahuma (1863–1921) described in *The Gold Coast Nation and National Consciousness* in 1911, as "Intelligent Retrogression […] 'Back to the Land' […] 'Back to the Simple Life' of our progenitors […] to rid ourselves of foreign accretions and excrescences"[24] and reactivation of the "African Personality", which "is […] defined by the cluster of humanist principles that underlie the traditional African society",[25] were very active within that tradition of resistance.

Stoking the Fire of Intellectual Resistance: Gold Coast African Intelligentsia and Cultural Nationalism

Apart from writing, lecturing and forming secular societies to publicise their nationalist ideas, other thinkers of the educated elite corps like J. B. Anaman

20 Kimble: *Political History*, p. 153.

21 Buah: *History of Ghana*, p. 96.

22 Casely Hayford: *Gold Coast Native Institutions*, p. 313.

23 See Sekyi: *The Blinkards*.

24 Attoh Ahuma: The Gold Coast Nation and National Consciousness [1911], cit. in Wilson: *Origins*, p. 266.

25 Kwame Nkrumah: *Consciencism*. London: Heinemann 1964, p. 79.

and Joseph William Appiah, alias Jemisimiham Jehu-Appiah, a former Wesleyan catechist, formed Independent African Churches as nationalistic schismatic movements to africanize the ecclesiastical bureaucracies and preach the promotion of aspects of indigenous values within the spiritual and devotional cultures of Christianity. Anaman and Appiah founded the Nigritian Church (c. 1907) and the Musama Disco Christo Church (M. D. C. C.)[26] (c. 1922) respectively. They promoted Fante and other local languages as liturgical languages and the M. D. C. C. frowned not on the indigenous practice of polygyny.[27] The tradition of schism continued into the post-colony moment. Its nationalist fervour inspired the Catholic priest Reverend Dr. Kwabena Damuah (1930–1992) during the second half of the 20th century to "Africani[z]e the worship of God, and promote Godliness and love according to the sacred traditions of Africa."[28] He therefore renounced Christianity and formed Afrikania Mission in 1982 to revive and revitalise indigenous "Theocentric" spirituality and reposition it among the major religions of the world".[29]

It was also prevalent for the early educated nationalists to petition irrational colonial legislation. Others demanded a system of formal schooling, which allowed a deeper study of African history and cultures. Hence many produced "defensive revisionist African historiography and arguments by refutation" to combat the biases of colonial historiography, set the records right about African histories, and highlight the relevance of African cultural values and pride. In support of this revision, Attoh Ahuma asserted in 1899 that "As a people we must grow our own authors."[30] Three other thinkers, who were also part-time historians, namely John M. Sarbah, Joseph E. Casely Hayford and Kobina Sekyi, whose works we would shortly come to inspect, argued for the imperativeness of the correction of the records about history, culture, and, as Casely Hayford put it to "simply say, 'Allow us to make use of our own Native Institutions, which we understand, and which from experience

26 For more on the M.D.C.C. and its founder see De-Valera N.Y.M. Botchway: *Prophet Jemisimiham Jehu-Appiah: The Man, his Vision and Work*. M.Phil Thesis, Department of History, University of Cape Coast, 2004.

27 Kimble: *Political History*, p. 164.

28 Kwesi I. Otabil: *Notes on West African Traditional Religion*, vol. 1. Fourth Edition. Winneba: Ghana 1994, p. 210.

29 Samuel Gyanfosu: A Traditional Religion Reformed: Vincent Kwabena Damuah and the Afrikania Movement, 1982–2000. In: David Maxwell / Ingrid Lawrie (eds): *Studies of Religion in Africa*, vol. 23. Leiden: Brill 2002, pp. 271–294, here p. 272.

30 Attoh Ahuma: By the Way. In: *Gold Coast Aborigines*, 27.05.1899.

are adapted to us.' We shall […] ask again, and, if […] not listened to, we shall hand on the legacy of legitimate and constitutional request to the next generation".[31] Sarbah posited that the impatient imposition, in a few years, of centuries-old European concepts and lifeways

> has generally neglected the duty to understand the African – his life, habits, cast of mind, institutions, and history. Europe has not studied the African, nor understood him […] Europe is apt to forget that Africans are human beings, with human aspirations and instincts, and they cannot for ever be treated like so many dumb-driven cattle[32] . . .
> The African must know himself, his country, and his destiny, and such knowledge […] will […] permeate […] outside until it fills his country with wonders […] his prospects will widen and become brighter as his mind is enriched.[33]

Casely Hayford averred that the correction was vital because, "on the Gold Coast, you are not dealing with a savage people without a past, who are merely striving to copy or imitate foreign institutions"[34], but "Here on the Gold Coast, you have to deal with an aboriginal race with distinctive institutions, customs and laws, which […] European writers may attempt to portray, but which they can never fully interpret to the outside world".[35] Moreover, Sekyi maintained that

> Europeans have been studying Africa, her institutions for years; but the result of such studies, when considered by Africans who can understand European modes of thought and expression, are not altogether satisfactory. A great deal of mischief was done through the hasty generalisations of past investigators and observers, several of whom were not in any way imbued with the scientific spirit […] A few of us in Africa are firmly of the opinion that the interpretation of Africa, of her institutions and ideas, of her various peoples, can best be achieved by the African himself.[36]

These were logical emphases that colonial subjects needed to "world" their locale by interpreting their historical and cultural realities to the outside world. This was their inalienable right. A powerful reminder these observations were that what history ought not to be or should be, within a colonial territory, should not be in the exclusive domain of the colonial power.

31 Casely Hayford, cit. in Wilson: *Origins*, p. 314.

32 John M. Sarbah: *Fanti National Constitution* (1906), chapter 6, cit. in Wilson: *Origins*, p. 281.

33 Ibid., p. 283.

34 Casely Hayford, cit. in Wilson: *Origins*, p. 314.

35 Casely Hayford: *Gold Coast Native Institutions*.

36 Kobina Sekyi: A Plea for the African Standpoint. In: *The Gold Coast Times*, 02.09.1935, p. 6.

Responding to Colonialism with Rhetoric, Ideologies, and History: A Survey of the Intellectual Resistance of Three African Gold Coast Intelligentsia

For elucidation, let us examine aspects of the intellectual resistance standpoints of Sarbah (1864–1910), Casely Hayford (1866–1930), and Sekyi (1892–1956). Their professional lives, and activities and thought trajectories usually did confluence in the realms of law, education, national politics, and philosophy. Although they received Western schooling, with all the three legal minds getting their university education in sterling institutions in England[37] where after studying classical Roman and Greek law and comprehending English legal and constitutional law were called to the English Bar, their foundational worldview was inherited from the indigenous deep thought and socio-cultural systems of their Akan-Fante ethnicity. Being inner members and relatives of some aristocratic families and ruling houses in the Akan-Fante states of the south of the Gold Coast, they were able to utilise these regal statuses and links to access and gather oral primary source materials pertaining to the genesis of the littoral and southern states, aspects of Akan-Fante laws and institutions of the Gold Coast for their historiographical and intellectual resistance to colonial wrongs enterprise. They therefore were advantaged because they understood the two worlds and could easily identify and genuinely criticise the loopholes and ineptitudes in the legal and political structures, and anthropological and historical definitions which the colonial regime obtained from the European world and standpoint and illegally imposed and haphazardly applied to the indigenous African socio-cultural terrain of the thinkers. Their nationalist contemplations therefore decided that tradition was vital and must play a role at least, equally as decisive as Western ideas, in shaping attitudes towards modernization even in the context of colonialism.

37 John M. Sarbah studied at the Wesleyan High School, Cape Coast, and Taunton School and the Inns of Court, England, where he, in 1887, gained admission into Lincoln Inn. Casely Hayford attended the Wesleyan Boys High School, Cape Coast, and Fourah Bay College in Freetown, Sierra Leone. He entered the Bar in the Inner Temple and also studied at Peterhouse, Cambridge, England. Kobina Sekyi studied at Richmond College of West Africa (the present Mfantsipim School), in Cape Coast, the University College, London, and the Inns of Court in England. He acquired a Bachelor of Arts, Master of Arts (Philosophy), and Bachelor of Laws. He became a member of the Inner Temple and Aristotelian Society in 1918. All three, after completing their studies, returned to Cape Coast and became legal practitioners, part-time historians, journalists and national politicians.

These men were subjects of an unfriendly imperial, colonial and capitalist regime, whose government and economics, regardless of petty reforms, fundamentally marginalised African aborigines mainly along racial lines, and exploited their natural, fiscal, and human resources. The illegal colonial enterprise of Europe "created the natural inferiority of the African race"[38] and used the technique of *Divide et Impera* to justify this cultural butchering and racial subjugation and facilitate colonial rule. Its early education and ecclesiastical adventures proselytised many notions that overtly or subtly implied that the European cultural landscape was the *Ultima Thule* in human development, and indigenous cultures, creativity, and cosmologies were substandard. This psychological "cultural butchering" removed many indigenes of the 19th and 20th centuries from their cultural moorings. But a vast, a sad, an increasing experience of the paradoxes in colonialism proved to many thinking Western educated Gold Coasters, so far as true contentment for them and their posterity and sacredness of culture were concerned, that these notions are unfounded. They started to rapidly arrive at an alteration of their earlier undeveloped ideas on the matter. Consequently, the reflections, travels abroad, and readings of the three thinkers, gave them a grasp of the underlying principles of the European colonial order and criticised them as not equal to their indigenous means of making sustainable groundwork for the standard requirements of all members of society, within the present and the future. This realization about the bareness and barren places of the colonial enterprise prompted them to question, from the periphery, the unnaturalness of the core of the colonial arrangement, and challenge improper colonial assumptions about aboriginal history and culture. They advanced coherent arguments to establish the veracity in indigenous jurisprudence, land tenure, social institutions, history and national consciousness.

Aspects of such arguments and rhetoric of order and reinterpretations of history and culture reflect in Sarbah's speeches and articles, like "Gold Coast when Edward IV was King" (1904)[39] and "Maclean and the Gold Coast judicial assessors" (1909)[40] as well as books like *Fanti Customary Laws* (1897),[41] and

38 Joseph E. Casely Hayford: *Ethiopia Unbound: Studies in Race Emancipation.* 2nd Edition. London: Routledge 1969, p. iv.

39 John M. Sarbah: Gold Coast when Edward IV was King. In: *Journal of the African Society* 3 (1904), pp. 194–197.

40 John M. Sarbah: Maclean and Gold Coast Judicial Assessors. In: *Journal of the African Society* 9 (1909–10), pp. 349–359.

41 John M. Sarbah: *Fanti Customary Laws.* London: W. Clowes and Sons 1897, reprinted by Frank Cass in 1968.

Fanti National Constitution (1906).[42] The nationalist ideas of Casely Hayford, a pan-Africanist and Garveyite knight,[43] corroborated many of the intellectual output of Sarbah, who he personally knew very well as a senior professional colleague in the law business and nationalist compatriot. His works included *Gold Coast Native Institutions* (1903),[44] *Ethiopia Unbound: Studies in Race Emancipation* (1911),[45] *The Truth about West African Land Question* (1913),[46] and *Gold Coast Land Tenure and the Forest Bill, 1911* (1912)[47]. His pamphlets included "United West Africa" (1919) and "The Disabilities of the Black Folk and Their Treatment: An Appeal to The Labour Party" (1929).

The ideological import of the works of Kobina Sekyi, the youngest of the three, was similar to those of the other two. After his university education in England in 1918, he dedicated two years to the study of the traditions of his people – the Fante – and became a member of Gold Coast National Research Association. He deepened his respect for African institutions and communal ethos. Thus his works, which were not bulky books but mostly newspaper and public lecture articles and plays, publicised the aesthetic and functional in African culture and philosophy and denounced colonialism. *The Blinkards* (1915), "Morality and Nature" (1915),[48] his M.A. dissertation "The Relation between the State and the Individual in the Light of its Bearing on the Concept of Duty" (1918)[49], "Our White Friends",[50] "The Future of Subject Peoples" (1917),[51] "The Parting of the Ways" (1925),[52] "A Comparison of Gold Coast, English and Akan-Fanti Laws in Relation to the Absolute Right

42 John M. Sarbah: *Fanti National Constitution*. London: Frank Cass 1906 (reprinted in 1968).

43 *Negro World*, 19.08.1922, quoted in Tony Martin: *Race First: The Ideological and Organizational Struggles of Marcus Garvey and the Universal Negro Improvement Association*. Dover, MA: Majority 1986, p. 116.

44 The first book of his was published in London by Sweet and Maxwell.

45 The second of his books, C. M. Philips published it first, in London.

46 It was published by C. M. Phillips in London.

47 Published in London by C. M. Philips in 1912.

48 It was first delivered as a lecture to the Philosophical Society of King's College, University of London, on January 19, 1915. Parts were subsequently published in *African Telegraph* and *Gold Coast Mirror*, on February 11 and 25, 1915.

49 See PRAAD, Cape Coast. Acc. 527/64 for a version of the work.

50 See PRAAD Cape Coast. Acc. 400/64 for a copy. The *Gold Coast Leader* published series of it in 1921 and 1922/23.

51 Kobina Sekyi: The Future of the Subject Peoples. In: *African Times and Orient Review*, Oct–Dec 1917. This work is reproduced in Ayo Langley (ed.): *Ideologies of Liberation in Black Africa, 1850–1970: Documents on Modern African Political Thought from Colonial Times to the Present*. London: Rex Collings 1979, pp. 242–251.

52 See PRAAD, Cape Coast, Acc. 464/64.

of the Individual" (1935),[53] "The Meaning of the Expression 'Thinking in English'" (1943),[54] and "The Best Constitutions are Born not Made" (1950)[55] were works that he produced.

Kobina Sekyi theorised in his dissertation that a state had a moral responsibility of influencing the morality of its people and its constitution of governance. Challenging Euro-Darwinist inspired unilateral theory of social development, where "progress", law and state represented the apogee of human development, he held the view that such a perspective confused civilisation with "progress" and "progress" with culture. Progress in his view was not essentially civilisation because that which was civilised was governed by morality. Thus he opined that the so-called "civilization" of Europe that produced the menace of colonialism, which immorally attacked African societies, cultures, and people as uncivilized, was one which suffered moral deficiency and was rather uncivilized. The European state and quest for social progress were therefore unsuccessful because it neglected adding to the morality of man. Challenging the colonial notion that African cultures generally debased women, he, using the Akan-Fante as case study in his dissertation, which also had a section that explored "The social systems of the peoples of the Gold Coast", showed in his argument that unlike Western forms, the indigenous forms empowered women to occupy high social and economic positions and allowed them active participation in politics. Drawing examples from the Akan-Fante customs, such as the Queen mother's status as the final authority to approve the nomination of a male paramount chief, he demonstrated how the rights of women were protected, roles defined and allowed to exercise important political functions. Similar to those in Sarbah and Casely Hayford, the cultural activist consciousness in Sekyi was critical of aspects of colonial educational, religious, and economic institutions, which it perceived inimical to the cultural survival of indigenous societies. Thus he refuted thorough "Anglicization and Christianization" as passports to "civilization" and progress. He also challenged certain interfering colonial ordinances. For example, he deemed the Marriage Ordinance of 1884 as anti-African, which bigoted

53 The PRAAD, Cape Coast, Acc. 659/64. This lecture series delivered in 1935 challenged British hegemony and law in Gold Coast. It compared indigenous Akan-Fante laws and English laws and favoured the former's application in Gold Coast. It called for reforms in the colonialist-colonist arrangement between England and Gold Coast.

54 See PRAAD, Cape Coast, Acc. 531/64 for "The Meaning of the Expression 'Thinking In English'" series.

55 Kobina Sekyi: The Best Constitutions are Born Not Made. In: PRAAD, Cape Coast, Acc. 423/64.

missionaries fashioned to disintegrate the African family, which allowed polygyny, and engender individualism and immorality.[56] "Wonders will never cease. What has marriage to do with the Government?"[57] was a succinct satirical expression of his disgust, through Old Fish, a character in *The Blinkards*, at the Marriage Ordinance of 1884. The colonial regimes interference in indigenous family life configurations and matrimonial arrangements, especially the plural marriage custom which was indigenously seen as an unfailing supply of population, and the imposition of English-oriented laws on the local terrain, in his view, was preposterous and unacceptable.

As a part-time revisionist historian Sekyi implored Western trained Africans to research and document the African past to liberate it from prejudiced European colonial historiography.[58] Hence his collecting of primary information about histories related to ancient African discoveries, origin, migration and collapse of some societies, and indigenous theology.[59] He condemned Africans who ended up being disloyal to the indigenous state, known in Akan-Fante as *Oman*, and its political weight, cultural norms, and moral values and practices because of their uncritical acceptance and application of certain foreign religious ideas and practices, like that of colonialism-inspired Euro-centric Christianity, which were antithetical to those of the indigenous milieu. Philosophically, he directed the Akan proverb *Oman so ho na posuban sim*, "The Company fence [of society] stands only so long as the state exists", to such converts, their ecclesiastical mentors, and the colonial regime. It was a reminder that the Oman was supreme and loyalty to it was to be paramount for all people and foreign institutions. Exposing the colonial institution's proverbial ignorance and critiquing its lack of respect for indigenous spiritual beliefs and practices of local communities, he explained that:

> our ancestors were above all things a religious people, with whom religion was no mere matter of form or weekly ceremony. Religion with our ancestors was interwoven with the

56 Sekyi: *The Blinkards*, p. xxv.

57 Ibid., p. 132.

58 Sekyi: A Plea for the African Standpoint.

59 See Fanti Nation Proverbs. In: PRAAD, Cape Coast, Acc. 549/64, and An African Political Hierarchy. In: PRAAD, Cape Coast, Acc. 555/64. See PRAAD, Cape Coast file Acc. 554/ 64 assembly of oral account traditions about the history of different ethnic groups. It contains accounts about the founding of Anomabu, origin of Wassa, genesis of Elmina, migration of Akyem Bosome, concept of God in Africa, Asante constitution, rise and fall of Takyiman and the migration of the Fante, arrival of the Fante on the coast, and highlights of Fante history and the oath of the paramount chief Cape Coast.

> whole fabric of their daily life; and therefore when the company system was established among them it was not without its religious concomitants.[60]

As a supporter of a renaissance of the rationality and dignity of the ancestors,[61] he opined that any Constitution that would govern the local national scene in the envisaged post-colony moment should essentially emerge from indigenous political philosophy and must respect the ancient sanctity of the *Oman.*[62] Following his exhortation that scientists, artists and artisans, and professionals, relying on the best of both local and foreign training and locale-friendly paradigms, should improve the local society with their knowledge and skills,[63] he worked closely with indigenous rulers and once served as counsellor to the chief of Cape Coast. He advocated for the sacred institution of chieftaincy to be upheld. As a believer of local modernization, dictated by local time and pace, he did not support externally (colonialism) generated political reforms that undermined the sanctity of time tested indigenous political traditions. He deemed such reforms and "new" constitutions young and inferior to endogenous political systems, and hardly useful to African reality, stability, freedom and especially indigenous political democratic and constitutional concepts, practices and systems. Like the other two thinkers Sekyi refuted the notion that colonialism, which was autocratic in politics, capitalist in commerce, and bigoted in culture and religion, was the Prometheus of political democratic ideas to indigenous Africa. The argument was that indigenous polities were essentially, in their unique ways, defined by democratic and constitutional elements. Sekyi viewed colonialism and its exploitative commercial and religious implications as the principal factors of social disintegration and economic retrogression to Africa.[64]

Generally, his ideas, which were fundamentally stimulated by the notion of "intelligent retrogression" and self-determination, were dually conservative and revolutionary like those of the other two thinkers. Conservative because they demanded a resurgence and repossession of all peripheralized, discarded and suppressed positive local values and institutions. Revolutionary they were because they urged indigenous populations to reconstruct such legacies to meet the needs of their day, and escape the mental oppression

60 Kobina Sekyi: The Parting of the Ways, reproduced in Ayo Langley: *Ideologies*, pp. 251–252.

61 Ibid.

62 See Sekyi: The Best Constitutions are Born not Made.

63 For example see Kobina Sekyi: Our Obligations. In: *Gold Coast Times,* 03.–10.01.1931.

64 See Sekyi: The Future of the Subject Peoples.

and embarrassment of unfettered Euro-philia and Anglo-mania, especially prevalent among the educated elites and "been-tos".[65] Thus in *The Blinkards*, a satirical comedy whose plot revolves around Mrs. Brofusem, the epitome of irrational Euro/Anglomania, whose brief travel to England produced in her the self-delusion that African culture is backward and must yield to "the finer values of the European", Sekyi exposed and admonished the colonial society's embarrassing mimicry of the ways of the "colonial master" and negative attitudes towards its indigenous customary values. Any borrowing by African societies, he counselled, should rationally take the high and functional and positive aspects of European culture, lest they embrace the unrefined low class ones. However, he like the two other thinkers, preached that caution should be taken in the surgery of cultural "grafting" because irrational hybridization of the borrowed, especially the vulgar, and indigenous systems would spawn a grotesque creature of an underdeveloped Euro-African culture of confusion and false values in Africa. He highlighted such a perverted situation in the caricatured lifestyle of Mrs. Brofusem.

He critiqued also the linguistic hegemony of English and sidelining of local languages in the colonial territory. To him languages as key markers of identity were also originally produced from and by unique socio-cultural milieu, therefore their effective intelligibility and application in creative thinking and processes were locale specific.[66] Many English words were deficient in conveying and defining African concepts satisfactorily. For example, he, in *The Blinkards*, challenged an erroneous colonial notion that the indigenous *etam* (shawl) left the wearer "naked". He argued that such an opinion was alive because the use of the word "naked", which in its proper English context connoted something entirely different, had been inadequate in conveying a local conception of bareness. He concluded that actually *etam* and other local garments left certain body parts "bare" not naked.[67] Reminding the colonial administration and indigenous peoples to make actual sustainable efforts to promote indigenous languages and develop their flexibility he brought into question the imposed status and acceptability of English as official medium of instruction in educational and administrative institutions in Gold Coast.

65 'Been-to' was a jargon used during the colonial time for Africans (especially rich illiterates) who had been to England. Satirically it referred to those who returned to their original homes with borrowed aspects of rudimentary English working class culture which they ignorantly imitated and cherished as high class English aristocratic culture.

66 See Sekyi: The Meaning of the Expression 'Thinking in English'.

67 Sekyi: *The Blinkards*, p. 53.

Proud of their origins and history, and convinced that goodness, morality, and sophistication resided in their cultural systems, the three thinkers deemed it their moral duty and destiny to use their mind, pen, and speech, to defend the human dignity and cultural fabric of their people and them from mockery and destruction by any people and force. Hence, John M. Sarbah observed:

> He who uses his opportunity to help raise the masses of his brethren to his own high level [of consciousness] is following his own destiny and cannot be engaged in a more nobler work. But when, from indifference or deliberate choice, an educated African becomes a tool of Europeans of the baser sort, and keeps back, directly or indirectly, the masses in ignorance and superstition, he becomes the greatest enemy of his down-trodden and long suffering race; and the greater his educational attainments and opportunities, the graver his fault and personal guilt.[68]

Consequently, as a brilliant lawyer and orator, Sarbah challenged unhealthy colonial policies. Perhaps the greatest that accentuated his national fame was that against the Land Bill of 1897, which gave so-called public land to the Crown. Challenging the legality of the Bill, he argued:

> another point which we have endeavoured to bring before this [Legislative] council is the definition of what is called 'public land'. In going through the Bill, we have endeavoured to understand the meaning of each closely and the meaning of the words in it. Looking at the definition of public land, our instruction are that the Bill seems to fall into error that every piece of land in this country except those enumerated in section 13 of the Bill is public land; [...] it is affirmed that every plot of land in Gold Coast has an owner whether inch, piece or plot, the waste land or forest land[69].

He boldly exposed the Bill as illegal and a violation that would "deprive the Aborigines of their [natural absolute] right in the soil of their native land", dissolve the different rights to land for individuals, families and community, weaken native authority, and break family bonds.[70] The Bill was withdrawn.

Spurred to use acts of defiance, rhetoric of order, arguments by refutation and defensive historiography to correct biases and inaccuracies in colonial laws, historiography and anthropological reports, the three thinkers argued with sociological and historical evidence that Africa had a glorious pre-colonial past and that unobstructed, its people could cause a cultural, historical

68 Sarbah: *Fanti National Constitution*, p. 249.

69 Extract of the Minutes of meeting of the Legislative Council on 27 May 1897, quoted in Azu Crabbe: *John Mensah Sarbah 1864–1910 (His Life and Works)*. Accra: Ghana UP 1971, chapter 3, p. 22.

70 Ibid., p. 23.

and intellectual renaissance for humanity's happiness and development.[71] In Sarbah's *Fanti Customary Laws* and *Fanti National Constitution* and Casely Hayford's *Gold Coast Native Institutions*, the unique features and relevance of some indigenous Gold Coast institutions and the role of the *Oman*, linguist (Okyeame), headmen, and the communal, commercial, and religious systems were highlighted with facts obtained from historical, ethnographic and ethnological researches. Apart from showing that citizens belonged to clans, which constituted matrilineal families, Sarbah outlined the development of the village community, the positions of the "Ohene" (chief) and "Omanhene" (paramount chief). The latter was the head of the nation and *primus inter pares* of the rulers of the people, who, by the unwritten constitutional provision of the Oman, collectively decided cases and legislature. Indigenous constitutions, he argued, were as old as the history of the people and naturally applicable to the people. Sarbah demonstrated knowledge about the complex legal processes and principles which regulated the government of the Akan-Fante social organizations, which he claimed was politically democratic.

In *Fante National Constitution*, Sarbah showed the beginnings of British jurisdiction in Gold Coast. Reiterating the view of Brodie Cruickshank, a British Gold Coast trader and official who stayed in Gold Coast from c. 1835–1854,[72] and on occasion acted as administrator and governor of the British settlements, that:

> indeed, we had no legal jurisdiction in the country whatsoever. It had never been conquered or purchased by us or ceded to us. The chiefs, it is true, had, on several occasions, sworn allegiance to the Crown of Great Britain but by this act they only meant the military services of vassal to superior. Native laws and customs were never understood to be abrogated or effected [sic] by it,[73]

he challenged British appropriation of Gold Coast. Offended by prevalent incorrect application of certain English words to define African realities, he criticized Cruickshank's misapplication of the word "allegiance" in his observation. Allegiance connoted a submissive position for the indigenous chiefs he made reference to, but they, Sarbah argued, did not regard themselves as such in the English sense of the word. Challenging the extension of British

71 Devine E.K. Amenumey, Professor of History: Lecture on Intellectual History of Ghana, delivered in October 2002, University of Cape Coast, Department of Arts, Cape Coast. (Notes in possession of the author.)

72 Brodie Cruickshank produced the two volumes *Eighteen Years on the Gold Coast of Africa*. London 1853 (Reprint: London: Frank Cass 1966).

73 Sarbah: *Fanti National Constitution*, p. 88.

laws beyond the limits of British settlements, he asserted that indigenous rulers did not confer any exclusive powers and rights on the British Crown. Petitioning the Secretary of State on June 5, 1889 on behalf of chiefs and peoples of Cape Coast, he showed the unfairness in and of British rule and logically averred that the Gold Coast territory was not *tabula rasa* obtained and settled on by British subjects through total conquest or cession. He said *inter alia* "today we are being ruled as if we had no indigenous institutions, no language and no national characteristics, no homes".[74] He implied that the British signed treaties of friendship or protection with indigenous inhabitants and sovereignties and therefore it was immoral for the former party to arrogate to itself a hegemonic status and treat the other with disrespect. He, like Sekyi, condemned the indiscriminate imposition and application of 'English' laws in Gold Coast. He disapproved the Marriage Ordinance of 1884 as anti-African in its disregard for indigenous marriage contract laws.

He further challenged an introduced English legal principle, that persons died interstate if they left no "written" wills to govern their property. He revealed that in the indigenous legal setting people did not expire on an interstate level, even in the absence of written wills about their assets. People often than not gave oral directions about their properties before dying. He called for the reforms of all clauses, within introduced English laws, which contravened indigenous laws and sentiments. As a natural member of a society that respected oral traditions, and a lawyer schooled in the way of English laws and the Austinian concept of Law, which supported documented statutory enactments, he argued that "law," whether written, like the British type of laws, or orally transmitted and mentally kept, like the Fante type, should be regarded as law no matter which cultural set-up it is coming from.[75] Hence, functional preserved Akan and Fante legal precepts, and African customary laws, which he deemed were naturally capable of advancement, should be suitably applied in contemporary times.[76] Customary laws, and their legal validity, efficacy and sacredness, he advocated, should be autonomous of colonial courts and the legal definition of English laws. Although his work largely focused on Akan-Fante systems and history, it revealed that Gold Coast indigenous polities and peoples had legal and political institutions, anchored by valid and dynamic democratic constitutions.

74 Crabbe: *Sarbah*, p. 102.

75 Ibid., p. 32.

76 Sarbah: *Fanti Customary Laws*, p. 6, 23.

On the issue of dress fashion, linguistic and naming culture heritage, Sarbah rejected unrestricted assimilations and prioritization of European garments, languages, names as markers of "civilization". He believed that the use of African ones did not connote backwardness. For example on language he argued "The fact that a man [/woman] (African) [can understand their language but] cannot read or write a foreign language is not a positive proof, that he[/she] is not astute in business, or [...] ignorant, or possesses not natural intelligence or ability for any useful work".[77] Consequently, it was in a quest to publicly broaden such cultural convictions, that he and some elites, who were "dissatisfied with the demoralizing effects of certain European influences, and were determined to stop further encroachment with their nationality"[78], formed the *Mfantse Amanbuhu Fekuw* in 1889 in Cape Coast. When it metamorphosed into the A. R. P. S. in the 1890s, which, according to Parker, was the "Gold Coast's first 'protonationalist' elite political organization",[79] it maintained its original mission and protected the right of indigenes to land[80], and strongly criticised those Africans it regarded as scornful of local culture heritage and customs. While it tolerated western educated Africans, it shunned Europeanized indigenes. The statement, "We simply want our education to enable us to develop and to improve our native ideas, customs, manners, and institutions",[81] highlighted in the *Gold Coast Aborigine*, showed the group's enduring orientation. The practical steps it took to collect, discuss, and compile a record of native sayings, customs, laws, and institutions[82] to deliberately revive the African culture, music, language, dress, and names, and promote history and culture, as instruments of political agitation, elicited a ready response in Cape Coast.[83] As a close monitor of colonial designs, it championed agitations for social and constitutional reforms right up to the 1930s.[84] The group's enduring demand for a formal schooling system that would teach subjects in African history, language, and culture to promote cultural awareness yielded gains. Governor Frederick Guggisberg acquiesced and

77 Sarbah: *Fanti National Constitution*, cit. in: Wilson: *Origins*, p. 295.

78 Ibid., p. xvii.

79 John Parker: *Making The Town: Ga State and Society in Early Colonial Accra*. Portsmouth, NH / Oxford: Heinemann and James Currey 2000, p. 201.

80 Kofi N. Awoonor: *Ghana: A Political History From Pre-European To Modern Times*. Accra: Ghana UP 1990, p. 91.

81 *Gold Coast Aborigines*, 08.02.1902, quoted in Kimble: *Political History*, p. 360.

82 Ibid.

83 Kimble: *Political History*, p. 150.

84 Buah: *History of Ghana*, p. 94.

"encouraged the teaching of African history and language".[85] Achimota College, established in 1927, began this process. This was the genesis of formal teaching of African history and aspects of culture in Ghanaian schools.

Sarbah and many members of the society practically took pride in speaking Fante, wearing the *etam*, in the indigenous throw-over-shoulder style, as part of their usual dressing, consigning their so-called Christian (European) names to the background and formalising their African names. It was this same matter with names that the likes of Reverend S. R. B. Solomon, William Esuman Gwira, Joseph William Appiah and Francis Nwiah became Attoh Ahuma, Kobina Sekyi, Jemisimiham Jehu-Appiah and Kwame Nkrumah respectively. Some "Europeanised" elites and colonial administrators scorned Sarbah and his colleagues, as "gone Fantee" adventurous who had tumbled into backwardness and the low level of the Tamfurafu (wearers of *etam*). Countering such name calling, Sarbah, who was the first African barrister in Gold Coast, wrote his certainty that it was better to be called by one's own name than be known by a foreign one and possible it was to acquire western learning without neglecting one's mother tongue. Furthermore, the African dress, he argued, was equal to Greco-Roman garbs and need not be thrown aside.[86] He therefore espoused the public wearing of African clothes. This position was also taken by Sekyi, who, making the indigenous Kente *etam* a common dress code of his,[87] suggested that Gold Coast African professionals, like lawyers, should be able to wear African dress and *etam* to perform their professional duties. Similarly, Casely Hayford argued that "the wearing of the native [sic] dress to the extent of suggesting that academic gowns should give way, in African Universities, to traditional garbs," because dress and habits matters "goes to the root of the Ethiopian's [a term he used for Africans] self-respect".[88]

Pioneering calls of this nature influenced some latter-day famous nationalists like Ephraim Amu, and Kwame Nkrumah. Amu, one of the country's celebrated music composers,[89] angered his employers – the Presbyterian Missionaries of the Akropong Teacher Training College, in the Eastern province of the colony – for preaching in Church while wearing the "pagan" *etam*. He

85 Boahen: *Ghana*, p. 114.

86 Sarbah: *Fanti National Constitution*, p. xvi.

87 Fred Agyeman: *Amu the African: A Study in Vision and Courage*. Accra: Asempa 1988, p. 60.

88 Casely Hayford: *Ethiopia Unbound*, p. xxviii.

89 Famous for the patriotic "Yen ara asaase ni" (This is our land) and the popular "[Asante] Bonwere Kente".

curtailed his interest to join the Presbyterian priesthood[90] after this cultural provocation. Acting with immense faith in the cultural revival and preservation cause, he boldly wore the shawl and promoted the use of some traditional musical instruments, which the missionaries deemed "heathen", in music composition and performance.[91] Eventually, the college and church in Akropong accepted such instruments for devotional purposes and "his work on African music, his pride in sensible and practical indigenous attire [...] inject[ed] new meaning and dignity into the muscles of Ghana and African culture and civilization".[92] Among other things Nkrumah, Ghana's premier president, also signified his African cultural nationalist thought through indigenous costumes. As interpreted by George Hagan, he usually wore *fugu* (smock) from the northern part of the country "as his battle [action] dress, as it was for some leaders in the olden days", and the Kente shawl, from the south, for non-belligerent "formal occasions". Nkrumah "used elements of cultural attire to show that customs from different ethnic cultures were merely different [microcosmic] aspects or manifestations of one [indigenous] cultural identity, the Ghanaian [African] identity".[93] All the nationalist thinkers reasoned to use aspects of world cosmopolitan culture, yet they found it beneficial and wise to endeavour to preserve and project African ones to maintain for themselves and posterity those cultural markers of their African identity.

Casely Hayford expressed some of his politico-cultural nationalist views in *Gold Coast Native Institutions*. On the validity of the indigenous system in governance, he espoused the view that officials at Downing Street, London, should partake in external administration, and leave the internal government of indigenes peoples "to develop upon the natural lines of their own institutions",[94] because the European, he averred, was not superior to the African. Thus calling for the destruction of all colonial schemes to submerge Africa, he iterated to the National Congress of British West Africa, in Lagos in December 1929, that unacceptable it was to remain nonchalant "while propagandists of another race are spreading abroad doctrines which may submerge our continent [Africa] and make the Black man perpetually a hewer of wood and drawer

90 Agyeman: *Amu*, p. 75.

91 Ibid., photo plates 4–9.

92 Ibid., p. 75.

93 George Hagan: Nkrumah's Cultural Policy. In: Kwame Arhin (ed.): *The Life and Works of Kwame Nkrumah*. Accra: Sedco 1991, pp. 1–26, here p. 15.

94 Casely Hayford: *Gold Coast Native Institutions*, p. 7.

of water."[95] While Casely Hayford denounced British patriarchal claims that imperialism and colonialism were in the interest of Africa and its peoples, and challenged British jurisdiction in Gold Coast, he consequently made demands for healthy British imperial policies for indigenous peoples and polities. Like Sarbah, he, as a reviser of colonial historiography, considered the historical fact of treaties of friendship and protection between Britain and indigenous rulers, and argued that Gold Coast was a Protectorate and not a Colony, a nomenclature which he faulted as inappropriate and misleading. Confirming the sovereign status of indigenous chiefs he averred that two treaties of 1831 and 1844 conferred on the British the status of "honest broker" for Asante and Fante. Thus, he argued, the two never relinquished their sovereignty, neither was Gold Coast captured or ceded to the British government. The British claim of political hegemony over Gold Coast therefore contravened the two treaties. According to him "the bond had no reference to territorial acquisition; it did not extend the Queen's Possessions beyond their former limits (the confines of the forts).[96] Therefore, "whatever authority by usage Great Britain may be able to extend in these parts we intently expect will be exercised with fairness, and full recognition of the historical facts relating to British relations with the Gold Coast".[97] In pursuance of his call for the British to be fair in their dealings with the aborigines, he challenged direct taxation and other taxes, which the colonial government unilaterally formulated and imposed on the local peoples. Such taxes, he, like the other two thinkers, described as anti-African and undemocratic. Aware that the taxed English commoners, had representatives in the House of Commons, he argued for significant African representation in the Legislative Assembly to provide adequate representation in the formulation and implementation of policies that would affect them. Hence, he asserted that

> Any important measure affecting the people must be passed with the consent and the direct co-operation of the chiefs themselves [and] [...] what the country requires most urgently to-day is a national assembly where all sections of the community will be adequately represented. This is the fundamental element of progress – the reform at which all thinking men must directly aim.[98]

95 Magnus J. Sampson (ed.): *West African Leadership: Public Speeches delivered by Joseph E. Casely Hayford*. London: Frank Cass 1969, p. 88.

96 Casely Hayford: *Gold Coast Native Institutions*, pp. 159–161.

97 Ibid., p. 167.

98 Ibid., pp. 164–165.

Among other issues, he also discussed colonial prejudices and errors about indigenous spirituality in *Ethiopia Unbound*, a novel-like "intellectual biography [...] that sought to rally Negroes [sic] throughout the world in defence of their culture, institutions and racial integrity."[99] Arguing that the designation "heathen" should not be used for peoples' religions and worldviews, he philosophically challenged any colonialism that engineered an assumed "right of [...] Christians to a monopoly of divine light"[100] and notions that the African landscape was spiritually bankrupt because beliefs and practices that defined their spirituality were vulgarly fetish and heathen. He opined through Kwamankra, the novel's protagonist,

> the word 'heathen' is a relative term, and perhaps your average Englishman has no right to call the average Ethiopian [African] heathen. Ours [spirituality] was the cradle of civilisation and that it had not the permanence that the Christian civilisation [European Christianity] is likely to have does not make it any the less a civilisation; and I, for one, feel nothing but pity for the kind of ignorance which scoffs at what it does not understand.[101]

Challenging the assumed superiority of Euro-centric Christianity he asserted that "I have studied our own Eastern [African spiritual] systems and compared them with the system you westerns [sic] have adopted [westernized Christianity] and find that one broad divinity [God] as well as humanity runs through them all".[102] He explained that indigenous cosmology accommodated a Supreme Being, the same Principle which the Anglo-Saxon and Teutonic called "God" and "Gutha" respectively. Linguistically interrogating the etymology of the Fante terms "NYIAKROPON" and "NYAMI" as names for that Principle, to elucidate the philosophical underpinnings of "African Theology", he argued that they were essentially the same as the Hebraic-Judeo-Christian notions of "YAHWEH" and "I AM".[103] He also denounced as spurious, the colonial claim derived from certain Eurocentric Talmudic Judeo-Christian traditions that Africa was spiritually ignorant with no knowledge of a renowned teacher like Jesus Christ. Hence, he declared, as a rebuttal, that since it was in Africa that Jesus Christ the Messiah found a safe haven,[104] then the African society and its people were destined to lead the physical and spiritual progression of Christianity and humanity.

99 Wilson: *Origins*, p. 40.

100 Casely Hayford: *Ethiopia Unbound*, p. 26.

101 Ibid., p. 27.

102 Ibid., p. 28.

103 Ibid., pp. 5–8.

104 Ibid., p. 9.

Negotiating resistance from the periphery, the three nationalist thinkers indubitably exposed the inadequacies of the colonial enterprise and revised inapt notions about indigenous history and human and cultural ecology so that the peripheralized aborigine would develop confidence in their unlimited possibilities to be self-determined. To this end, Sarbah, who declared that "The African must know himself, his country, and his destiny"[105] also asserted in an attempt to explain their intentions, actions and efforts that "[t]he[ir] [subject African's] ambition to excel in whatever is of good report is not insolence, neither is the determination to cultivate self-respect and to cherish a manly independent spirit, nor is pride of race in the African a sign of disloyalty".[106]

Conclusion

All in all some of the methods, particularly intellectual arguments and discursions, which some indigenous elements in Gold Coast, especially those of J.M. Sarbah, Kobina Sekyi and J.E. Casely Hayford, employed to manifest cultural nationalism against European, especially British political and cultural hegemony in that colonial African environment, were examined in the present article. Crucial was the protection of indigenous history and culture because they were the *force vitale* of African consciousness and identity. In the post colony moment of globalization, the complex dynamic indigenous cultures are susceptible to adjustments. Modifications should however be internally generated and conscientiously guided by indigenous ethos and rationality in a way that would allow the complex to retain its basic values and identification. Blind imitation of the rudiments of foreign cultures would be detrimental to the dignity of the African's sense of cultural uniqueness and verve, because "any human relationship cast in the model imitator mould tends towards a superior-inferior stratification of attitudes. It is psychologically difficult for a model to regard an imitator as his equal". [107]

105 Sarbah: *Fanti National Constitution*, pp. 234–235.

106 Sarbah, cit. in Wilson: *Origins*, p. 301.

107 Coleman: *Nigeria*, p. 147.

Constructions

Transcending the Spatialized Other in and through Jeanette Winterson's *The Stone Gods*

Solveig Lena Hansen / Cathrin Cronjäger

Introduction

"Already we've got an Us and a Them. Seems like you've turned into a Them" (199), a companion says to Billie Crusoe, the female protagonist of Jeanette Winterson's *The Stone Gods*.[1] This marks the moment when Billie deserts her home, located in so-called 'Tech City,' and deliberately becomes a social outcast by entering its far side, so-called 'Wreck City.' Both are metropolises of the Central Power state, a totalitarian, capitalist and fully mechanized regime run by one major company, MORE Corporation. To produce and carefully control its own hegemonic cultural identity, the Central Power has discursively established its global opponent, the Eastern Caliphate, as thoroughly Other: uncivilized, underdeveloped, and fundamentalist.

Winterson's negotiation of difference is surely not new to her literary agenda, as she has paid attention to its effects right from the beginning of her writing career. In *Oranges Are Not the Only Fruit*[2], for instance, a teenage girl struggles with her same-sex desire while growing up among fundamentalist Evangelists in a small town in England. This *Bildungsroman* is reminiscent of Winterson's own maturation process, being adopted and brought up by Pentecostal Evangelists in the small English town of Accrington in the 1960s and 1970s. Contemplating this theme in later publications, Winterson introduces a number of thoroughly postmodern figures, taking Otherness to an extreme by making them real and surreal at once, e. g. the Dog Woman in *Sexing the Cherry*[3] or the enigmatic figure of Villanelle in *The Passion*.[4]

While alterity and its effects have always played a crucial role in her writings, *TSG* captivates its readers through its centrality. Even the planets in this science fiction novel are structured by their potential to be appropriated and alienated as soon as they are exploited and made useless. The currently inhabited planet, the Red Planet, is at the brink of becoming fully disintegrated

1 Jeanette Winterson: *The Stone Gods*. London: Penguin 2007. In the following, we will abbreviate the novel as *TSG* and quote from it only in the main text.

2 Jeanette Winterson: *Oranges Are Not the Only Fruit*. London: Bloomsbury 1985.

3 Jeanette Winterson: *Sexing the Cherry*. London: Bloomsbury 1989.

4 Jeanette Winterson: *The Passion*. London: Vintage 1987.

and hostile to any kind of life, thereby undergoing the discursive process of becoming alien. This is when the most valuable, i.e. richest class is about to leave for a new, pristine planet, called Planet Blue. This place is subjected to the diametrically opposed process, i.e. the discursive conversion of something unknown into something known. In *TSG*, the status and negotiation of social/cultural difference is thoroughly interwoven with spatial practices that add up to a dystopian depiction of a humanity caught in an eternal loop of degeneration and destruction. Winterson's use of the sci-fi genre is thus marked by an exploration of Otherness and its correlation with processes of discursive and spatial exclusion. *TSG* suggests that to have an effect on the hierarchical relation between center and periphery means to start focusing on the most personal level. As much as the story depicts a dystopian humanity, it does formulate a utopian solution: When Billie falls in love with the post-human female 'robo sapiens', Spike, a pivotal moment of personal growth sets in. The conscious action of getting involved with an entity so different from her hints over and over again at a possible liberation from the infinite cycle of human destructiveness.

Following the novel's claim that Othering is ethically problematic since it is the basis for stigmatization, exploitation, and hostility, we intend to analyze *TSG* as a negotiation of both individual and collective spatial practices that influence the protagonists' lives and their immediate surroundings. Using *TSG* as a scenario for a thought experiment, we want to scrutinize the moral relevance of encounters with Others, arguing for a practice of 'giving each other space' instead of 'spatializing the Other' as a contribution to a good life. Furthermore, we want to explain how queer sci-fi novels like *TSG*, itself a particular literary genre, can contribute to the political and cultural critique of Othering.

Thereby, we use 'Other' (with a capital 'O') as a reference to colonized and marginalized subjects in order to "connote an abstract and generalized but more symbolic representation of empire's 'others'"[5], while we use the word 'other' to denote an entity different from the self in a non-hierarchical sense.

5 Bill Ashcroft / Gareth Griffiths / Helen Tiffin: Othering. In: Bill Ashcroft / Gareth Griffiths (eds): *Post-Colonial Studies. The Key Concepts*. London / New York: Routledge 2013, pp. 156–158, here p. 156.

Spatializing the Other

As scholars of the spatial turn point out, the category of space is essential to the analytical differentiation of all entities, e.g. discerning one identity as 'separate' from one's 'own.'[6] While in this case the separation of entities is the *result* and space the analytic *tool*, the process of political Othering firstly produces social hierarchies, stigmata, and stereotypes.[7] Postcolonial scholars especially argue that "[t]he existence of others is crucial in defining what is 'normal' and in locating one's own place in the world"[8]. Here, 'Other' "can refer to the colonized others who are marginalized by imperial discourse, identified by their difference from the center and, perhaps crucially, become the focus of anticipated mastery by the imperial 'ego'"[9]. Within this process, spatial demarcations can be conceptualized as an *outcome* of previously constructed differences.

While 'space' can be seen as a category to dissect distribution and difference, 'place' refers to concrete localities and constellations of entities.[10] In *TSG*, separate places are generated on numerous levels: the universal, the global, the local, and even the interpersonal one. In all these places, the position of the Other is a peripheral one – in the background, at the border, on the margin, in the wilderness, etc. Moreover, the more pronounced the Other, the lower their status in a society that pushes them off-center into spaces of (graded) difference.

This depiction is similar to the work of Zygmunt Bauman. In *Wasted Lives*, he argues that the production of '"human waste"', i.e. of the marginalized Other, is a notable effect of modern "*order-building*" and "*economic progress*"[11]. In that way, the creation of places for the Other can be understood as an effect of Western capitalist history. Interpreting spatialization this way, the material structure of places (i.e. topography) and their social, relational

6 Michael Pinsky: *Future Present. Ethics and/as Science Fiction.* Madison / Teaneck: Fairleigh Dickinson 2003, pp. 30–39.

7 Gayatri Chakravorty Spivak: The Rani of Sirmur. In: Francis Barker / Peter Hulme / Margaret Iversen / Diane Loxley (eds): *Europe and Its Others.* Colchester: University of Essex Press 1985, pp. 128–151, here p. 132.

8 Bill Ashcroft / Gareth Griffiths / Helen Tiffin: Other. In: Ashcroft / Griffiths (eds): *Post-Colonial Studies. The Key Concepts*, pp. 154–156, here p. 154.

9 Ibid., p. 155.

10 Benno Werlen: Körper, Raum und mediale Repräsentation. In: Jörg Döring / Tristan Thielmann (eds): *Spatial Turn. Das Raumparadigma in den Kultur- und Sozialwissenschaften.* Bielefeld: Transcript 2008, pp. 365–392, here p. 383.

11 Zygmunt Bauman: *Wasted Lives. Modernity and its Outcasts.* Oxford: Polity 2011, p. 5 (italics in original).

structure (i.e. topology) are dynamically linked by means of human action and influenced by historical factors. The distribution of space together with the (self-)positioning of individuals can thus be understood as a powerful dialectic between social actions and social structures.[12] This taxonomy makes it possible to consider the materiality of places in direct relation to their social settings and to analyze the "'negotiation of spatiality'"[13]. In *TSG*, Billie's first recognition of social demarcations through space happens on the (literally) universal scale when she understands the full dimension of the mission to Planet Blue:

> 'Spike – what exactly is the plan for Planet Blue?' 'Destroy the dinosaurs and relocate.' 'That's the official story. What's the real story?' 'The rich are leaving. The rest of the human race will have to cope with what's left of [Planet Red], a planet becoming hostile to human life after centuries of human life becoming hostile to the planet. [...] MORE is building a space-liner called the *Mayflower*. It will take those who can afford it to Planet Blue, where a high-tech, low-impact village will be built for them. MORE is recruiting farmers from the Caliphate to make a return to sustainable mixed farming to feed the new village.' (73–74)

Here, the material order of the new, unexploited, and 'maiden-like' planet is contrasted with the old Red Planet, which has been destroyed by what humans call progress and has been turned into a place fully hostile to human life. While the Red Planet has a projected remaining life span of fifty years, the MORE Corporation is planning to conquer new spaces in order to relocate the rich elite of the Central Power to Planet Blue. This topologically separated society, with a topographical segregation as its outcome, illustrates the hierarchy on the Red Planet, which then pre-(s)elects the privileged rich and leaves the rest of the human race to die. By calling the ship for the colonization of the new planet *Mayflower*, Winterson quite obviously refers to the process of the first European settlement of the United States in 1620, which is but one cutting remark towards the role major Western democracies have played within destructive processes. In addition, the accumulation of intertextual references to both literary history and historiography establishes a network that alludes to the West's utopian rhetoric of conquering new spaces and, of course, to the West's utopian tradition of imagining the 'non-existing', yet 'perfect' place. Criticizing this tradition, feminist scholars have pointed out that this new and

12 Anthony Giddens: *The Constitution of Society. Outline of the Theory of Structuration*. Oxford: Polity 1984, pp. 121–127.

13 David Harvey: *Spaces of Hope*. Edinburgh: Edinburgh UP 2000, p. 180.

perfect place never was a utopia for everyone,[14] something that dystopias such as *TSG* have repetitively demonstrated by narrating the perspective of non-privileged subjects at 'hidden places'.
This kind of spatial practice becomes most obvious in the process of Othering between different nation states, as Edward Said has pointed out.[15] Along these lines, the recruiting of children from the Eastern Caliphate for the sex industry in *TSG* can be translated into a topographical division with its concomitant topological power distributions of the more influential, i. e. richer Central Power:

> The Central Power is a democracy. We look alike, except for rich people and celebrities, who look better. That's what you'd expect in a democracy. So, sexy sex is now about freaks and children. [...] Kids under ten are known as veal in the trade. [...] [They] are Caliphate kids. We buy them. We wouldn't do it to kids in the Central Power because (a) it's illegal and (b) we're civilized. (23)

Here, arguments of Otherness are ironically pushed to the extreme by separating one's 'own', i. e. civilized and valuable children from the 'Others', bought from Other places and imported, not as humans, but as mere goods into one's 'own' system.
Similarly, practices of spatialization are narrated as a process within national boundaries, i. e. on the local level. Here, the effects of Othering in correlation to space become doubly apparent because the factor of "order-building"[16] is introduced. In the beginning of the novel's third part, for example, Billie offers an elongated description of her surroundings: "Curfew Zones. Routine military patrols in 'areas of tension'. CCTV on every street [...]. Right to enter homes and business without warrant. [...] To distract from all this, the Government built a super-casino in every city" (156). Following Bauman, these spatial constellations appear more as a result of Tech-City's orders, which require control and surveillance as well as a limited mobility of its citizens. Again, an interdependence of topography and topology is visible: The agency of its citizens is limited as is their mobility in the public sphere, exceeding the demarcation of their homes. Thus, 'artificial' demarcations such as boundary posts, walls or watchtowers can be understood as expressions of topological relations.

14 Elisabeth Grosz: *Architecture from the Outside. Essays on Virtual and Real Space.* Cambridge, MA / London: MIT 2001, pp. 132–137.

15 Edward W. Said: *Orientalism.* London: Routledge & Kegan 1978.

16 Bauman: *Wasted Lives*, p. 30.

As Bauman further claims, any process of 'ordering' necessarily entails the spatializiation of 'waste': "Where is design, there is waste. No house is really finished before the building site has been swept clean of unwanted leftovers. When it comes to designing the forms of human togetherness, the waste is human beings. Some human beings who do not fit into the designed form nor can be fitted into it."[17] This interdependency of ordering and spatialization as well as its seemingly endless potential to come up with depictions of the Other come to yet another local and pivotal point in *TSG's* last chapter, where Billie enters Wreck City. This place used to be highly evolved but has been exploited, destroyed, and abandoned by the rich and is now being inhabited by what Bauman calls 'human waste'. Wreck City consists of other smaller places such as "the Dead Forest" (192), a radioactive field. This topographical area is introduced as "Tech City's big secret [...]. The incurables and the freaks are all in there. They feed them by helicopter" (203). This area can be understood as topologically structured; the social outcasts in this special place are a result of Tech City's capitalistic practices of ordering. As Bauman writes:

> Chaos is the order's alter ego, an order with a negative sign: a condition in which something *is not* in its proper place and *does not* perform its proper function [...]. That 'something' with no abode and no function strides the barricade order separating order from chaos. Its excision is the last act of creation before the completion of order-building labours.[18]

Briefly applied to *TSG*, Wreck City can be seen as Tech City's alter ego, spatialized in the course of progress and order-building. Wreck City is the chaotic place Bauman theoretically designates, the place of outlaws without any social function. In the novel, a turning point sets in when Billie understands that the full seclusion of these individuals was an intentional and reckoned action by MORE. Thus, the topographical setting, enforced by social order, triggers her recognition. This, in turn, leads Billie to critically examine the workings of Othering.

Love as an Intervention

As seen above, the negotiation of spatiality on the local, global, and universal scale comes along with a critical examination of instances of Othering and degrees of Otherness. Winterson's handling of the Other is one

17 Bauman: *Wasted Lives*, p. 30.

18 Ibid., pp. 30–31 (italics in original).

that is characteristic of the sci-fi genre as a whole, oscillating between what Darko Suvin introduced as "estrangement and cognition."[19] The novel, *TSG*, is itself an 'Other,' evoking our imagination with new futuristic life forms, fully estranged of our presently known and lived reality.[20] Literature, thus, forms part of the discourse about Othering itself: It cannot only stimulate the debate but also propose alternatives to social orders. This strategy also applies in *TSG* when the Other is introduced on the local and henceforth most intimate level. When Billie meets the female-gendered android,[21] Spike, she explains:

> Robo *sapiens*.
> [...] [Humans] have no need for brains so our brains are shrinking. Not all brains, just most people's brains – it's an inevitable part of progress. Meanwhile, the Robo *sapiens* is evolving. The first artificial creature that looks and acts human, and that can evolve like a human – within limits, of course. [...] They remember everything [...]. Ask them what you ate at your wife's first G party and they have the menu off by heart. Except that they don't have hearts. (17)[22]

Reconsidering *TSG's* spatial practices, it comes as no surprise that this encounter takes place on the journey between two worlds, i. e. from the nearly exploited Red Planet to the new place of hope, Planet Blue. The journey can be read as an analogy to Billie's growing critical awareness regarding her own society's cultural norms and mores. The process of falling in love with a post-human being leads Billie to recognize that the concepts that have structured her reality are becoming obsolete. The category that has been considered the most 'natural,' i. e. humanness as a biological entity, must be reassessed in the face of human-like artificial intelligence[23] and, reversely, the fact that

19 Darko Suvin: On the Poetics of the Science Fiction Genre. In: *College English* 34,3 (1972), pp. 372–382, here p. 373.

20 Nina Köllhofer: Bilder des Anderen: das Andere (be-)schreiben – vom Anderen erzählen. In: Karola Maltry / Barbara Holland-Cunz / Nina Köllhofer / Rolf Löchel / Susanne Maurer (eds): *genderzukunft. Zur Transformation feministischer Visionen in der Science Fiction.* Königstein i. T.: Helmer 2008, pp. 17–68, here p. 33. Köllhofer adverts to the social critique underlying especially feminist science fiction in the depictions of the Other in its most abhorrent, i. e. socially dreaded form. No other genre offers such an imaginary leeway effecting the confrontation between a culture and its expelled Others.

21 An android refers to a humanoid robot, while cyborg refers to a human being who has been technologically altered. Thus, Spike is an android who turns into a cyborg.

22 'G party' refers to the day where persons are genetically fixed, thereby interrupting the aging process.

23 This critical assessment of the rather futuristic category of post-humanness can be regarded as an analogy to contemporary debates around sex, gender, and sexuality by confronting us with 'the Other' symbolically. In an era of gender mainstreaming and Civil Partnership Act, a

humanity becomes increasingly artificial by what is considered technological progress:

> 'It's obvious – cut me and I bleed.' 'So blood is the essential quality of humanness?' said Spike. 'And the rest! The fact is that you had to be built – I don't know, like a car has to be built. […]' [Spike responds:] 'Every human being in the Central Power has been enhanced, genetically modified and DNA-screened. Some have been cloned. Most were born outside the womb. A human being now is not what a human being was even a hundred years ago. So what is a human being?' (77)

Billie then states, "'I accept that you are a rational, calculating, intelligent entity" and suggests, "[b]ut you have no emotion' […] 'So your definition of a human being is in the capacity to experience emotion?' asked Spike. 'How much emotion? The more sensitive a person is, the more human they are?'" (78) Emotions and Billie's acknowledgement that they are a valid, even an incommensurable source of trust and knowledge, is the pivotal recognition within a plot that ends in extinction every time rationality is set up as the epitome of human intellect and genius. Billie, despite having (rational) second thoughts, eventually gives into feeling love towards Spike, i. e. the Other: "The strange thing about strangers is that they are unknown and known. There is a pattern to her, a shape I understand, a private geometry that numbers mine. […] She is a stranger. She is a stranger that I am beginning to love" (107).[24]

While Neta C. Crawford points out that the themes of "love, sex, and empathy are a means by which alienation is analyzed and bridged"[25] in feminist science fiction, it is empathy and sympathy which range among the key features Martha Nussbaum regards as essential to the functioning of modern democracies.[26] Arguing that educational systems in Western nations have increasingly become an instrument to teach students to function neatly in capitalist economies, Nussbaum calls for a re-emphasis on humanist ideas taught in the liberal arts and literature at all levels of the educational curricula. It is

cyborg is an obvious Alterity, reminding us of historic or current cultural 'Others' of various kinds.

24 This statement can likewise be read regarding both humanness and gender, i. e. Billie understands Spike's shape due to the fact that Spike resembles a human being in general and a woman in particular.

25 Neta C. Crawford: Feminist Futures. Science Fiction, Utopia, and the Art of Possibilities in World Politics. In: Jutta Weldes (ed.): *To Seek Out New Worlds. Science Fiction and World Politics.* New York: Palgrave Macmillan 2003, pp. 195–220, here p. 203.

26 Martha C. Nussbaum: *Not for Profit. Why Democracy Needs the Humanities.* Princeton: Princeton UP 2010, p. 96.

about the capacity to imagine and empathize what others feel, which enables humans to respect and accept Otherness, which, in turn, builds the basis for democratic citizenship.[27]

TSG, though remaining dystopian in its vision, draws on exactly this emotional potential: Being empathetic towards the Other and its difference in a benevolent sense brings about a deepening of affections between Billie and Spike. Behind this dystopia thus lies the claim for the importance of "love as an intervention" (83, 217, 244), as *the* key to disrupting the vicious cycle of humanity's self-destructiveness. It is, the texts suggest, the capacity to respectfully take the position of the Other in order to understand oneself and one's own being more fully.

TSG appears in some ways like the fictional counterpart to Nussbaum's factual argument, postulating the cultivation of imagination and tolerance inherent in literature. When Billie hopelessly asks, "Poetry didn't save us, did it?", Friday answers ambiguously, "Not once, but many times" (95).[28] Fittingly, it is the confrontation with poetry, love, and sex, which causes Spike's transformation to a human-like form. Even though she was programmed for the improvement of humankind to make decisions unaffected by emotions, she quite paradoxically develops the capacity to feel because she is also programmed *to evolve* (cf. 210, 216): The evolutionary process sets in because she is unable to understand a line of John Donne's poetry due to its 'incorrect' grammar and figurative language. Spike solves this problem by choosing to feel it (cf. 80–81). And because she is unable to rationally understand love, she chooses to trust this emotion until she, eventually, becomes a cyborg by developing a beating heart (cf. 110). What appears contradictory at first becomes evident in the end: Though Spike was developed to be humanity's greatest achievement in the fight against the flaws induced by "emotionalism" (cf. 169), it is her *choice* to experience emotions, and this allows her to evolve them. Spike suggests that this is also possible for humans: "'I merely observe that this is a quantum universe and, as such, what happens is neither random nor determined. There are potentialities and any third factor – humans are such a factor – will affect the outcome.' – 'And free will?' – 'Is your capacity to affect the outcome'" (215). In short, despite her programming, Spike evolves abilities humans want to do away with by all means. To allow for empathy,

27 Ibid., pp. 108–109.

28 Billie contemplates: "Neither art nor love fits well into the economics of purpose, any more than they fitted into the economics of greed. Any more than they fit into economics at all." (169).

love, and affection, the text repeatedly suggests, even (or especially) in the face of Otherness, are at least as important a source of knowledge as rational objective reasoning. Above all, the former serves as the key to humanity's liberation from the destructive cycle. These developments take place on every cycle of destruction, i. e. chapter of the novel, independent of time and space. So it is important to note that the repeated decision to choose love regardless of the time-space axis underscores positive emotions as the possibility to overcome those structures that are marked by rationalism and spatialized Others. The solution, *TSG* suggests, lies in humanity's capacity to intervene in randomness by opting for love, leaving us with the rhetorical question "A quantum universe – neither random nor determined. A universe of potentialities, waiting for an intervention to affect the outcome. Love is an intervention. Why do we not choose it?" (244)

Giving Each Other Space

TSG repeatedly brings society to an end, stating on humanity's inability to either fully grasp the effects of their actions or effectively change their behavior. Finally, Billie understands that the ubiquitously created and re-created rhetoric of hope for a better world and a second chance is futile: "[T]he future of the planet is uncertain. Human beings aren't just in a mess, we are a mess. We have made every mistake, justified ourselves, and made the same mistakes again and again. It's as though we're doomed to repetition." (216) As much as the idea of an eternal repetition might be considered unpromising, it contains a very important idea also spelled out by theorists:

> Only infinity is fully and truly all-inclusive. Infinity and exclusion are incompatible; and so are infinity and exemption. In the infinity of time and space everything may happen, and everything must happen. Everything that was, is and yet may come into being has its place. It is only the idea of 'no room' that has no room in infinity. The idea that infinity absolutely cannot accommodate is that of redundancy – of waste.[29]

Here, Bauman shows that the idea of infinity is a possibility to think without borders. Spatializing the Other is of course impossible when no borders can be reached, or, in the words of *TSG*, when "[e]verything is imprinted for ever with what it once was" (246). Anticipating eternity, chaos can neither be ordered nor even be recognized as chaos. This idea, articulated as a thought experiment by Bauman, is of course utopian and fictional, but still, in the words of Jeanette Winterson, "[o]nly the impossible is worth the

29 Bauman: *Wasted Lives*, p. 94.

effort" (110). Nevertheless, it is precisely the idea of infinity where spatialization is impossible that hints at a practice of giving each other space: "Even creating the smallest place is a moral act, for it involves not only creating but also destroying, and including and excluding. This place we are in right now prevents other things from taking place, and it has arisen by transforming and destroying what existed here before."[30] Thus, a novel like *TSG* can be seen not only as a place to negotiate Othering and its spatial effects, but also as a scenario of "giving hospitality, constructing welcome"[31]. Unsurprisingly, the claim that Winterson herself makes on the book seems to point to a very similar direction:

> Stone Gods isn't a pamphlet or a docu-drama or even a call to arms, it is first and foremost a work of fiction, but I am sure that change of any kind starts in the self, not in the State, and I am sure that when we challenge ourselves imaginatively, we then use that challenge in our lives. I want the Stone Gods to be a prompt, but most of all, a place of possibility.[32]

According to this (and Nussbaum), literature possesses the ability to act like a prompt leading to cathartic changes in the self in terms of a more tolerant and trustful attitude. The main characteristic of Billie is not stoical persistence but curiosity and vigilant spontaneity, i.e. the 'change of self' Winterson adverts to, which affects the reader due to the story's autodiegetic narration.[33] Considering the repetitive claim of 'love as an intervention,' we can clearly perceive the concept of emotionality and respect for one another beyond this catastrophic vision. However, the important idea in *TSG* is that change should start on the interpersonal level since it is, first and foremost, the encounter with the concrete o/Other that requires a decision between 'spatializing' or 'giving space'.[34] In accepting the counterpart as *o*ther (not as Other), in not spatializing them but giving them space, lies – so we argue in accord with Winterson's scenario – a possibility for a good life. The metaphor of 'giving each other space' then means "tolerance of those who do not do as you do" (208). Moreover, the eudemonic idea of love as "concern *for the*

30 Robert David Sack: The Geographic Problematic: Moral Issues. In: *Norsk Geografisk Tidsskrift* 55,3 (2001), pp. 117–125, here p. 117.

31 Jonathan Darling: Giving Space: Care, Generosity and Belonging in a UK Asylum Drop-in Centre. In: *Geoforum* 42,4 (2011), pp. 408–418, here p. 410.

32 Jeanette Winterson: The Stone Gods. http://www.jeanettewinterson.com/book/the-stone-gods/ (accessed 15.05.2014).

33 Autodiegesis, as a narratological term, denotes a story told and focalized by an 'I'.

34 Pinsky: *Future Present*, p. 39.

other for the other's own sake"[35] receives a very political message in *TSG* since not the 'other' but the 'Other' is loved for its own sake. After Spike's death on Planet Blue, Billie remembers, "We were each other's conquered land." (242) The colonized places the novel often refers to are here replaced with a metaphor of a 'conquered' yet deeply loved other, who provides "a place" (243) for the self. The cathartic effect of *TSG* consists of the recurring implication that the purification itself is laying in positive emotions towards the concrete Other on an interpersonal level.

However, facing the effects of modernization described by Bauman, such a change is not only relevant for interpersonal relationships. In order to negotiate Othering on a political level, reading novels like *TSG* might be a starting point to critically reflect upon effects of spatialization in an era of globalization and capitalism. At this very juncture, Iris Marion Young argues for an enhanced model of deliberation, formulating a feminist critique on discourse ethics. "Considering difference as a resource"[36], Young writes, is necessary for political justice and should replace the presumption of formal equality in the political discourse:

> If we are all really looking for what we have in common – whether as a prior condition or as a result – then we are not transforming our point of view. We only come to see ourselves mirrored in others. If we assume, on the other hand, that communicative interaction means encountering differences of meaning, social position, or need that I do not share and identify with, then we can better describe how that interaction transforms my preferences. Different social positions encounter one another with the awareness of their difference.[37]

Only if we admit the existence of Otherness and find a way to deal with it respectfully and productively through communication, a "collective social wisdom not available from any one position"[38] is possible. According to Young, stories are one way of popularizing this difference. It is through stories that we understand the location, i. e. the history, emotions and incitements of our counterparts: "Narrative exhibits subjective experience to other subjects. The narrative can evoke sympathy while maintaining distance because

35 David O. Brink: Eudaimonism, Love, and Friendship, and Political community. In: *Social Philosophy and Policy* 16,1 (1999), pp. 252–289, here p. 252 (italics in original).

36 Iris Marion Young: Communication and the Other: Beyond Deliberative Democracy. In: Seyla Benhabib (ed.): *Democracy and Difference. Contesting the Boundaries of the Political.* Princeton: Princeton UP 1996, pp. 120–135, here p. 126.

37 Ibid., p. 127.

38 Ibid., p. 132.

the narrative also carries an inexhaustible shadow, the transcendence of the Other, that there is always more to be told."[39]

TSG, we lastly argue, offers an important fictional contribution to this debate: On the interpersonal level, it formulates a solution for the daily encounter with others. By confronting Billie with an 'alien' life form, the novel displays the interdependence of the personal and the political. For the political communication and negotiation itself, *TSG* sharpens our awareness that the practice of 'spatializing the Other' could be replaced by the practice of 'giving each other space'. In that sense, as also argued by Young, difference (i. e. the *o*ther, not the *O*ther) is a resource for reflection and a more balanced political discourse. As much as 'transcending the Other' is necessary, it becomes obsolete when we encounter difference in a non-hierarchical way proposed by Young. The obstacles faced by global humanities (as described by Bauman) could be solved in the discourse Young adverts to. Thus, a novel like *TSG* hints at the imperative of sorting out problems for the sake of global justice, by giving its readers a clue to focus on interpersonal relationships.

39 Ibid., p. 131.

Disrupting the Center

Toward a Theory of Global Aesthetics

Kyle J. Wanberg

> Wir waren kompliziert genug, die Maschine zu bauen,
> und wir sind zu primitiv, uns von ihr bedienen zu lassen.
> Wir treiben Weltverkehr auf schmalspurigen Gehirnbahnen.
>
> [We were complicated enough to build the machine,
> and we are too primitive to let it serve us.
> Global traffic travels in model trains of thought.][1]
>
> *Karl Kraus*

The final line from Franz Kafka's short story, *Das Urteil* (translated into English as "The Verdict" or "The Judgement"), is "In diesem Augenblick ging über die Brücke ein geradezu unendlicher Verkehr."[2] ["At that moment, the traffic going over the bridge was nothing short of infinite"[3]]. It is morning, and the bustle of the city is at full throttle, moving in infinite impervious flows which do not alter as a man falls to his death. Georg, the son who has just taken his life after being sentenced to death by his father, is effaced by the final word of the story, *Verkehr* [traffic], a word also suggestive of communication.[4] Encompassing forms of interconnection that are made up of flows within a topography of fluctuation and translation, we can use this image to think about developments that have transpired in the world and within debates about literary production itself since Kafka's own death. Here I wish to consider the traffic of aesthetics under the rubric of globalism and its attendant flows.

1 The German text is from Karl Kraus: Aphorismen: Zeit [1909]. In: *Project Gutenberg – DE*. http://gutenberg.spiegel.de/buch/aphorismen-4692/3 (accessed 29.05.2014); the English translation from Karl Kraus: *Dicta and Contradicta,* trans. from the German by Jonathan McVity. Chicago: University of Illinois Press 2001, p. 46.

2 Franz Kafka: Das Urteil [1913]. In: *Project Gutenberg – DE*. http://gutenberg.spiegel.de/buch/franz-kafka-erz-161/6 (accessed 29.05.2014).

3 Franz Kafka: The Judgement: A Story. In: *Kafka's Selected Stories,* trans. from the German by Stanley Corngold. New York: Norton 2007, p. 12.

4 The word is also suggestive of sexual intercourse, and Kafka admitted that when writing the line he was thinking of "a violent ejaculation" (Max Brod: *Franz Kafka: A Biography*, trans. from the German by G. Humphreys Roberts. New York: Schocken 1960, p. 129).

In *Das Urteil*, the image of traffic supercedes the death of the main character, demonstrating his insignificance. The infinite traffic represents the indifference of modernity and its profusion of exchange networks in urban capitalism. Eclipsing Georg's human particularity, the frailty of his body falling from the bridge, the stream of traffic emphasizes the triviality of his death. This is a symbol of the category of the universal that prevails over the particular. In literary studies, a similar tension arises between complex particularities and a series of universalisms, each in its turn eclipsing the particular voices that are rendered silent in its wake.

This study explores the often crowded significations of the global and its traffic by exploring its recent co-articulation with literary and oral aesthetics. I focus on how the aesthetic articulation of the universal (in various forms) can been seen to cooperate with or critique the strictures of world literature. In so doing, I offer a critique of the global. At the same time, I will explore how the global may be imagined as a process and methodology for undermining Eurocentric epistemologies of world literature. In order to fill out what such a critical postcolonial methodology of global aesthetics might look like, I end the paper with a discussion of orature.

Far from denoting a transparent field, world literature continues to be constituted by structures of uneven distribution, translation, and an overall disparity in linguistic capital across the globe. The universalism inherent in the field's designation has recently provided for much scholarly debate. Emily Apter has called attention to the (un-)translatability of world literature,[5] while David Damrosch adopts a broadly applicable conception of world literature as "a mode of circulation and of reading,"[6] repudiating ambitions towards mastery over the field.[7] Eric Hayot has discussed the formation of aesthetic worlds in order to undo the systemic 'Eurochronology' of modernism.[8] While each of these critics provide valuable explorations into the limits of universalism in world literary study, in what follows I examine how global aesthetics might offer a substantively different epistemology from practices of reading literature designated by the shifting universals: the nation, the world, the planet. Each of these universals creates its own spatial constellation of borders or boundaries between a center and a periphery. The concern of this essay is

5 Emily Apter: *Against World Literature: On the Politics of Untranslatability*. New York: Verso 2013, p. 7.

6 David Damrosch: *What is World Literature?* Princeton: Princeton UP 2003, p. 5.

7 Ibid., p. 299.

8 Eric Hayot: *On Literary Worlds*. New York: Oxford UP 2012.

to illumine and critique these shifting orientations through which literature and other cultural productions have been approached while also examining the emergent discourse of global aesthetics. I begin by tracking the changing idiom of world literature in disciplinary frameworks and in view of processes of globalization. In conversation with these shifts, I argue for global aesthetics as something that reconfigures residual colonial geographies and the "aesthetic feudalism"[9] that developed concurrently with occidental literary traditions.

The Equivocality of the Global

From its earliest dissemination, world literature circulated as something that transcends the limits of national literatures. Yet it was never entirely disarticulated from the cultural frameworks, networks of dissemination, and cosmopolitan desires inherent in the imaginary formation of the nation-state. If a truly global aesthetics is possible, it will have to make a significant epistemological break from the universalistic systems of aesthetic valuation in both national and world literary studies. It is not enough for these disciplines to allow a few more non-Western texts into the canon while retaining their basic structures if those structures are fundamentally flawed.

My focus in this paper is the globality of aesthetics, rather than the aesthetics of globality.[10] The idea of globality betokens a radical kind of equivocality. Over the last fifty years the global has come to seem ubiquitous, from the appearance of the "global village"[11] to current discursive formations such as global warming, global networks, and global security systems. In the United States, the global has crept into the rhetoric around international politics and determinations about foreign policy. By 1975, Henry Kissinger was discussing the birth pangs of a "truly global society,"[12] and in 2003, Donald Rumsfeld declared the existence of a "global war on terror."[13] The term implies the

9 Ngũgĩ wa Thiong'o: *Globalectics: Theory and the Politics of Knowing*. New York: Columbia UP 2012, p. 63.

10 An exploration of the global within the history of aesthetics could provide an important complement to this study, but this is outside of aims of this short study.

11 Marshall McLuhan: *The Gutenberg Galaxy: The Making of Typographic Man*. Toronto: University of Toronto Press 1962.

12 Quoted in Adam Curtis: Baby It's Cold Outside, segment. In: *The Power of Nightmares: The Rise of the Politics of Fear*. BBC Documentary Film 2004.

13 Donald H. Rumsfeld: Global War on Terrorism. Quoted in full in: Rumsfeld's War-on-Terror Memo. In: *USA Today*, 20.05.2005. http://usatoday30.usatoday.com/news/washington/executive/rumsfeld-memo.htm (accessed 29.05.2014) (memo dated from 2003).

teleological bent of de-territorializing processes that expand capitalism's frontiers and can serve as a universal diagnostic for anything from a greater sense of communitarianism to justifications for world-wide violence. Part of my argument in this paper is the idea that the global can also be deployed against these diagnostic processes, in order to take shape as a critical concept.

I have already argued elsewhere towards a conception of "global literature" that included oral forms of cultural production.[14] This concept was intended as a departure from the constitutive exclusions of world literature, which neglects the study of non-written forms of expression such as orature. However, since then I have grown increasingly less easy with the concept of global literature as denoting a significant break from that of world literature. Substituting the global for the world cannot produce a fundamental epistemological break from earlier forms of world literary study for which my work aims. This is not only due to the above-mentioned equivocality of the global, but also because exclusions already inhere in the term "literature." Literature, describing written forms of production, forecloses on works of cultural production in non-literate language communities and predominately oral societies.

Given the sheer weight of the language that surrounds interpretive reading practices, the descriptive terms for what is studied under the rubrics of 'nation,' 'world,' 'globe,' and 'planet' further complicate matters. We may very well ask: what are the significant changes to the material studied under each of the subsequent rubrics in this list? If it is simply a matter of 'rebranding' old knowledge formations with new terminology, then what are the consequences for the discipline? Just as Johann Wolfgang von Goethe's way of imagining world literature as a new international horizon demonstrated the extent that the concept was grounded in German-European cultural rivalries, naming "global literature" a new form of study may yet reflect the extent to which we are still caught up in the European enlightenment tradition that produced world literature. Reconsidering our practices of reading in the light of globalism may emphasize the extent to which such practices of naming effect a double-bind. While the intentions of such projects may be broad-minded and inclusive, conjuring up new regimes of practice with terminology whose implications have not been fully understood jeopardizes their success.

This problem is especially disquieting given the free-floating field of reference of the global, with its opaque sets of relations. When it is deployed today,

14 Kyle Wanberg: A Moving Pedagogy: Teaching Global Literature through Translation. In: Masood Raja / Hillary Stringer / Zach Vande Zande (eds): *Critical Pedagogy and Global Literature: Worldly Teaching.* New York: Palgrave Macmillan 2013, pp.113–130.

the global seems to allude to everything without denoting anything in particular, summoning to mind sinister associations with globalism and globalization. Moreover, the wide-spread adoption of the concept within the academy is symptomatic of the university's growing interconnection with global flows of capital and transnational economic exchange. For example, the ongoing construction of the "global university" (a seeming redundancy) has so far failed to promote popular critique of forms of inequality and injustice around the world.[15]

A stunning example of this is the contradictions that haunt New York University's lofty ambitions. Having dubbed itself the "global network university," NYU has built eleven international academic centers for study abroad and two independent degree-granting institutions. One of the latter establishments, NYU Abu Dhabi, imports vulnerable contract labor from poor countries. This newly built hub has received attention recently for their brutal and extortive rights abuses of foreign construction laborers. The realities that these workers have faced stand in stark contradiction to the guarantees that NYU has made about the fair treatment of workers in the 2009 "statement of labor values."[16] The term 'global' is haunted by these economic and social realities that are conditioned by increasing incentives to expand the scale and increase the rate at which goods and ideas circulate. The confidence crisis NYU now faces because of the rights abuses that were recently exposed at its Abu Dhabi site underscores the extent to which the global is not a transparent category. Rather, what is so deeply disturbing about this catchword is that it conceals the way it operates by promoting some rights and privileges at the expense of others' rights and privileges.

As the process of globalism develops, forms of communication and information join in the commodification process and require circulation (traffic) just like material goods. Not surprisingly, these flows often take place in the same economic networks that have been developed and secured by the material-capital exchange markets. As New York University has so far demonstrated, becoming global means to create a progressively itinerant institution to insure this circulation. This requires the grooming of a large faculty population whose positions are increasingly insecure and easily replaceable (from

15 Spivak discusses the ambitions of the globalist university to minimize the humanities and social sciences in the name of globalization in her new book. Gayatri Spivak: *An Aesthetic Education in the Era of Globalization.* Cambridge, MA: Harvard UP 2012, p. 2.

16 Ariel Kaminer / Sean O'Driscoll: Workers at N.Y.U.'s Abu Dhabi Site Faced Harsh Conditions. In: *New York Times*, 19.05.2014, p. A1.

the university's perspective), and hence one that is also mobile and deployable around the globe. Ideas can now be ordered online and be trafficked according to their consumers' caprice, while those aspects of this global traffic that are more sticky, such as support for unfair labor practices, get pushed out of sight. Under the broad rubric of the global, these networks generate new peripheries that become increasingly neglected and opaque. As Achille Mbembe has remarked, these spaces, bounded off from flows, are left for dead and become part of a vast topography of death-worlds through the operation of a form of power he terms necropolitics.[17] These broadly political concerns with the traffic of globalism set the stage for thinking about aesthetic production because its power works through the very institutions and spaces where literature and art are studied. Globalism in this sense is eminently relevant to how works of literature and aesthetic production are imagined, evaluated, and disseminated. For these reasons and others, it is important to think towards a critical concept of the global that can help deconstruct these formations from within.

Literature as a Rough Map

In his captivating work on Comparative Creoles, George Lang discusses the early formation of European national literary traditions during the Renaissance. Connecting these historical formations with the much more recent phenomenon of the emergence of written creole traditions, Lang offers a picture of how the then-emergent national literary traditions depended on the existence of a pre-existing tradition in dominance against which they vied for legitimacy. He writes:

> National literatures in Western Europe were founded on the same dynamics [through which the ethnotext asserts itself as a legitimate form of representation in a literary discourse]; as against an alien but legitimate language and literature (usually Latin), writers chose a vernacular as literary vehicle and projected a new literary realm, mobilizing the rhetorical possibilities of the new vehicle, all the while borrowing from the rhetorical repository of the previous tradition.[18]

Pascale Casanova has argued that literary traditions have been in contest since the sixteenth century, helping to determine the uneven distribution of what she calls "literary capital." Despite her Eurocentric bias, her point that

17 Achille Mbembe: Necropolitics. In: *Public Culture* 15,1 (2003), pp. 11–40.

18 George Lang: *Entwisted Tongues: Comparative Creole Literatures.* Atlanta, GA: Rodopi 2000, p. 141.

national literary traditions never developed in complete isolation, but in an environment of cultural competition is well-taken and complements Lang's argument above. As she writes:

> International literary space was formed in the sixteenth century at the very moment when literature began to figure as a source of contention in Europe, and it has not ceased to enlarge and extend itself since. Literary authority and recognition—and, as a result, national rivalries—came into existence with the formation and development of the first European states. Previously confined to regional areas that were sealed off from each other, literature now emerged as a common battleground.[19]

These arguments emphasize the extent to which power relations and the prestige of particular nation-states were at stake in the establishment of European national literary traditions. Moreover, the specter of nationalism continues to haunt the space of world literature, just as, in a certain way, the international was always haunting the development of national literature. Goethe's ideas about *Weltliteratur* represent an important shift in perspective from the projects set forth by European nations to promote their own literary cultures. However, this shift does not take place so much in terms of method (in terms of the actual practices of differentiation and contestation) than in scope. The appearance of the world literature horizon did not precipitate an entirely new day for aesthetic valuation in Europe. Traditions of national literature had long been seen as the major lens through which to understand the relative cultural achievements of European political rivals.[20] World literature helped to open up provincialized Eurocentric literary perspectives to nations and civilizations beyond their own purview, worlds already exposed to the expansionist ambitions of Europe's colonial projects. Moreover, it helped to promote and expand the existing networks of translation. Thus, world literature has come to be seen as a cosmopolitan form of literary aesthetics, one that is not entirely circumscribed by the nation form.[21] Yet Goethe did not renounce the kind of international competitiveness that characterized national literary perspectives. In the same breath that he introduces the concept of world literature, remarking that "the epoch of world literature is at hand," Goethe

19 Pascale Casanova: *The World Republic of Letters*, trans. from the French by M. B. DeBevoise. Cambridge, MA: Harvard UP 2004, p. 11.

20 Ibid., pp. 9–12.

21 This becomes the focus of the idea of *Weltliteratur* as it is considered by Karl Marx and Friedrich Engels in *The Communist Manifesto:* as a newly emergent intellectual commodity with its own circuits of production, translation, marketing, and consumption. Karl Marx / Friedrich Engels: Manifesto of the Communist Party. In: Karl Marx: *Later Political Writings*, ed. by Terrell Carver. Cambridge: Cambridge UP 1996, pp. 1–30, here p. 5.

recommends his fellow Germans to enhance their literary endeavors through wider reading practices for the enhancement and progress of German literary culture alone. Here is the oft-cited quote in context:

> But, really, we Germans are very likely to fall too easily into this pedantic conceit, when we do not look beyond the narrow circle which surrounds us. I therefore like to look about me in foreign nations, and advise every one to do the same. National literature is now rather an unmeaning term; the epoch of World literature is at hand, and every one must strive to hasten its approach. But, while we thus value what is foreign, we must not bind ourselves to anything in particular, and regard it as a model. We must not give this value to the Chinese, or the Servian, or Calderon, or the Nibelungen; but if we really want a pattern, we must always return to the Greeks, in whose works the beauty of mankind is constantly represented. All the rest we must look at only historically, appropriating to ourselves what is good, so far as it goes.[22]

Since the time it was first invoked,[23] and despite Goethe's assertion of the incoherence and anachronism of national literature, world literature has not at all supplanted national literary traditions. The struggle represented by the history of world literature is significantly different from these (often) older traditions, but such different forms of aesthetic valuation continue to exist alongside one another, emphasizing the divergent ideological functions each reading practice continues to serve. Moreover, as is clear from the passage quoted above, Goethe was still very much engaged in the project of developing a privileged cultural heritage that was distinctly European in the sense of being reliant upon certain established chains of patrimony. Hence particularities such as the Serbian or Chinese tradition do *not* constitute proper models, however much can be learned from them. On the other hand, the Greeks do provide such a model because the beauty of mankind is constantly represented in them. And this must particularly concern Goethe's fellow Germans.[24]

22 Johann Wolfgang von Goethe: *Conversations of Goethe with Johann Peter Eckermann,* trans. from the German by John Oxenford. Cambridge, MA: Da Capo 1998, p. 165.

23 Spivak distinguishes between Goethe's method of framing the horizon of world literature as something yet to come and Marx's way of diagnosing it as something already secure. Spivak: *An Aesthetic Education*, p. 461.

24 My point here is that the universal that Goethe conceptualized, that is, the "world," is both expansive and yet narrow, liberal and conservative at the same time, an inclusive idea yet with a select ideal. He validates one universal with yet another: the world is that which may be represented by the representation of mankind. Yet at every juncture, these representations concern particularities and the aesthetic valuations of a particular cosmopolitan with distinguishing taste (Goethe in this case), provincializing national traditions based upon the horizon of the universal and translations into German of Serbian, Persian, and Chinese poets.

Moreover, Goethe's growing conviction that poetry had now become the "universal possession of mankind"[25] did not automatically render national literary perspectives null and void. While the promotion of world literature did incite a major shift in the possibilities afforded within literary study, allowing for the reception of minority voices (including what Deleuze and Guattari have called "minor literatures"),[26] the fact remains that the very cosmopolitanism of Goethe's perspective compromises its seemingly inclusive ethos. In spite of his international perspective, Goethe found it necessary to moor *Weltliteratur* to the greater glory of German letters on the one hand and to the increasingly independent spirit of a growing international market on the other. He held literary works up to measures of civilization, progress, and development. In so doing, Goethe was privileging a new kind of imperialism of occidental culture, anchored in Europe's traditions of enlightenment.[27] While the study of literature expanded (an analogical relation could be drawn to the concurrent expansion of European imperial power) to include voices that would previously have been considered unimportant or marginal, the ideology of world literature remained closely tied to such notions as progress and the development of so-called great civilizations. In other words, even as world literature disentangled literary production from the ideology of a singular "national character," it also created cultural and national hierarchies within its new international scope.[28] Meanwhile, it tacitly excluded alternative forms of literary and cultural production, including orature.

One of the legacies of Goethe's great cosmopolitan vision for world literature has been that the spaces where colonialism and other imperial ambitions have thrived are marked as peripheral even where they are central to these ambitions. The worldly perspective Goethe put forward allowed Europeans greater access to non-Western literary traditions, but this was wholly in the service of the expanding of a European enlightened consciousness. The defining characteristic of this expansive consciousness was not its sensitivity to the

25 Goethe: *Conversations*, p. 165.

26 Gilles Deleuze / Felix Guattari: *Kafka: Toward a Minor Literature*, trans. from the French by Dana Polan. Minneapolis: University of Minnesota Press 1986.

27 Goethe: *Conversations*, pp. 160–168. Interestingly, Goethe's praise of a Chinese novel engenders remarks on the thoughts and behavior of the Chinese people, extending to speculation about the reasons for the longevity of the Chinese empire, relating the production of literature to the crafts of state.

28 Sandra Bermann / Michael Wood: *Nation, Language, and the Ethics of Translation*. Princeton: Princeton UP 2005.

cultures for which European imperial projects had dire consequences, but rather its capacity to forget, perhaps willingly, these very consequences. While the West has been entirely the product of an imaginary that created maps to expand its spheres of influence and exploit resources in faraway places, it has nevertheless a locus with real effects even if it itself cannot be found upon any map. And perhaps this presence is most deeply inscribed in aesthetic productions by artists from the so-called non-Western periphery who respond to European aesthetic traditions while challenging the supremacy of the European enlightenment.[29] While the West/Rest dichotomy has no geographical indices, and cannot begin to capture the complexity that is at stake in the works that engage with these traditions, it is discursively active and produces effects that do not remain only discursive. What is at stake in the dichotomy is an aesthetic sensibility that places the occident as the seat of high culture that sets the standards of what is good art (or what can even be considered aesthetic). If works that respond to this hegemony or call attention to the injustice of the colonial projects that subtended Europe's historical enlightenment formation are still understood from the vantage point of world literature, is this not reifying the ideological function of this formation while forgetting its entanglements? If we are to understand such works on their own grounds, how can we without doing them violence?

Comparative Globalism

In comparative literature, a series of vigorous debates takes place every ten years or so over how the discipline imagines itself and its future. This ongoing conversation has been a process of self-definition by comparatists, offering accounts of their unique contributions to various disciplines. Developing out of a post-war need in the US, to engage with ideas and literatures beyond the borders of the US, comparative literature was originally conceived as a mix of philological and structuralist methodologies. In the American Comparative Literature Association's (ACLA) 1975 draft of its Report on Standards, the work of comparatists is specifically distinguished from world literature. Instead of a world literature grounded in the study of the occident, the report looks forward to a new conception of global literature and its study:

> There has [...] arisen widespread and growing interest in the non-European literatures—Chinese, Japanese, Sanskrit, Arabic, and many others less familiar, as well as those oral

29 For instance, see Camara Laye: *Le regard du roi*. Paris: Plon 1954; Yambo Ouologuem: *Le devoir de violence*. Paris: Seuil 1968.

> "literatures" of illiterate communities which are not properly described by our most basic term but for which we have no alternative. A new vision of *global* literature is emerging, embracing all the verbal creativity during the history of our planet, a vision which will soon begin to make our comfortable European perspectives parochial.[30]

Kwame Anthony Appiah argues that this appeal for greater inclusion of non-European written and oral aesthetic production reflects anxieties over the maintenance of the discipline's European heritage. Without unfairly dismissing forms of study devoted to this heritage, he calls for its integration with "the multiple comparisons and the scores of languages in which the study of literature and orature flourish."[31]

In response to the ACLA report of 1993, Mary Louise Pratt identifies three major historical trends in the academic study of literature and culture: globalization, democratization, and decolonization. Defining globalization as "the increased integration of the planet, the increasingly rapid flows of people, information, money, commodities, and cultural productions, and the changes of consciousness which result,"[32] Pratt's conception of the transformations of the field seems overwhelmingly optimistic.

More than twenty years later, with the advantage of hindsight, we can reconsider Pratt's conclusions. Globalization has indeed proved to bear out the greater mobility of *certain* people: realizing this greater freedom of movement just for a rather small elite. Meanwhile, large-scale migrations, while signifying transnational flows of people around the globe, are largely made up of refugees fleeing economic and/or material violence and wreckage wrought by the large-scale circulations of goods and capital. Such border-crossing tends to be accompanied by highly exploitative labor conditions and the separation of family members from one another. Other populations have had greater restrictions placed on their movements. In the history of liberal economic reform, we have witnessed an increase of the flow of capital beyond national boundaries on a massive scale, often motivated by efforts of large transnational companies to escape from restrictions imposed at the national level. But what does all this mean for the study of global aesthetic productions?

In her recent work on the effects of globalization on the humanities, Gayatri Spivak presents a rather bleak outlook. Referring to her proposal of the planetary as an alternative mode of universalism to the global, she describes the

30 Charles Bernheimer: *Comparative Literature in the Age of Multiculturalism.* Baltimore: Johns Hopkins UP 1995, p. 30.

31 Ibid., p. 57.

32 Ibid., p. 59.

problem with the contemporary obsession with discourses of globality and all things global in these terms:

> Globalization is achieved by the imposition of the same system of exchange everywhere. It is not too fanciful to say that, in the gridwork of electronic capital, we achieve something that resembles that abstract ball covered in latitudes and longitudes, cut by virtual lines, once the equator and the tropics, now drawn increasingly by other requirements—imperatives?—of Geographical Information Systems. The globe is on our computers. It is the logo of the World Bank. No one lives there; and we think that we can aim to control globality. The planet is in the species of alterity, belonging to another system; and yet we inhabit it, indeed are it. It is not really amenable to a neat contrast with the globe.[33]

Yet what if the straight lines weaving this grid can be subverted (rather than controlled) from within the episteme of the global? This would require that the concept be turned against the historical processes with which it has come to be associated, and which Spivak summarizes so incisively. While I share her concerns, I do wonder if the planetary really offers the kind of alterity she proposes. The planet, the place we live, is another universal (like the world and the globe) and its substitution does not guarantee that a radical epistemological shift take place. It runs the risk of being co-articulated with yet another abstract particularity (the biosphere) and "new age" ideas about its place as a concrete universal within the general universe (the cosmic). Global aesthetics, on the other hand, indicates a historical conjuncture (the global) that, turned against itself, could open onto the deconstruction of the rigid cosmopolitanism of world literature. Moreover, the very shape of the globe challenges the notion of a single center. Rather than relying on old colonial geographies, where the "West" was considered a privileged seat of culture, the global subverts aesthetic hegemonies of the center.

The ubiquity of the global as diagnosing contemporary states of affairs or even its use as a catchphrase should raise questions about what exactly is being indicated or described when the term is bandied about. The problem with using a term like this is that it is yet another placeholder representing the universal. But, as I have sought to demonstrate with my exploration of its precursors in this field, in particular those of nation and world, there is always some such placeholder (we could just as easily have examined, for example, the universals of society or culture), and it is this reality that presents the problem that needs to be addressed. In other words, universality itself presents a problem in the study of literary and aesthetic production, because it tends to collapse important differences. The global, without denoting anything in

33 Spivak: *An Aesthetic Education*, p. 338.

particular, does have the advantage of indicating something general about space. There is no center, or else the center is always moving. Without a center, there can be no necessary privileging of it over the periphery. Yet the truth is, as we have seen, that the networks of globalism do, in practice, create contingent peripheries based on the topography created by amassed capital. Hence the thing to do is to explore how the global may be disarticulated from the economic regime with regard to aesthetic production. I would suggest that the modifier of the global should remain provisional and strategic. Only so long as it provides a way to deconstruct and dislocate the center does the global offer the study of aesthetics a productive category. Global aesthetics may differ from world literature in this sense. Moreover, the traffic implicit in the modifier should allow students of global aesthetics to think about and respond to forms of cruelty and exploitation that beset globalism and globalization.

Perhaps one more thing that may help distinguish the global from the post-Enlightenment conceptions of the world is its radical sense of heterogeneity, encompassing vast networks of difference and exchange. For example, there can be no critical notion of the global without translation.[34] As a counterpoint to ideas of progress celebrated as the conquest of the earth, the inequality of languages,[35] and the disparity of literary capital across cultures, a truly global aesthetics will undermine the hierarchies structuring the history of literary study by forging new routes of translation between writing and orality. The global networks that bring together language, translation, and the distribution of works of cultural production are neither entirely static nor fluid: as structures, they tend to reproduce themselves, but they have moving parts. And hence they can be reimagined and reconstituted in different constellations from the way they currently operate.

The Global Aesthetics of Orature

I am arguing for an appreciation of aesthetic production that follows the shape of the globe with no center and hence no periphery. This is an ideal image that stands in direct conflict with current economic realities. The historical roots of the current disparities of cultural capital unevenly distributed across the globe can clearly be linked to the legacies of European imperialism

34 For a detailed discussion of translation in the context of globalism, see Wanberg: *A Moving Pedagogy*, pp. 113–130.

35 Talal Asad: *Genealogies of Religion.* Baltimore: Johns Hopkins UP 1993, p. 156.

and its colonial projects. Writing on these legacies with respect to their effects on aesthetic appreciation, Ngũgĩ wa Thiong'o argues that colonialism has created a lasting form of feudalistic thinking:

> Aesthetic feudalism, arising from placing cultures in a hierarchy, is best seen in the relationship between oral and written languages, where the oral, even when viewed as being "more" authentic or closer to the natural, is treated as the bondsman to the writing master. With orality taken as the source for the written and orature as the raw material for literature, both were certainly placed on a lower rung in the ladder of achievement and civilization.[36]

Global aesthetics must run counter to such structures that hierarchize forms of aesthetic production. From indigenous perspectives of oral societies, the superiority of written cultural forms is nonsensical.[37] In light of this, a comparative study of indigenous literature must have a well-established place within any truly global aesthetics, and this is deeply tied to the problem of how to approach the study of orature.

Orature (a neologism denoting oral culture) was originally coined by Pio Zirimu in the 1960's, and taken up as a critical call for decolonization in Anglophone African universities.[38] Emerging from this anticolonial context, it is a ripe form for thinking about how global aesthetics can work against dominant forces of representation. Moreover, orature can raise critical questions about translation that tend to be excluded from discussions of world literature, since in addition to linguistic translations; it often also entails translations from a performative idiom to graphic representation.[39]

Indigenous language systems have historically been rooted out as a perceived threat to dominating powers, since they represent forms of knowledge and cultural capital to which the colonizing forces did not have access.[40] Taking such colonial legacies into consideration, global aesthetics have an opportunity to explore the legal and political implications of oral traditions that

36 Ngũgĩ: *Globalectics*, p. 63.

37 For example, Elicura Nahuelpán argues that *oralitura* is central to how art and knowledge continue to be shared among the Mapuche in Chile. Elicura Chihuailaf Nahuelpán: *Message to Chileans*, trans. from the Spanish by Celso Cambiazo. Victoria, BC: Trafford 2009, p. 77.

38 Ngũgĩ wa Thiong'o: *Penpoints, Gunpoints, and Dreams: Towards a Critical Theory of the Arts and the State in Africa*. Oxford: Clarendon 1998, pp. 105–128.

39 Such processes tend to involve a wider margin of "intercultural transference," or interpretive errors, than most literal acts of translation. Gabriele Schwab: *Imaginary Ethnographies*. New York: Columbia UP 2012.

40 Ngũgĩ wa Thiong'o: *Decolonizing the Mind: The Politics of Language in African Literature*. Portsmouth, NH: Heinemann 1986, pp. 10–33.

remap the globe with alternative geographies and systems of economic distribution to those set up under colonialism.[41]

Recently, signal efforts to find alternative ways to explore aesthetics across non-Western traditions have been made that suggest a future for the study of global aesthetics in the sense I have been laying out. For example, in his book *Trans-Indigenous*, Chadwick Allen brings Native American literature and art into conversation with indigenous Maori cultural productions, in order to develop a way of reading across these traditions. Allen examines different non-Western traditions by directly bringing them into conversation, without using European or American literature as the standard against which all other cultural productions are measured and evaluated. Allen's approach firmly asserts that orature and other non-written art forms can take center stage, subverting the highly mediated and institutionalized discourses around Native American and Aboriginal Studies that mark them as peripheral or specialty discourses.

Ngũgĩ's and Allen's efforts help provide helpful clues to what a critical discourse of global aesthetics might entail. But they are not the only progressive voices seeking to reimagine literary and aesthetic studies from a divergent and non-hegemonic perspective. Perhaps one of the most exciting voices in the ongoing conversation around non-canonical literary studies has been that of Édouard Glissant. Faced with the challenge of linking disperse aesthetic productions within the African diaspora, across the vast geography of territories where plantations operated in the United States and the Carribean, Glissant traces what he calls a poetics of relation. As he writes:

> It is not just literature. When we examine how speech functions in this Plantation realm, we observe that there are several almost codified types of expression. Direct, elementary speech, articulating the rudimentary language necessary to get the work done; stifled speech, corresponding to the silence of this world in which knowing how to read and write is forbidden; deferred or disguised speech, in which men and women who are

41 Some efforts to think about globalism and literature remain fixed within a linguistic paradigm such as Anglophone studies, by focusing on the routes of economic exchange set up in the 19th and 20th centuries under colonialism. For example, Shameem Black: *Fiction Across Borders*. New York: Columbia UP 2010, and Paul Jay: *Global Matters: The Transnational Turn in Literary Studies*. Ithaca, NY: Cornell UP 2010, complicate the center-periphery model in cultural and literary studies as they have been taken up in the discipline of English. Yet they remain limited in scope. Globalism is generally not a matter that concerns a single language, but one that involves linguistic as much as economic exchange. While I share some of the concerns of these writers about how violence may be linked to representation and globalization, I believe that translation has to be a central part of the conversation about global aesthetics.

> gagged keep their words close. The Creole language integrated these three modes and made them jazz.[42]

The idea of global aesthetics must be open to exploring such poetics of relation that link cultural productions across space and time without having recourse to the discourses of colonialism and civilization that justify or prop up cultural or ethnic supremacies. Rather, it may very well have the potential to decenter the seat of debates around aesthetic value and perhaps even eliminate the feudalistic forms of thinking that are anchored in the contrast between center and periphery. New questions can and should be raised by considering works of aesthetic production in relation to more than one tradition.

Although world literature was originally envisioned as a universal remedy for the narrow definition of national literary traditions, practical and ideological limitations challenged the realization of this vision. Without critical frameworks to rethink its implication in the expansion of empire, the discourses that privilege occidental aesthetic sensibilities will reproduce the mystifications that continue to ensure its cultural hegemony. Counter-narratives to these forms of occidental domination that subscribe to nebulous colonial geographies fall into the trap of constructing monolithic and stable entities that conceal the complex, shifting, adaptive systems of power and its networks of exchange. Historically, such narratives have reinforced widespread neglect of non-written sources. As a counterpoint to the world literary view, global aesthetics might offer ways to study works of cultural production inspired by creolization, folklore, performance, and song. The traffic that Kafka refers to in *Das Urteil* is indifferent, infinite, overwhelming. It cancels out the particular (the music and gesture of a performance, for example) rather than carrying it forward. Global aesthetics, if it is to help us think about literary and artistic works without holding them to some old standard of value inappropriate to them should no longer travel in 'model trains of thought,' as Karl Kraus suggests in the epigraph above, but in thoughts without pre-established itineraries that allow for variety of form.

42 Édouard Glissant: *Poetics of Relation*, trans. from the French by Betsy Wing. Ann Arbor: University of Michigan Press 2010, p. 73.

A Revolutionary Myth

Border Crossing, Nostalgia and Identification in Robert Rodríguez's *Machete* (2010)

Julia Brühne

Robert Rodríguez's *Machete* is yet to attract much attention in the scientific community. One could simply see it as another borderland film dealing with the Mexican-American border problem within the conventions of the splatter movie genre. But I want to argue that *Machete* actually proposes a deeper reflection on the problem of the *chicano* identity in the United States. By creating the anachronistic superhero Machete, Rodríguez not only shows that the need for foundational novels, as found in 19th century Mexico, is still topical, but he also dissembles his own hero as well as the possibility of a revolution by depicting Machete as a 'myth' in the tradition of Roland Barthes.[1] Thus, the aims of this article are to show that the relevance of *Machete* goes far beyond the Mexican and American borders and that the film is well worth examining via cultural and literature studies. To achieve this, I will first examine the connections between *Machete* and a 19th century Mexican novel in order to define the type of revolution and border transgression *Machete* depicts. In a final step, I will try to analyze the identification with Rodríguez's eponymous hero and how it is accomplished.

I

Machete, released in 2010,[2] deals in a quite peculiar way with the problem of illegal border crossing from Mexico to the United States. The film starts with the introduction of the hero, an apparently coarse, scarred Mexican federal agent code named 'Machete' (Danny Trejo), because he uses an enormous bushwhacker instead of a service revolver. Machete and his colleague are on

1 Barthes' definition of myth implies that myths are second-order semiological systems. This means that the 'classic' combination of signifier and signified (producing the "sign") becomes dilated: The product of signifier and signified, the sign, receives a new implicit meaning beyond the original. This new meaning constitutes the myth, which obviously is not recognized as such, but is taken as a natural fact. In our case, the 'sign' 'Machete' is emotionally laden as a revolutionary hero, respectively as a prototypical Mexican criminal, and can hence be classified as myth. For details, please see my discussion below.

2 *Machete* (USA 2010, D: Robert Rodríguez).

their way to arrest the notorious drug lord Torrez (Steven Seagal), a former federal agent who used to be Machete's partner and now has changed allegiance. Machete's frightened colleague unsuccessfully tries to deter his boss from the mission and dies only seconds later after Torrez's men open fire. Machete's supervisor tries to stop the operation, calling him via cell phone to try and convince his agent to stay back, but Machete refuses. As we learn later, the supervisor himself is in cahoots with Torrez, benefitting from the drug money and in return protecting Torrez from the police. But that is not the only unpleasant surprise Machete faces during his mission. After his colleague is shot, Machete crashes the car into a former hotel that seems to be where Torrez holds young girls prisoners by drugging them. He breaks into various different rooms, beheading and mutilating the criminals with his machete. Finally, he finds an allegedly kidnapped beautiful young woman lying on a bed, naked. As she refuses to put on her clothes, he picks her up and carries her into another room, where she nestles up against him, flirting provocatively. Machete is unresponsive to her offers, since his only interest is to save the girl and find Torrez. Suddenly, the 'victim' grabs Machete's machete and castrates him. Then, she hauls out a cell phone that was hidden inside her vagina and calls Torrez to tell him her mission is completed. Together with Machete's traitorous supervisor, Torrez enters the room. His Asian girlfriend (Cheryl Chin) shoots the decoy in the head, as she is no longer of any use to Torrez, and brings in Machete's wife, who has been kidnapped previously. The wounded and horrified Machete cannot help but watch his former partner beheading his wife. After Torrez informs Machete that he has also killed his daughter, he sets fire to the hotel to put Machete to a dishonorable death (in contrast to the 'honorable alternative' of being beheaded). The sequence ends with an unresolved cliffhanger. The next scene takes place three years later in Texas, at a day labor site where illegal – mostly Mexican – immigrants try to earn their living as day laborers. Machete, unemployed and homeless, and with no way to either acquire legal papers or go back to Mexico, has become one of them. He meets Luz (Michelle Rodríguez), a legal *chicano* immigrant who works as a taco seller at the day labor site. She has founded a network that aims to help fellow *chicano* immigrants without papers gain a foothold in the United States. The supposed head of the network is an ominous figure named Shé. We later learn that this is a made-up identity invented by Luz to encourage the members of the network, whose work is difficult, dangerous and hard to accomplish without a strong financial background. Sartana Rivera (Jessica Alba), a young C. I. A. agent, also of Mexican descent, is investigating Luz, whom she believes to be Shé. Her mission is to break up the network and stop its activities, which are illegal, at least in the eyes of U.S. immigration law. While observing Luz's taco stand, Sartana one day spots Machete, who fascinates her with his unusual appearance but whom she also identifies as a potential threat. As she is sitting in her car, taking pictures of Luz and Machete, a *chicano* approaches and asks her if she needs a gardener – a question Sartana dismissively answers only by showing him her identity disk. The camera zooms to the disk, showing us the inscription "U.S. Immigration and Customs". What follows is a kind of content match cut, as the setting abruptly changes and shows us a borderland region and a facilitator who kicks a group of immigrants out of a van, even though they are still far from a city where they could seek refuge. Only seconds after the van leaves, a private border patrol (also called the 'vigilantes') headed by Von Jackson (Don Johnson) sets upon the immigrants. Von Jackson accuses them of "trespassing on my daddy's land"[3] and shoots a pregnant young girl. Her boyfriend, in turn, gets shot by Senator John McLaughlin (Robert De Niro), a conservative hardliner who plans to build an electric border fence in order to fight illegal immigration. McLaughlin promotes his plans by applying an explicitly racial rhetoric to his election campaign in order to secure his reelection. After shooting the pregnant woman's boyfriend, he turns to one of the 'vigilantes' who has filmed the brutal procedure with a video camera and asks him to burn him a DVD, as his supporters would love to see their senator like that. What follows is a promotional commercial where McLaughlin classifies the illegal immigrants as parasites and promises the voters to protect them from the "infestation"[4] the immigrants have ostensibly brought to the country. As the commercial ends, we are back at the day labor site. Machete is asked to take part in some kind of fight, in which he can win 500 dollars if he defeats his opponent. The scene depicts Machete as a figure of moral integrity as he wins the fight effortlessly by simply stepping aside whenever his opponent attacks him, then rejects the prize and only takes five dollars to pay back Luz, who had earlier served him a taco for free. Later that day, Machete meets Michael Booth (Jeff Fahey), an obscure, rich business man who hires him to assassinate McLaughlin. Booth tells Machete that the Senator must be killed because eliminating illegal immigrants from the U.S. job market would endanger the economy, as wage levels would rise if only regular American citizens were available for employment. Machete refuses to kill McLaughlin, but Booth pressures him using his status as an illegal immigrant, threatening him

3 *Machete*, 00:10:19.

4 For the promotion commercial see ibid., 00:11:30–00:12:00.

with deportation back to Mexico. Machete finally agrees, and Booth offers him a broad variety of weapons to choose from to commit the murder. He picks a sniper rifle and, to Booth's surprise, a machete, thus equipping himself with a substitute for his lost 'service revolver'. Booth pays Machete a hundred and fifty thousand dollars cash for the assassination: money which Machete directly hands over to Luz in support of the network. But again, Machete has been cheated: while he is waiting for the right moment to carry out the assassination during a campaign event, someone else shoots McLaughlin and gives him a rather superficial wound to the leg. At the same time, Booth's men chase Machete to make him the scapegoat for the assassination attempt. Booth's hiring of Machete turns out to have been part of a propaganda campaign to help McLaughlin secure reelection: if the candidate who promotes harsh immigration politics is wounded by one of those immigrants, his plan for an electric border fence would gain new support. Thus, Booth's actual intention is not to prevent the new fence but to support its construction, not because he wants to reduce the crime rate and drug dealing in the United States, but because he wants to help Torrez (his true boss whose drug money financed McLaughlin's campaign) to monopolize his drugs racketeering in the U.S. border regions. After the failed attempt on McLaughlin's life, Machete gets caught several times, but always manages to escape, often with help from members of the network, especially from Luz, who hides him in her cottage. But Booth's men seek him out and burn down Luz's house. Machete manages to escape, only to be immediately caught again, this time by agent Sartana, who interrogates Machete to find out who incited him to the assassination. Machete refuses to answer, overpowers her and forces her to drive to her flat with him. There, he hands back her pistol and begs her to trust him to bring her the man who hired him. Sartana actually begins to trust him and also starts to identify with the network's goals. Machete forces his way into Booth's house to find evidence for his racketeering. There, he encounters Booth's wife June and his daughter April (Lindsay Lohan), a drug addict hoping to become a (pornographic) model. Booth's relationship with April is special since he fosters passionate forbidden feelings for her. He confesses these regularly to a Catholic priest, who happens to be Machete's brother. Machete accepts an erotic invitation from mother and daughter, who, both naked, were about to create an erotic video for April's internet audience just as Machete showed up. Machete kisses both women while bathing in the pool, then drugs them, searches Booth's office for evidence that proves the intrigue, leaves the camera with the erotic recording for Booth to see and transports the women to his brother's church so he has leverage against Booth. When he returns to Sartana, they check the CDs and are happy to find there is enough evidence to bring Booth, McLaughlin, Torrez, and Von Jackson to trial. The next morning, Von Jackson and one of his men find Luz and apparently kill her by shooting her in the right eye. Simultaneously, Booth, furious about the video, attacks the church together with contract killer Osiris Amanpour (Tom Savini), who was hired to finally get rid of Machete. After a firefight with the priest, they crucify and kill him. To his misfortune, Booth did not know that the church was monitored by cameras, allowing Machete and Sartana to hand the recording together with the other evidence they found on the CDs from Booth's office to a journalist, who shows the recording at an official press conference. McLaughlin flees from the conference in his limousine and shoots Booth for having "jeopardized"[5] his career. Machete, while searching for Torrez in order to kill him, learns that Luz has been shot. The people from the network urge him to become their leader in the war (Luz earlier called it "La revolución") against Torrez and the 'vigilantes'. They want him to become Luz's substitute, a mythical leadership figure. Machete refuses at first but is finally persuaded. At the same time, Sartana definitely changes allegiance: She tells the people at the day labor site that laws that do not offer justice are not laws and must be overturned. Celebrated by the immigrants, she tells them it is time to show McLaughlin and the people like him what "true law" means. She ends with the words: "We didn't cross the border – the border crossed us!"[6] In the remaining 25 minutes, a bloody battle is waged between *chicanos* and the members of the border patrol. The *chicanos*, led by Machete, attack the members of the border patrol with the help of their lowriders, who have been prepared with top notch on top of the engine hoods.[7]

5 *Machete*, 01:14:35.

6 For the whole scene, see ibid., 01:19:41–01:20:19.

7 The lowrider culture in the US has its origins in the first third of the 20th century and is closely linked to the so called *pachucos* – young Americans of Mexican descent, adopting a special habit that distinguishes them from "authentic Americans" (*norteamericanos auténticos*), according to Octavio Paz. Paz describes the *pachucos* as ambiguous beings, who neither want to be fully assimilated into North American culture and society nor wish to return to their Mexican origins. They are "instinctive rebels" (*rebeldes instintivos*) against the discrimination they face in the U.S.-society, but at the same time wish to maintain their difference from both societies. Outwardly, this difference appears via a certain kind of clothing, and special language and behavior. See Octavio Paz: *El laberinto de la soledad*. Mexico: Fondo de cultura Económica 1973, pp. 9–25, esp. pp. 12–14. The lowrider culture occurs in this special environment (it was actually part of the "zoot suit" fashion of the 1930s, which was not an entirely Mexican-American phenomenon, but included other cultures as well; however, the Mexican-American "zooters" were identical to the *pachucos*; see *Lowrider History book*. http://www.lowridermagazine.com/historybook/0000lrm_history1/ (accessed 29.09.2014)). Lowriders were a new means of

Surprisingly, Luz also joins in, suddenly reappearing with no sign of injury except for an eye patch. As she is asked how her eye is, she only replies "What eye?" Together with some of her men, she saves McLaughlin from Von Jackson, who now considers the former an enemy for having spoiled their mission thanks to the DVD recordings shown at the press conference. They interrupt McLaughlin's execution and help him by dressing him up like a Mexican so that he can fight on their side against his former allies. Equipped with machine guns, pistols etc., both parties fight each other in a furious final battle, during which Von Jackson and many of his men are shot. Disguised as a nun, Booth's daughter April also joins the *chicanos* and shoots McLaughlin, whom she knows to be responsible for Booth's death, with the words "In the name of *my* father … I forgot the rest". Ultimately, Machete comes into final confrontation with his arch-enemy Torrez. At first, it looks like Torrez is winning. Then, Machete manages to drive his machete into Torrez' stomach. Torrez, accepting his defeat, commits a kind of hara-kiri, spits blood and dies. The fight is over. Machete now climbs the roof of one of the lowriders and raises his arm, holding up his machete. His allies, including April, raise their guns, confirming Machete and Luz as their chiefs. The film ends with a more or less classic romantic happy ending: We see Machete on a motorbike, slowly driving down a highway. A police car follows him and tells him to stop. Sartana hands him a passport and papers so that he can start over again in the United States, this time as a legal immigrant. But Machete does not show much interest in the papers, so Sartana climbs onto his lap, huddles against him and tells him she wants to come with him wherever he is planning to go. They kiss and drive off together.

The last thing that comes to mind while watching *Machete* is that there might be a connection between this tough, eccentric, bloody yet simultaneously shocking and exhilarating exploitation movie[8] and a Mexican national

showing and performing difference: "The car, the clothes and the language were all badges of pride for a generation caught between cultures, struggling to find their own identity." (Ibid.) Bearing in mind the importance of revolution in *Machete*, it is well worth noting that the lowriders and their drivers, suddenly being able to get from A to B easily, were considered as potentially dangerous intruders by the Anglo-American population, who feared the *pachucos* could 'conquer' traditionally Anglo-American areas instead of staying within the boundaries of their communities like the first Mexican immigrant generation (see ibid.).

8 An exploitation movie can be defined as a "film designed by its producers to 'exploit', via clever marketing and promotion, the notoriety of certain sensational current events and trends. […] Exploitation films are usually low-budget and calculatedly commercial, venturing into parts of the market neglected by mainstream film making. The term also implies an objective on the part of the producer to 'exploit' base audience desires to see more explicit descriptions

romance written towards the end of the 19th century. I refer to the novel *El Zarco*, written in 1888 by the indigenous author Ignacio Manuel Altamirano for educational purposes.[9] *El Zarco* belongs to the so-called "foundational novels", a term coined by Doris Sommer in *Foundational Fictions*, her seminal book on Latin American 19th century fiction. The romances written during that period, she argues, mirror the socio-political conflicts of the time in the erotic sphere. Through heterosexual love and marriages between, for instance, antagonist groups, they "provided a figure for apparently nonviolent consolidation during internecine conflicts at midcentury"[10]. In *El Zarco*, however, the proposed marriage between Manuela, a white girl of European descent, and Nicolás, an Indian proletarian, fails due to Manuela's disgust at the indigenous wedding candidate whose affectionate courtship she rejects, very much to the grief of her mother, in favor of the similarly Europeanized eponymous hero: the blue-eyed bandit El Zarco. The latter is the head of a ruthless robber band (the *plateados*) that terrorizes the population, stealing jewels and murdering families – a 'profession' that attracts the bored, adventure-seeking Manuela, who uses it to meet El Zarco in clandestine rendezvous. However, when they finally run away together from Yautepec, Manuela's rural hometown, to Xochimanchas, an old Aztec ruin in the mountains the bandits have chosen as their hideaway, she soon becomes disappointed and disenchanted by the rude everyday life among the robbers, which completely lacks the romantic atmosphere she had hoped for. Nicolás, begged by Manuela's mother to bring her daughter back, accepts the challenge, but is caught by soldiers who arrest him for accusing them of not fulfilling their duty to fight the bandits. Manuela's adopted sister, the shy, honest mestiza Pilar, who has been secretly in love with Nicolás for a long time, overcomes her timidity and adopts a temporary, masculine political agency in order to save him from prison. She succeeds in freeing him, and Nicolás, realizing that Pilar is actually the object

of sex, violence, or drug abuse than are available in other films and media. […] Sexual liberation in the 1960s fostered the rise of the US sexploitation film, which emphasized sex and nudity. […] A further variant, blaxploitation, consisted of low-budget exploitation films aimed at black urban audiences in the US." (Exploitation Film. In: Annette Kuhn / Guy Westwell: *A Dictionary of Film Studies*. Oxford: Oxford UP 2012, pp. 149–150. *Machete*, in this respect, could be called a 'mex-ploitation' film.

9 Ignacio Manuel Altamirano: *El Zarco, The Blue-Eyed Bandit. Episodes of Mexican Life between1861–1863* [*El Zarco* (*episodios de la vida mexicana en 1861–1863*)], trans. from the Spanish by Ronald Christ. Santa Fe, NM: Lumen 2007.

10 Doris Sommer: *Foundational Fictions. The National Romances of Latin America*. Berkeley: University of California Press 1991, p. 6.

of his true love and desire, asks her to marry him. Meanwhile, Manuela starts to regret her rejection of Nicolás, especially when she learns about his marriage to Pilar, whom she considers an inferior rival. But Nicolás joins forces with Martín Sánchez Chagollán. Don Martín is a mestizo rancher who seeks revenge for the brutal murder of his father and son committed by the *plateados*. He has been authorized by President Benito Juárez to fight against and kill every member of the *plateado* gang, since the government military forces are unable to fight them because they are all needed in the war against French invaders. Martín is characterized as an equally strong-willed and ethical person who shows no mercy for those who, in his eyes, do not deserve to be spared, but who never kills for sport or arbitrary reasons. As such, he serves, together with Nicolás, as a role model for a modern, accurate masculinity. On the day of Nicolás and Pilar's wedding ceremony, Don Martín captures the bandits and Manuela, who is witness to El Zarco's execution: he is shot and then hanged from a tree. Spewing blood, Manuela dies the death of the traditional romantic heroine,[11] collapsing dead beside the gallows tree.

Sommer refers to *El Zarco* as a domesticizing foundational novel: Manuela symbolizes monarchist (creole) Mexico that wishes for the return of a "European prince" to replace the "Indian prince" (Benito Juárez) they have as president.[12] El Zarco, with his blond hair and blue eyes ("zarco" meaning "blue"), represents this European prince who poses a threat to Mexico. In the historical context in which the novel is set, Mexico faces French invasion under Napoleon, who would establish the Habsburg archduke Maximilian as Mexican emperor Maximilian I (1864–1867). The conservative, monarchist Mexicans are thus blamed for 'prostituting' themselves to foreign exploiters, a factor the novel transfers into the figure of Manuela, who is blamed and punished for 'prostituting' herself to El Zarco. The latter equally receives punishment for his ambition to rule the country via terror and murder: Just like the historical Maximilian I, he is executed. The idea that El Zarco is actually the fictional surrogate for the unwanted emperor becomes even more plausible if we consider that his name-giving blue eyes correspond to the extraordinary blue eyes the historical Maximilian I was famous for.[13] Altamirano uses the

11 See Juan Pablo Dabove / Susan Hallstead: Pasiones fatales. Consumo, bandidaje y género en El Zarco. In: *A contra corriente* 7,1 (2009), pp. 168–187. http://www.ncsu.edu/acontracorriente/fall_09/articles/Dabove_Hallstead%20.pdf (accessed 15.06.2014), here p. 183.

12 Sommer: *Foundational Fictions*, p. 226.

13 I owe this thought to Professor Stephan Leopold, who brought up this connection between Maximilian I and El Zarco in a graduate seminar at the Johannes Gutenberg University (Mainz) in spring 2013.

novel as a didactic instrument to encourage the population to strive and fight for the ideal of a "liberal indigenous republic"[14]. It deals with the question of Mexican national identity and with the imagery of the perfect autochthonous democracy – a utopia finally realized in the peaceful village of Yautepec, where the Indian Nicolás, as an honorable and respected blacksmith, represents the ideal of a new, courageous but also modest, rational, and production-oriented masculinity that overpowers the colonial, cruel and consumerist (European) masculinity represented by El Zarco.[15] Returning to *Machete*, it seems more than likely that this film continues the foundational novel's quest for national identity while mirroring the problems of a state suffering from industrial and economical regression while still struggling with the consequences of the Mexican-American War (1846–1848). This war, which not only deprived Mexico of half of its national territory but also marked the beginning of the border problems between the two states, was a national trauma that led to the so-called Chicano Movement in the 1960s and 70s. The movement developed in part as a result of the 1950s Civil Rights Movement, where African Americans demanded equal rights, equality, and acceptance within American society. The Chicano Movement reached its peak in 1969 when the National Chicano Youth Liberation Conference formulated *El plan spiritual de Aztlán* (spiritual plan of Aztlán), a desire to restore the "stolen homeland"[16] they called Aztlán.[17] The Aztlán ideology conveyed the desire to restore the antebellum status quo. The *chicanos* claimed the U.S. southwestern territories were originally Mexican and demanded a genealogical right to live there, as the

14 Sommer: *Foundational Fictions*, p. 224.

15 For the two antagonizing masculinities and their characteristics which are at stake in the novel, see Dabove / Hallstead: Pasiones fatales.

16 Ramón A. Gutiérrez: Aztlán. In: Vicky L. Ruiz / Virginia Sánchez Korrol (eds): *Latinas in the United States. A Historical Encyclopedia.* Bloomington / Indianapolis: Indiana UP 2006, pp. 71–73, here p. 73. See also Maricela DeMirjyin: Aztlán. In: Lee Stacy (ed.): *Mexico and the United States.* New York: Marshall Cavendish 2003, pp. 70–71.

17 *Aztlán*, translated either as "the place of whiteness" or "the lands to the north" was the original home of the Aztec peoples and therefore holds great historical significance. A legend about Aztec leader Montezuma finding Aztlán with the help of the goddess Coatlicue, who made him and his men believe it was the place of eternal youth, adds a mythological dimension to Aztlán; see ibid., p. 70. The lowriding culture I talked about previously also developed in the *Aztlán* region (the Southwest of the U.S.); see Michael C. Taylor: Lowriders. In: *The New Encyclopedia of Southern Culture*, vol. 14: Folklife, ed. by Glenn Hinson / William Ferris. Chapel Hill: University of North Carolina Press 2009, (without page numbers).

land had originally belonged to Mexico.[18] This seemingly radical concept can be seen as a reaction to the ambivalent American attitudes towards Mexican immigrants: on the one hand, there was the *bracero* program, which started in 1942, a deal that brought approximately 5 million Mexican guest workers to the United States.[19] The idea was that the workers would only stay for a year before returning home; however, many of them stayed or came back illegally after being deported and tried to get their jobs back. This situation led to massive protests against the program and illegal immigration. The border was no longer a mere transit line but started to become a symbol for national integrity and sovereignty. In 1954, the protest culminated in "operation wetback", a campaign where the army, the border patrol, police forces, and others organized the deportation of hundreds of thousands of workers back to Mexico. The operation was called an act of 'repatriation'. It was also in the 1950s when the American media almost exclusively spread a homogenous image of Mexican immigrants, classifying them as "illegal hordes" who were the authors of a "wetback invasion". Even today, the attitude towards (illegal) immigrants is shaped by this ambivalence between the need for cheap workers and laws designed to restrict immigration.[20] The events of 11 September 2001 also led to more restrictive immigration laws and interrupted negotiations for a new amnesty law and the naturalization of "undocumented aliens"[21].

In *Machete*, the aggressive rhetoric of certain groups against (illegal) immigrants is obvious, as is the *Aztlán* concept: The latter becomes clear in the speech Sartana gives to the day labor *chicanos* towards the end of the film, just before the bloody '*chicano* revolution' reaches its peak. Standing on the roof of her car, Sartana, finally disenchanted with the way her supervisors are handling immigration, convinces the other *chicanos* that she is one of them, willing to fight on their side against Von Jackson and his men. By shouting, "We didn't cross the border – the border crossed us!"[22] she evokes the *Aztlán* discourse, stating that the territory the Americans want to remove them from is originally Mexican. Living there is therefore a natural, genealogical right

18 See for instance Conrad Solloch: *Performing Conquista: Kulturelle Inszenierungen Mexikos in europäischen und U.S.-amerikanischen Medien im 20. Jahrhundert.* Berlin: Erich Schmidt 2005, pp. 164–165.

19 Ibid., p. 160.

20 Ibid., p. 161–163.

21 Ibid., p. 164.

22 *Machete*, 01:20:13.

for Mexican citizens. For Altamirano, the French, allegorized as the bandits, especially El Zarco, had to be removed from Mexico to be able to create a free, prosperous, and autochthonous Mexican republic. In *Machete*, the borderland has to be reconquered from the foreigners to become legal territory under immigrant control in the sense of the *Aztlán* ideology. In order to achieve this goal, the *chicanos* need a strong, virile, mythical figure, someone who can take over the leadership. This is Machete, the scarred, strong, honorable and ethical combatant the *chicanos* put all their hopes and trust in. So far, the analogy to *El Zarco* seems to hold water. Both works are of foundational character, both deal with the problem of foreign intruders on national territory. Both end in a utopia that became reality, and both present an unforgettable masculine hero who is practically unbeatable and functions at the same time as a role model for morality and a certain kind of wisdom. Machete could easily be construed as a twenty-first century Don Martín, who kills 'in the name of justice' and takes revenge for the brutal deaths of his wife and daughter, but who usually spares innocent 'civilians'. Like Don Martín, Machete is incorruptible. His antagonist Torrez, in turn, strongly resembles the bandit and assassin El Zarco, as neither shows signs of pity or mercy. They are primarily interested in power and personal gain, not justice. Just as El Zarco decorates his clothes and horses with excessive silver ornament (*plateado* derives from *plata*, meaning 'silver'), Torrez always surrounds himself with beautiful young women in bikinis to show his supremacy.

Yet, these parallel binary opposites are not assignable to the whole movie, as *Machete,* unlike *El Zarco,* does not stick to the inner border or the inner conflict between Mexican citizens. The border and the conflict are transferred to the outside, as Torrez is not Machete's only antagonist; the characteristics attributive of El Zarco are not exclusively transferred to Torrez, nor are they not completely depicted in negative terms. The various binary oppositions of *El Zarco* are instead intertextually adapted to *Machete* in many different – at times contrasting – ways. To make this clear, we must first look at the other binary oppositions that exist in *El Zarco* and *Machete*.[23] In *El Zarco*, we find

23 Dabove and Hallstead as well as, e.g., Max Parra underline the various binary oppositions as constitutive elements of *El Zarco*. For Dabove and Hallstead, the opposition between the two concepts of masculinity represented by El Zarco and Nicolás is of major importance as it shows the emergence of a new capitalist order (Dabove / Hallstead: Pasiones fatales, p. 173–176). Parra stresses the antagonism of the new rational people (*pueblo racional*) and the mob (*populacho*), the latter of which has to be annihilated in order to create the new Mexican republic. Max Parra: 'Pueblo', bandidos, y Estado en el siglo XIX mexicano. Notas a partir de El Zarco de Ignacio Manuel Altamirano. In: *The Colorado Review of Hispanic Studies* 4 (Fall 2006),

the basic opposition between barbarism (the bandits and as well Manuela, for desiring their leader) and civilization (the population of Yautepec, especially Nicolás, as well as Benito Juárez and Don Martín). Along with these antagonisms comes the opposition between vices, respectively irrationality and virtue/rationality, an opposition marked especially by the two central couples, Manuela/El Zarco and Pilar/Nicolás. There is also an opposition between dissipation and consumerism on the one hand and canniness coupled with a sense of production and manufacture, symbolized in Nicolás' profession as a blacksmith, on the other. Still further, there is the opposition between a premodern, colonial masculinity[24] that only serves to consume goods without producing anything and commit bloody assassinations, and the favored new masculinity consisting of strong morals, rationality, self-control, and a certain ability for tenderness and devotion. Altamirano grants the latter to the indigenous man or the *mestize*, while he depicts the European or Creole encoded bandits as representatives of an outdated masculinity that must be overcome. The *mestizes*, together with their president Juárez, are supposed to lead Mexico into a new future characterized by a working capitalist system and an almost Calvinistic work ethic[25], backed by the classic distribution of male and female fields of work: The wife, like Pilar, should stay at home as *ángel del hogar* (angel of the hearth) and give birth to the new citizens of the new state, whereas the husband works hard to earn a living for his family.[26]

In *Machete*, we can also see the binary opposition between nature and culture, between technical civilization and a pre-technological 'barbarism'. Yet, the sympathies are allocated differently here. Machete's technological unawareness, or rather his rejection of technical achievements, is not barbarism or ignorance to be annihilated. Instead, it forms a significant feature of his depiction as an ever virile, unbeatable superhero. In the introductory scene, one of Machete's first acts is to destroy the walkie-talkie his supervisor uses

pp. 65–76. http://spanish.colorado.edu/sites/default/files/images/stories/pdf/colorado_review_pdfs/Volume_4/004005Parra.pdf (accessed 15.06.2014). For a discussion of the basic opposition between civilization and barbarism, see José Salvador Ruiz: El laberinto de la aculturación: Cuidadanía y nación mestiza en El Zarco de Ignacio Manuel Altamirano. In: *Revista de Crítica Literaria Latinoamericana* 31,6 (2005), pp. 23–36.

24 See Dabove / Hallstead: Pasiones fatales, p. 173.

25 See ibid. and Ruíz: El laberinto, p. 28.

26 See Christopher Conway: Lecturas: Ventanas de la seducción en El Zarco. In: *Revista de Crítica Literaria Latinoamericana* 26,52 (2000), pp. 91–106, here p. 98. http://www.jstor.org/discover/10.2307/4531123?uid=3737864&uid=2129&uid=2&uid=70&uid=4&sid=21103864366751 (accessed 15.06.2014).

to tell him to cut short the operation. When he enters the Torrez residence by chopping off the heads of Torrez's guards, he always uses his machete. Even when he finds one of the chopped off hands still carrying a gun, he leaves it in favor of his machete. Later, when Sartana criticizes him for not getting in touch with her via text message, he replies: "Machete don't text."[27] While in *El Zarco*, Nicolás and Don Martín fight against barbarism in the name of progress and a capitalist encoded new order, *Machete* turns back to an original kind of masculinity: The protagonist uses a traditional Mexican bushwhacker to fight perverse technological progress that enables people like Senator McLaughlin to build an electric border fence to punish every illegal immigrant directly via electrocution. Thus, in *Machete*, a rather conservative, 'pre-modern' masculinity, represented by Machete, is favored over a 'modern' American masculinity that has nothing in common with the rational, moralistic code which Altamirano craved. The modern masculinity represented by Booth, McLaughlin, and Von Jackson now stands for corruption, immorality, and also for sterility, or at least an unhealthy sexuality, as Booth wants to sleep with his own daughter. The progressive, capitalist, production-oriented system Altamirano had in mind is presented here in its nightmarish excrescent: The modest business suits that Booth, McLaughlin, and Torrez are wearing become the symbols of corruption, greed, and unscrupulousness, while Machete's initially scary appearance proves to be a sign of his moral integrity. On the other hand, Booth, McLaughlin and the like are the ones who characterize the illegal immigrants (to whom Machete himself belongs), to a certain degree in the same way Altamirano characterized the bandits: Where Altamirano calls on his readers to support social cleansing measures and to get rid of the bandits who are terrorizing the country, the political right in Rodríguez's film tries to agitate the audience to expel the illegal immigrants they depict as "parasites". What is interesting here is that *El Zarco* alludes to the dictatorship under Porfirio Díaz. Díaz wanted to get rid of the bandits to guarantee safety to foreign investors who intended to come to Mexico to build a railroad network in the country.[28] *Machete* parallels this historical fact ironically, giving us a political right who want to banish illegal immigrants from the United States in order to allow drug lord Torrez to monopolize his racketeering without the fear of illegal immigrants bringing cheaper drugs into the country. In this respect, one could also acknowledge,

27 In the subsequent film *Machete Kills*, he says in a similar situation: "Machete don't tweet."

28 See Parra: Pueblo, p. 69.

as Max Parra does, that the bandits in *El Zarco* embody a certain kind of social climber[29] that again parallels them with the Mexican immigrants. However, the figure who is actually portrayed by Altamirano as a social climber is Nicolás, who, born an Indian, became mestize not through the intermarriage of his parents but through acculturation. As Altamirano emphasizes, he was not "a contemptible, servile Indian; rather, a cultured man ennobled by his work, and well aware of his strength and worth."[30] So in the Jurij Lotman sense of the word, he crosses a conventionally uncrossable border, that is to say, the symbolic border between his indigenous origin (we might again say 'barbarism', in quotation marks, naturally) and the world of 'civilization'.[31] But Manuela and El Zarco are also transgressive subjects, as they respectively enter each other's subspace: El Zarco invades Yautepec in order to meet Manuela, who in turn, follows him to the bandits' repository in Xochimanchas, a place where she normally never would have gone.[32] But Manuela and El Zarco's transgressions of each other's border are not permanent: Both die, directly or indirectly at Don Martín's hand. The *sujet* (event) which their transgressions constitute is therefore restitution: The status quo is restored, as the transgressive intruders have died or been killed. The *sujet* of Nicolás's transgression has, in turn, the character of a revolution: As the novel seems to fulfill the utopia of a bandit-free "autochthonous democracy", the social norms and rules have changed to his advantage; his transgression of the

29 Ibid., p. 71.

30 Altamirano: *El Zarco*, p. 64.

31 For Lotman, literary spaces are always subdivided into two semantically opposed subspaces. Between these subspaces, there runs a boundary that basically cannot be crossed. A classic example would be a forest as subspace 'A', which is semantically encoded as uncivilized and natural, and a city as subspace 'B', encoded as a place of civilization and culture. The boundary between the two spaces could be, for instance, a river. Now, Lotman categorizes literary texts into two groups: The ones where no border crossing takes place and where the established order of each space remains intact: Those texts would be defined as presenting no event, in Lotman's terms *sujet*. The other group, on the contrary, is defined through the border crossing event (*sujet*): The character that crosses the normally uncrossable border, the "hero", provides an event which means a threat to the established order of the subspace in which he intrudes through his transgression. The reaction to this transgression can now be either revolutionary or restitutive. In the first case, the hero manages to break up the order of subspace 'B' and establish a new order. The second case means the hero dies, is punished or sent back to the subspace 'A', or he becomes absorbed by the subspace 'B', meaning he is allowed to occupy a place, a position within the social order, but is unable to break it up. See Jurij M. Lotman: *Die Struktur literarischer Texte*, trans. from the Russian by Rolf-Dietrich Keil. München: Fink 1972.

32 Conway depicts Manuela convincingly as a victim who has to be sacrificed in order to restore the social order that she had formerly broken by following El Zarco instead of marrying Nicolás and becoming an angel of the hearth just like Pilar. See Conway: Ventanas, p. 98.

symbolic border is both successful and enduring. In *Machete*, the subspaces constituting the *histoire* seem quite obvious, even more as there actually exists a border in the literal sense of the word. Subspace 'A', in Lotman's terminology, is Mexico, and subspace 'B', the United States. The Mexican subspace is – from the white, middle-class American point of view – encoded as poor, underdeveloped, rather uncivilized, a place of drug use and a drug war ruled by corrupt politicians. The United States, in contrast, is depicted – both by Americans and Mexican immigrants who desperately try to get there – as hyper-developed, a place to find jobs and earn money, a place of incorruptible, righteous laws.[33] In fact, there is no clear distinction between the two subspaces. We learn quickly that drugs, violence, and corruption permeate both spaces, as they are far from being exclusively Mexican problems: It is well-known that Mexico is the most important transit state for drugs transported to the U.S.; the United States is also a large customer for Mexican drugs.[34] The symbol of this permeability is Torrez, the former Mexican federal agent who speaks almost exclusively in English and provides his American clients with the drugs they need. The laws and the people who made them are just as corrupt as Machete's Mexican supervisor, and they apply the same brutality as he does. So, the semantic oppositions that primarily characterize the subspaces are completely relativized. The border persists and continues to be theoretically uncrossable, separating the Mexican periphery from the United States as the center of financial interest. As a consequence, the illegal immigrants who succeed in crossing it and thus constitute a *sujet*, normally do not succeed in taking possession of the other subspace. Instead, they are absorbed by subspace 'B' as they become immobile day laborers caught in in-betweenness. The *sujets* generated by those subjects are thus solely *sujets* of restitution – the revolution never comes, meaning that a character who transgresses the border succeeds, for instance, in overthrowing the order that constitutes space 'B' and creating a new space, following a new order and new

33 When Sartana captures Machete, she initially tries to convince him to trust the American law, which she believes to be different from the Mexican one, designed only to be broken by those who hold political power: "I know what they did to your family. And if I were you, I wouldn't trust anyone either, but it's different here. Laws are enforced. And people control them, not drug lords. The system works here." (*Machete*, 00:41:28–00:41:43).

34 A scene which perfectly illustrates the parallels between Mexican and American drug problems is the one where Booth violently breaks into a drug dealer's house, shooting several men in order to bring the drugged April home (ibid., 00:19:47–00:21:05). This sequence mirrors the introductory scene where Machete breaks into the old hotel and kills at least a dozen of Torrez's men in order to save the allegedly kidnapped girl (ibid., 00:02:16–00:03:26).

rules. This seems to change in *Machete*: the protagonist, himself initially hardly more than a broken illegal day laborer, brutally deprived of his job and family, becomes the leading figure in the revolution the other *chicanos* seek. They want to leave their in-between spaces, turn the *sujet* of restitution into a *sujet* of revolution and pick Machete as their chief and hero. Speaking in terms of the *Aztlán* plan, they plan a revolution to bring their lost territory back and undermine the border. The film's ending implies that the revolution has been successful – in my opinion, this is not quite the case. There cannot be a 'real' revolution, because the two usually disjunctive spaces are no longer disjunctive. They have become mixed and contingent, and thus form what David Baguley might call an "entropic vision"[35]: The two semantic characteristics of each space have been weakened as the negative aspects ascribed to the Mexican subspace have permeated the American subspace. Both spaces thus form entropy where no revolution is possible because the achievement it desires is practically nonexistent – the antebellum status quo, meaning the territorial distribution before the Mexican-American War, is not restorable. There also is no consistent, integrative *chicano* identity, or one loyal group fighting for the same goal. Two scenes perfectly illustrate this circumstance: The first takes place in the kitchen of a restaurant where two dishwashers, one American, one Hispanic, watch the news of the attempt to assassinate the senator. The Hispanic man says they should close the border and detain the illegal immigrants. When the other asks if he had not once crossed the border himself, he replies: "Well, I'm already here. Fine with me if they close it."[36] This disloyalty to his fellow Hispanics is the counterpart of McLaughlin's pragmatic opportunism we see during the final 'revolution' battle, when the Senator, noticing that Von Jackson has sided against him, shows no compunction about changing allegiance and allowing Luz to dress him up as a Mexican (with a hat and a checked cardigan) to fight on their side against the border patrol. Together with Torrez, who practically has become an American (or at least, controls American politicians and shows no mercy for his compatriots), this shows how easy it actually is to switch from the periphery to the center and vice versa, to 'become' either Mexican or American. Conversely, it shows how difficult it is to identify one stable identity on which a revolution could build its premises.

35 The author applies this term to 19th century naturalist novels. David Baguley: *Naturalist Fiction. The Entropic Vision*. Cambridge: Cambridge UP 2005.
36 *Machete*, 00:33:08.

In the next section, I argue that if the revolution taking place at the end of the film is nothing but a myth, the revolutionary figure must also be a myth, at least in Roland Barthes's sense of the word.

II

Barthes exemplifies his definition of myth via a cover picture from the magazine *Paris Match*:

> On the cover, a young Negro in a French uniform is saluting, with his eyes uplifted, probably fixed on a fold of the tricolor. All this is the meaning of the picture.[37]

According to Barthes, in analogy to Ferdinand de Saussure's definition of a linguistic sign, this picture consists of a signifier and a signified. The signifier is what we see when we look at the picture before assigning it a meaning: A black man in French uniform, saluting. The signified in this primary linguistic system would be a French soldier inside the French colonial empire saluting (his eyes being probably fixed on the Tricolor). As we see, the signified in this model implies a certain kind of biography, a personal history of the person whose picture has been taken. This system of signifier and signified presents a certain wholeness, and together they create what Barthes calls "meaning". This "meaning" is the point where the myth starts. A myth is a second-order semiological system that partly covers the primary linguistic system. In the mythological system, the "meaning" becomes "form": The mythological system drains the linguistic system of its "meaning" – what remains is the "form" that has to be filled again, this time with the new, mythological meaning. This means that the facts about the young black man, his biography, have to be spared in order for the picture to be filled with a mythological meaning which becomes a second signified: All sons of France are equal, there is no repression; the French imperialism is something natural. This naturalization is the primal characteristic Barthes applies to his definition of the myth. The myth transforms ideology into nature:

> We reach here the very principle of myth: it transforms history into nature. [...] everything happens as if the picture naturally conjures up the concept, as if the signifier gave a foundation to the signified: the myth exists from the precise moment when French imperialism achieves the natural state: myth is speech justified in excess.[38]

37 Roland Barthes: *Mythologies*, trans. from the French by Annette Lavers. London: Vintage 2000.

38 Ibid., pp. 129–130.

Looking at *Machete* again, something very close to Barthes's example of the "young Negro" seems to occur. Booth uses Machete to naturalize American immigration politics, more precisely, McLaughlin's plans for an electric border fence. To follow Barthes, without any mystification in the primary semiological system, the signifier of Machete, i. e. the picture of him given to us by the camera, could be put as follows: A muscular, scarred, long-haired Hispanic with a large tattoo on the chest, looking for a job. The signified would require his history: Why is he scarred, what has made him into a probable illegal day laborer who has experienced tough times? Booth mystifies Machete as he drains the "meaning" from the linguistic sign – he uses Machete's body and his outer appearance as a mere form and fills it with the myth of the brute and barbaric Mexican who represents all the other illegal Mexican immigrants McLaughlin has declared war on. He activates the alleged binary oppositions between Mexicans and Americans we saw above and makes them look 'natural'. He chose Machete for the fake assassination because his body presented the ideal form to be filled with the myth of the dangerous Mexican immigrant who has to be eliminated from American soil. The myth suggests that the illegal Mexican immigrant presents a natural threat to the country's sovereignty, so every measure to protect the citizens from this potential danger is non-negotiable, as it is 'nature'.

Paradoxically, the *chicanos* mystify their hero Machete in much the same way. They take the myth of the dangerous, virile, and violent Mexican and use it for their own purposes – yet without considering its 'constructedness'. Just like the white middle-class American citizens whose votes McLaughlin wants to win, they take the myth at face value. Thus, they reinforce the binary oppositions between white America and the *chicanos* inscribed on Machete's body. Just like Booth uses him as proof for the natural dangerousness of illegal immigrants, the *chicanos* proclaim Machete's hero status as being 'natural'. Both sides fetishize Machete: the United States in order to preserve their stereotype of the Mexican brute who 'naturally' had to be deprived of his territory in 1848 and who now 'naturally' has to be expulsed from the country; the network in order to convince themselves that their earlier failures in the fight against American repression and dominance happened for a reason and were only the forerunners of something bigger. Machete as a myth, for the network, means coming to terms with contingency. If Machete is a 'natural', heaven-sent hero, representing 'original' Mexican virility, morality, and courage, then the many fellow immigrants who are dead or missing can be given a certain amount of meaning. The liberator can only be someone with the outer appearance of Machete, who knows how to handle a giant bushwhacker and who rejects the accomplishments of the technological world, which is always already corrupt.

However, Rodríguez seems to be quite aware of the mythmaking on both sides; he subtly and repeatedly deconstructs the very possibility of such a myth during the film and shows us the myth believer's naiveté. The introductory scene contains the first attempt at categorizing Machete as a mythological figure: Machete's colleague shows uncompromising loyalty towards his "jefe", telling him (not without a considerable degree of pathos), "Estoy contigo … ¡jefe!" ("I am with you … boss!"). As a reply, Machete holds up his bushwhacker, replying gloomily, "This … is the boss!"[39] Machete knows that he, putting it in terms of Jacques Lacan, can never actually *own* the phallus – he can just temporarily acquire a phallic symbol (the machete). But he himself will never *be* the phallus, as the power associated with the concept of the phallus is always borrowed; it never actually forms a permanent part of someone's body.[40] It is thus naïve and inappropriate to believe that Machete's phallic power might come 'naturally'. Rodríguez makes this even clearer when Machete is castrated by the beautiful traitor: From now on, he is literally castrated, so he needs the machete even more as a phallic symbol in order to fill this gap. The Machete-myth is further fueled but at the same time ironized by the cliffhanger: How could Machete possibly manage to survive this desperate situation and escape from Torrez despite his severe injury? The myth of the unbeatable superhero is invoked but at the same time ironically undermined by exaggerating a cinematographic convention. Sometime later, when Machete hides in Luz's residence after the failed assassination attempt, he implicitly warns her not to construct him as the hero they all have been waiting for. Luz calls him 'Machete', showing him that she knows who he is:

> MACHETE: You know me?
> LUZ (chuckling): I know the legend.
> MACHETE: Maybe the legend's better.
> LUZ: I'll be the judge of that.[41]

39 *Machete*, 00:01:44–00:01:52.

40 For the concept of the phallus as a symbol of power nobody ever actually can possess, see Jacques Lacan: *The Signification of the Phallus*. In: Id.: *Écrits: A Selection*, trans. from the French by Alan Sheridan. New York: Norton 1977, pp. 281–291.

41 *Machete*, 00:35:07–00:35:15.

Apart from the obvious erotic intentions of this conversation, it is clear that Machete is striving for the deconstruction of his own myth.[42] The hypothesis that he is created as a myth, in the Barthesian sense, is further supported if we consider Luz's invention of 'Shé' as the alleged leading figure of the network. Luz confesses to Machete that Shé does not exist: "Unfortunately, Shé's a myth. Just someone I made up. To lead the network."[43] Shé is a myth, but in the sense we would usually apply to the notion: Something not real, a story people made up for other people to believe or because they did not know better. Apparently, Shé has not worked properly: she is no longer able to protect the immigrants from the border patrol; the Shé concept is not strong enough, or, in Barthes' words, the 'form' 'Shé' has not been filled with an accurate mythological meaning, a new signifier. That's why Machete is needed: He has to fill the 'form' (some kind of revolutionary hero) with a 'natural' meaning. His outer appearance, the rumors about him, his "don't fuck with me, I won't fuck with you attitude"[44] fits the form perfectly, as heroism can 'naturally' be inscribed onto him. This scene also reveals that the *chicano* 'revolution' had always already been built on a myth – it does not have any authentic concept it could refer to; the movement can define itself only on behalf of a myth, that is, a 'naturalized' ideology. But, as Barthes tells us, once revolution has become ideology, it is no longer revolutionary. It is a myth on the left and, as equally ideological as the one on the right.

Of course, Rodríguez also deconstructs the Machete-myth of the right. He achieves this deconstruction in two ways. In the first place, the myth, serving to strengthen the usual stereotype of the barbaric, violent Mexican, is turned against itself: Machete is not only dangerous, he is also apparently unbeatable

42 For Barthes, a revolution is normally the counterpart to the bourgeois myth: "The revolution is not a myth because it names itself, whereas the bourgeoisie is eager not to name itself but to make its existence seem the 'natural' state of existence for humankind" (Barthes: *Mythologies*, pp. 145–146; pp. 137–142). However, the network talks about inciting a revolution: But by making Machete the revolutionary hero, they are embroiled in ideology right from the start. The revolution is thus not a revolution, but a myth on the left. Machete, who several times tries to escape that myth, surrenders to it in the final scene, when he tells Sartana, "Why would I wanna be a real person, when I'm already a myth?" By rejecting the papers, which Sartana contends would allow him to be a real person, he ultimately rejects being "named" and thus definitely proves the revolution to be a myth (*Machete*, 01:35:45). If we argue with Jacques Rancière, we could say that the network's revolution is not a revolution because it uses the same 'language' (hence the same myth) the Americans use against the Mexicans. This parallels Rancière's analysis of the language of the French Revolution, which was in fact the language of the monarchy. See Jacques Rancière: *Politique de la littérature*. Paris: Galilée 2007, p. 30.

43 *Machete*, 00:34:10–00:34:17.

44 Ibid., 00:08:43.

and repeatedly castrates the white American, while the stereotype, as Homi Bhabha put it,[45] should actually banish the constant threat of castration. So, the Machete-myth on the right is two-fold: On the one hand, Machete perfectly conforms to the stereotype, being scarred, strong, and rowdy. On the other hand, precisely these characteristics allow him to block his antagonists in a permanent run of castrations. Every time he chops off heads or other body parts, he symbolically castrates the victim and thus deprives the white American of his predominance.[46] The second way Rodríguez manages to deconstruct the myth on the right is meta-reflexive in nature. As mentioned above, Booth regularly visits Machete's brother, the priest, to confess his forbidden, incestuous passion for April. Every time he came for confession, the priest made a record of it. Before he dies by Booth's hand, he hands the DVDs over to Machete. The recording allows the latter to crack the password on Booth's computer – "I love April" – and hence read his files and find evidence of Booth and Torrez's scheming. Similarly, the video cameras in the church reveal the brutal murder of the priest and thus provide evidence to show at the press conference, which ruins McLaughlin as a politician. The media of 'film' and 'press' which formerly helped McLaughlin and Booth to propagate their racist positions now turn against them: the stereotypical characteristics originally applied to Machete (as representative of all illegal immigrants), now prove to also be the characteristics of the allegedly reliable, ethical politicians and businessmen. Thus, the myth that the Texans built around Machete and respectively the immigrants via film and press is in turn deconstructed via film and press. But this refers self-referentially to the fact that the myth the immigrants have built around Machete is also destructed by the film director himself. The self-referentiality serves to deconstruct not only the myth on the right, the 'easy' myth, but also the revolutionary myth on the left, with which we would normally identify.[47] This leads to my concluding

45 For Bhabha, the colonial stereotype is two-fold: It works as a fetish by which the colonizer is able to maintain the differences between him and the colonized, but by which he also denies that difference because, following Freud, acknowledging the difference would mean castration. The difference is thus suppressed but always threatens to erupt, hence the traumatic depictions of the colonized subjects as cannibals, anarchists etc. See Homi K. Bhabha: The Other Question: The Stereotype and Colonial Discourse. In: Jessica Evans / Stuart Hall (eds): *Visual Culture. The Reader.* London: Cromwell 1999, pp. 370–378. Machete is the embodiment of the bursting out of the repressed fear of castration.

46 For the chopping off of body parts as a symbol of castration, see Sigmund Freud: Das Unheimliche [1919]. In: Id.: *Psychologische Schriften* (= *Studienausgabe*, vol. IV), ed. by Alexander Mitscherlich et. al. Frankfurt am Main: Fischer 1970, pp. 242–274.

47 A further idea about how easily myth-building works on both sides (right and left) is

question: Does the spectator identify with Machete? And, if so, how and why does this identification take place?

III

As Barthes argues, a myth can become irrelevant if it ceases to be understood by its audience by becoming outdated or unnecessary. For instance, in today's postcolonial times the cover title with the black soldier would probably no longer present the myth of the naturality of French imperialism; the mythological system would be reduced back to the primary linguistic system. This is exactly what threatens the Machete myth. We, the contemporary 21st century audience, cannot possibly identify with the hero of an exploitation movie, as the heyday for exploitation movies was in the 1980s. Nevertheless, such films are still popular, and *Machete* proved so successful that Rodríguez made a sequel.[48] My hypothesis, therefore, is that we need a proxy to identify with Machete, just like the other characters do. The notion of 'proxy' I want to apply here derives from Slavoj Žižek, who uses the term to define the "nature of the gaze" in film. Žižek argues that, for a contemporary audience, the fascination of *film noir* consists not of the featured story plot, but of the assumption that there was once a spectator living in the 1940s who was actually able to identify with the universe of the film noir, whereas today's spectator is unable to identify with the plot and unable to believe the story presented on screen. Something similar occurs with the film *Shane*, "a pure Western *at a time when pure Westerns were no longer possible*, when the Western was already perceived from a certain nostalgic distance, as a lost object."[49] *Shane,* therefore, is a meta-Western (André Bazin), shot at a time when the genre was practically dead already. Thus, the viewer of *Shane*, in order to identify with the eponymous hero, needs a proxy, someone who is actually able to identify with Shane and lets us partake in this fascinated identification with the hero. In *Shane*, the proxy is the young boy from whose perspective the film

provided by the scene where Sartana speaks to the *chicano* masses from the top of her car: Having formerly despised her for being a representative of the American law, the listeners very quickly start to embrace and applaud her just as if she always had been 'one of them'. The scene paradoxically parallels the attitudes of the American voters who are just as easily convinced to vote for McLaughlin as against him.

48 The sequel is called *Machete Kills* (2013). A further sequel, *Machete Kills Again … in Space!* is being planned.

49 Slavoj Žižek: Looking Awry. In: Robert Stam / Toby Miller (eds): *Film and Theory. An Anthology*. Malden, MA: Blackwell 2000, pp. 524–538, here p. 529.

is shot: "In *Shane*, [...], we can be fascinated by the mysterious apparition of Shane only by proxy, through the medium of the 'innocent' child's gaze, never immediately."[50] What happens in *Machete* reveals many parallels to Žižek's interpretation of *Shane*. Structurally, both productions have a lot in common, being both part of a genre that no longer existed at the time they were shot. Also, both feature an eponymous hero, one whose appearance does not fascinate us and allows us to identify with him right from the start, but only by proxy. While in *Shane*, it is a child providing us with his gaze, in *Machete*, it is a young woman with a rather childlike appearance and attitude: Sartana, who is fascinated by the considerably older Machete from the first time she sees him and very soon falls in love with him – a kind of complementary, incestuous father-daughter-love, mirroring the relationship between April and her father. She huddles against him and wants him to cuddle her and give her the kind of security she could also want from a father; she praises him for his bravery and honorable conduct and believes steadfastly in his ability to fight the antagonists. For her, he is a bulletproof superhero destined to save the world.[51] The depiction of Machete as something between father and lover is repeated in the April character, who, after having lost her beloved father, turns to Machete as a new, strong father figure who helps to avenge the death of her biological father. In this respect, it is equally worth noting what Luz says when asked about her eye: Her counter question "what eye?" can be paronomastically changed to "what I?" If Luz questions her own existence (as a subject), while putting herself under the leadership of Machete, it might be argued that she gives up her subjectivity (in Lacanian terms, her place in the symbolic order[52] where she was previously defined and positioned as Shé). Giving up the 'Shé' myth in favor of constructing the 'Machete' myth, Luz also gives up a certain symbolic existence and clings to the powerful father figure whose myth promises to save the *chicanos* from their misery.

But why do we, as spectators, nostalgically wish to be able to identify with an anachronistic superhero like Machete? I would argue that we want to

50 Žižek: Looking Awry, p. 529.

51 Interestingly, the name 'Sartana' refers to a male Italian Western hero – the connection to the Western genre and its subgenres is therefore already installed in the name.

52 The symbolic order, for Lacan, is the linguistically structured world ruled by the symbolic father: The name of the father (*nom-du-père*). The symbolic order is diametrically opposed to the imaginary: the place of the original, happy mother-child dyad. Every subject has to enter the symbolic order in order to find his or her place in the world, to occupy a certain position, to be symbolized as a 'subject'. See for instance Slavoj Žižek: *The Sublime Object of Ideology*. London: Verso 1989, pp. 16–23.

identify with him and thus with the network, because it allows us to believe in the temporary possibility of a revolution, the possibility of correcting the wrongs of the world, while comfortably seated in a movie theatre. Machete as a superhero is a way to quell the "entropic vision". The Machete myth and the convictions of the network enable us to believe in a world where clear and explicit binary oppositions between good and evil, right and wrong, hero and villain still exist. It is nostalgia for an allegedly lost world where we could still easily attribute clear characteristics to the various subspaces and where the contingency was never big enough to prevent the ultimate victory for the heroes.

A similar phenomenon seems to occur with *Sherlock*, a BBC television series which has been broadcast since 2010. Here, too, an anachronistic, this time intellectual, superhero is reactivated and made into a Barthesian myth. Like Machete, Sherlock occasionally tries to convince people that he actually is no hero, and that turning him into a hero shows the ideological function of the Barthesian myth.[53] In the final episode of season two, Sherlock's enemies actually try to destroy the myth via the press: The press who had contributed a good deal to mythifying him in the fictional world now deconstructs its own myth by suggesting that Sherlock's "science of deduction" is nothing more than a lie. The angry deconstruction of the intellectual superhero by the middle class is the attempt to classify his intellectual abilities. They want to prove that he is just an ordinary human being like 'us' and that such a superior brain does not exist.[54] But John Watson refuses to believe them and so do we: We do not actually need Watson to be able to believe in Sherlock's superiority, that is to say, we do not need Watson as a proxy like we needed Sartana. The

53 For example, in the last episode of the first season, Sherlock tells John: "Don't make people into heroes, John. Heroes don't exist and if they did, I wouldn't be one of them."

54 Among Barthes' examples of everyday myths, what probably corresponds best to the apparently paradoxical attempt to demystify Sherlock Holmes is "The brain of Einstein": "Perhaps because of his mathematical specialization, superman is here divested of every magical character; no diffuse power in him, no mystery other than mechanical." (Barthes: *Mythologies*, p. 68.) Thus, even when they try to demystify Sherlock, they are still confirming the myth. The myth Sherlock represents for the audience, in turn, matches better with Barthes' "Steak and Chips" myth, food symbolizing the French national character: "Commonly associated with chips, steak communicates its national glamour to them: chips are nostalgic and patriotic like steak. *Match* told us that after the armistice in Indo-China *'General de Castries, for his first meal, asked for chips'*. […] What we were meant to understand is that the General's request was certainly not a vulgar materialistic reflex, but an episode in the ritual of appropriating the regained French community. The General understood well our national symbolism; he knew that *la frite*, chips, are the alimentary sign of Frenchness." (Ibid., pp. 63–64.) Just like the chips, Sherlock is an emblem of Britishness.

Sherlock-myth captures us unmediated; it is a bourgeois myth that still works. Why does it work? I would argue because if we can 'keep' the Sherlock-myth, we can also keep the myth about 'being British': even though Sherlock rebels against the British government (incarnated in his brother Mycroft), does not show much respect for the British monarchy, and does not conform to social and political hierarchies, he seems to embody perfect 'Britishness'. In a world of globalization, of EU politics trying to standardize what it means to be "European", Sherlock is the embodiment of nostalgic resistance. He disdains politics and intelligence services as well as the no-smoking rule, but he sticks to the traditional cup of tea, the London cab, the fireplace and the dusty books, and he even manages to unite those traditions with the latest technological advances. Thus, *Sherlock* also helps us to cope with the "entropic vision": Not only does he make us believe there is a superior brain able to solve every logical problem (hence rescuing us from contingency), but he also gives us the possibility of individuality, tradition, and patriotism. Hence, what we need here is not a proxy to identify with Sherlock; we need Sherlock to be our proxy, our medium of interpassivity[55] who allows us to enjoy through him the cornerstones of 'Britishness': An enjoyment (*jouissance*) that seems more and more impossible in an almost fully globalized world.

Thus, the problems of borders and entropies, center and periphery, do not stop at the Mexican-American border: It is a global subject, and to deal with it, some kind of proxy is necessary. So, if Rodríguez has chosen an 'outdated' splatter genre to tell his story about the Mexican-American border problem, he has diagnosed the symptoms of his time just as precisely as the BBC producers who reactivated the Conan Doyle superhero and set him in today's 'globalized' London.

55 Žižek uses this term, explaining that enjoyment often works through interpassive activities: If we, for example, record a movie, even if we never have time to watch it afterwards, it seems like the video recorder had the pleasure (*jouissance*) of watching it – the machine carries out the enjoyment for us. Hence, interpassive enjoyment means to enjoy something via a representative, in our case Sherlock. See Slavoj Žižek: *Lacan. Eine Einführung*. Frankfurt am Main: Fischer 2008, pp. 36–40.

Reviews

Julia Bamford / Franca Poppi / Davide Mazzi (eds):
Space, Place and the Discursive Construction of Identity.
Bern: Peter Lang 2014.

Kevin Rigg

This book provides a compilation of papers presented at a 2012 conference in Naples discussing space, place, and the discursive construction of identity. It provides a platform for an extended dialogue about the way an individual's identity can be structured and recognized using different approaches to the morphological study of how identity is fashioned when we research, contemplate, compose and analyze its relevance in respect to space and place.

By default, the publication is of significance to linguists; however, due to the eclectic nature of the problems explored and the range of subject matter analyzed, it is also relevant to those engaged in a multitude of other academic disciplines. In particular, social researchers, historians, philosophers, writers, and those with an interest in interpreting literature in its many guises will find it both engaging and thought-provoking. It is particularly relevant to academics who aim to discover and determine the human identity of those with whom they engage, study, and write about, both in contemporary and historical studies.

The book outlines recent research on modern-day issues such as immigration and the status of identity in an increasingly globalized and de-traditionalized world. For example, it comments on how immigrants adapt their identity to be more easily absorbed into their new surroundings whilst developing a nostalgic view of their place of origin (Davide Mazzi, pp. 177–178). It also recognizes the significance of the use of technology to communicate in virtual time using social media as we interpret, communicate, and express ourselves when describing or detailing our perceptions (Silvia Cacchiani, pp. 195–196; Giorgia Riboni, pp. 217–218).

The work provides an overview of many topics that add to our understanding of the complex nature of identity, its status and existence, particularly when considered from an individual's perspective of place and space. It applies an interdisciplinary approach, whilst maintaining an emphasis on linguistics, to create the means to develop a clearer understanding of the impact of space and place when deliberating identity in the modern world. It argues, using clear examples, how each of the component parts of space and place persuade and influence the way we consciously and subconsciously locate the essence of human identity, including our own. Further, it offers a broader discussion of how aspects of identity are distinguished using an analysis of written sources, interview transcriptions, and the way in which academic writing evolves in tandem with the author's experience base. It provides an assessment of the individual's standpoint from a number of perspectives, including providing a critique of aspects of theatrical performances, and the expression of expectations when using social media and quality review blogs. It therefore offers a wide application of linguistic analysis to support the examination of identity when considered in the context of actual and abstract concepts of space and place.

Each of the 14 contributors presents an introductory section that describes the particular theoretical application relevant to their work. They clearly outline their methods and findings, and identify areas for improving the academic underpinnings with suggestions for specific further research. However, the greatest addition to scholarship the book brings is the ability to plumb new depths of thought when considering the question of human identity. In our efforts to recognize individual characteristics that form and create our cultural, historical and personal identity, this work provides a refreshing series of conundrums to consider, and in so doing enhances the application of academic thought into the topic.

Historians are constantly seeking an elusive truth about the originality of the material they study; including the accuracy and interpretation of narratives found in documentary and oral sources. Consequently, I found the chapters depicting the analysis of social research interviews (Greg Myers / Sofia Lampropoulou, p. 23), how people characterize architecture using metaphor (Rosario Caballero, p. 107), the analysis of text and space in 17th century newspapers (Nicholas Brownlees, p. 135), and the assessment of live media broadcasting of attacks on the World Trade Centre on 11th September 2001 (Charlotte Danino, p. 157) of particular interest. Nonetheless, the entirety of the work is worthy of full consideration as it provides a rounded discussion of the issue of identity from unique and different perspectives. The findings include valuable insights into how contemporary methods of communication create virtual, instantaneous arenas for social intercourse and how humans interpret their world and establish their place within it. It highlights how achieving a greater understanding of the construction of identity will let us attain an enhanced comprehension of our social world and the changes occurring within it. It is easy to find present day applications of this process from the material presented within each of the chapters.

Linguists are the main contributors to this work; it therefore contains a lot of their scholarly language and theoretical arguments. Nevertheless, the overall style of presentation imparts clarity to the topics under discussion, the methods used to research them, and the findings. This approach allows for those more comfortable in other academic disciplines to glean a strong understanding of the impact, value, and contribution that the study of language makes to improving the knowledge of how we use, create, and interpret written and oral data when considering identity.

Margarita Díaz-Andreu: *Archaeological Encounters: Building Networks of Spanish and British Archaeologists in the 20th Century.* Newcastle upon Tyne: Cambridge Scholars Publishing 2012.

Miquel Carandell Baruzzi

Before archeologists started posting on their Facebook and Twitter accounts, personal correspondence was the major source of information for historians of archeology. Needless to say, when the prominent Catalan scientist Lluís Pericot García (1899–1978) built an astonishing archive of thousands of letters received from colleagues at home and abroad during more than 50 years of professional activity, he preserved a piece of history. And now the Spanish historian, Margarita Díaz-Andreu, working through more than seven hundred letters from the archive, has interpreted a portion of that past. In particular, Díaz-Andreu has explored the relations between Spain and Britain using Pericot's letters in her book *Archaeological Encounters: Building Networks of Spanish and British Archaeologists in the 20th Century*. To do so, the author has used the "Geographies of Knowledge" historiographical framework, which inquires how the locations of researchers or sites can influence the way that knowledge is produced and circulated. Her description of Pericot's correspondence shows convincingly how scholars' locations clearly shaped their research. Her analysis draws both countries' scientific networks in great detail. Furthermore, she shows how the way they were built was related to interests, power, negotiations, and – crucially – social interactions.

Although Díaz-Andreu also analyzes the role of the troubled mid-twentieth century political context in how these interactions worked, in my opinion, she partially fails to highlight how individuals' political beliefs and positions also played a crucial role. Pericot, for instance, is pictured in the book as a politically neutral figure. However, from his correspondence, we learn that, while he initially considered going into exile during the most repressive period of Franco's regime, Pericot became, in Díaz-Andreu's words, an "important member of the political-cultural elite in both Barcelona and Spain." So even if Pericot really wanted to stay apolitical, did he really do so, or did he have a complex capacity for redefining his political position?

The same goes for the Australian Marxist scholar, Gordon Childe (1892–1957), one of Pericot's English correspondents. Although he frequently visited the USSR and raised "tensions" in his Spanish visits, "in daily practice, [Childe] separated politics and academia". While Díaz-Andreu successfully disassembles the myth that Childe could not have relations with the scholars working in fascist Spain, her labeling of scientists as "neutral" or "separated from politics" does not allow a further analysis of how these individuals acted in relation to the wider European politics. Why and how did a Marxist scholar visit a country ruled by fascists? How did Pericot relieve these "tensions"? What strategies did all these scholars use to be successful in such political contexts? Were these any different from those used by other historical actors? In this respect, how different was archeology from other cultural manifestations?

The well-chosen "Geographies of Knowledge" approach allows Díaz-Andreu to explore the complexities of the assumed relations between a supposedly dominant and imperialist England and an assumed underdeveloped and nationalist Spain. Pericot's interest in the Catalan-speaking area, his mastering of the English language at a time when most of his colleagues had learned French, the differences between the reactions to his lectures in Oxford, Cambridge, and London, and the English archaeologists' cordial relations with their Spanish colleagues demonstrate the extent to which these assumed notions of imperialists and nationalists are false and must be further explored. In the same direction, Díaz-Andreu persuasively dismantles Neustupný's (1997–1998) closed notions of minority and mainstream archeology, showing that these categories could change depending on the observer's point of view. To expand this point, the author was able to take advantage of the work done by the research group Science and Technology in the European Periphery (STEP). Since its formation in 1999, STEP has tried to better understand the complex notions of center and periphery in the context of the circulation of knowledge.

To sum up, this book is a very useful tool for those interested in the history of 20th century Spanish and English archeology. It is also an interesting work for all those concerned with the relations between scientific elites in different countries during this convulsive period.

Valerie Hansen: *Silk Road: A New History.* Oxford / New York: Oxford UP 2012.

Hang Lin

Being an artery of contact between China and the West since as early as 2,000 BCE, the Silk Road is probably best known for bringing the Chinese Han (206 BCE–206 CE) and Tang (618–907) dynasties and the Roman and Byzantine empires into (remote) contact in the first millennium of the Common Era. Coined by the German geologist and explorer Ferdinand von Richthofen in 1877, the Silk Road is one of the most evocative names for many travel romantics, conjuring up images of deserts and dunes, caravans and camels laden with luxury silks, and dusty marketplaces. But in *Silk Road: A New History*, Valerie Hansen, an established historian on early China and its neighbors, moves away from the timeless and exotic images to portray a historical picture of peoples and their lives along the Silk Road. Unlike most previous works on the Silk Road, which concentrate chiefly on art and visual culture, Hansen constructs her account around a wide array of new written sources recently discovered in China and Central Asia, most of them rendered in a multitude of languages including classical Chinese, Sanskrit, Sogdian, and Khotanese, and shifts her focus onto the actual lives of peoples to "identify the main actors, the commodities traded, the approximate size of caravans, and the impact of trade on localities through which goods passed" (p. 4).

Hansen takes up for her narrative seven places where local, written documentation is available, no matter how fragmentary and chronologically narrow it may be, and accordingly assigns each of the seven main chapters to an individual place: the kingdom of Kroraina (Chapter 1), Kucha and the Caves of Kizil (Chapter 2), Turfan (Chapter 3), Samarkand and Sogdiana (Chapter 4), historic Chang'an (Chapter 5), the Dunhuang Caves (Chapter 6), and Khotan (Chapter 7). For each chapter, Hansen also carefully chooses an explanatory heading to guide the reader to the most significant characteristics of the region. In Chapter 5, for instance, Hansen illustrates a lively and rigorous illustration of historic Chang'an, the capital of the Tang and the cosmopolitan eastern terminus of the Silk Road. In Chapter 6, the reader joins Hansen on a trip through the magnificent treasure trove of Buddhist art encapsulated in the caves at Dunhuang on the Gansu Corridor. The chapters proceed in a loose chronological and geographic order, though the author frequently takes the reader on excursions to parallel stories and modern discovery.

Throughout the book, Hansen exhibits an enviable ability to delve into the mélange of some of the most exotic (and unfortunately mostly extinct) languages of Central Asia and to elicit a haunting depiction of real life from the often extremely fragmentary records. Hansen's erudition is admirable, but more admirable is her impressive generosity in acknowledging her obligation to many scholars better versed in Central Asian and Indo-European languages. The scope of sources she utilizes for her study is striking, ranging from court histories, tax receipts, commercial contracts, inventories, travel passes, to diaries of envoys and even records by cooks. So we read, for example, from an excavated fourth-century letter the swearword of a woman whose husband left her and saddled her with his debts, in which she complained "I would rather be a dog's or pig's wife than yours" (p. 118). Such written evidence, as Hansen rightly admits, is "scant and often missing crucial sections," yet she also reminds us that these genuine firsthand materials are "the only way that understanding of the history of the Silk Road will advance" (p. 238). Despite the wide expense of sources of various languages and some tongue-twisting names of ethnic groups and sites, Hansen's clear writing style and solid structure make the book easily accessible to undergraduate students and general readers. Certainly, the densely annotated notes following the chapters also indicate that this is a meticulous scholarly study based on substantial research (although a bibliography is unfortunately not appended). Several detailed line maps and many high-quality color plates of archaeological finds vividly visualize her narrative and thus further enhance the joy of reading.

There is no doubt that Hansen succeeds in reaching her book's primary aim to "sketch the main events in the history of each oasis community, describe the different groups who resided there and their cultural interactions, outline the nature of the trade, and ultimately tell the flesh-and-blood story of the Silk Road" (p. 24). But more demanding readers may wonder why Hansen's narrative is geographically limited only to the area extending from Chang'an in the east to Samarkand in the west. If the Silk Road can be divided into two major sections, then the whole of the west section which ranges from Sogdiana to the Byzantine and Roman empires is not at all covered in the book. In this sense, some earlier yet seminal studies such as Luce Boulnois' *Silk Road: Monks, Warriors & Merchants* (Hong Kong: Odyssey 2005) and Christopher I. Beckwith's *Empires of the Silk Road: A History of Central Eurasia from the Bronze Age to the Present* (Princeton: Princeton UP 2009) are warmly recommended to be read in conjunction. Those who thirst for more in-depth insights into primary sources assembled from the Silk Road can turn to Xinru Liu's recent book *The Silk Roads: A Brief History with Documents* (Boston: Bedford / St. Martins 2012).

In general, *Silk Road: A New History* takes us a step forward toward a more interactive, and less bounded, history of peoples and communities along the Silk Road. Valerie Hansen should be loudly applauded for providing a painstaking and inspiring analysis of the multifaceted history of the Silk Road. Full of intriguing observations and thought-provoking syntheses, it is bound to become an indispensable book which will inspire future researchers on this perennial topic in Asian and world history.

James E. Kitchen: *The British Imperial Army in the Middle East. Morale and Military Identity in the Sinai and Palestine Campaigns, 1916–18.* London: Bloomsbury 2014.

Frank Jacob

James E. Kitchen's book deals with one of the forgotten wars of the Great War: forgotten because the campaigns fought in the Middle East ranged far away from the public interest at home and seemed to have no tremendous impact on the history of the First World War as a whole. However, the battles in the Sinai and Palestine offer several levels of interpretation: they could be seen as crusades, imperial defenses, or simply a sacrifice of British troops (p. 2). Kitchen's account considers the problem of morale during these campaigns, and it helps to understand the decisive factors of modern warfare (p. 5). Therefore, the "aim of the book is to address morale in the British imperial army that fought in Egypt and Palestine" (pp. 6–7). Kitchen, consequently, looks at the role of "endurance, combat performance, and the construction of military identities" (p. 7). Of special interest for the military historian will be the daily life of the common soldier, particularly those in the Middle East, where a multinational and multi-ethnic force was fighting against the Ottoman army. This has been neglected for far too long. For decades, it was only the generals and decisive politicians who formed the focus of historical accounts that dealt with this theater of war. As a consequence, Kitchen's new book is extremely valuable in several ways.

In the first chapter (pp. 25–60), he describes the nature of the Great War in Sinai and Palestine and shows that, in contrast to the Western front, warfare remained fluid there even though the number of causalities was as many as on the European battlefields. The soldiers had to wage a war against their environment (pp. 27–33), where being wounded was even worse than dying; against modern technologies (pp. 38–46), in that they faced both artillery and aircraft, especially after 1917; and against diseases (pp. 53–59). The "industrialized slaughter" (p. 59) finally reached these battlefields as well, and the Great War "in the Middle East displayed many aspects and utilized many of the tools of a twentieth-century military campaign, but in the end, it was the traditional enemy of armies throughout history – disease – that emerged victorious" (p. 60).

The second chapter deals with the depiction of the campaigns in Palestine as a twentieth-century crusade (pp. 61–99), because the liberation of Jerusalem from the Ottomans seemed to resemble the medieval crusade. Such romanticism was even strengthened by the heroic figures of this theater or war, e. g. Lawrence of Arabia (p. 61), through whom the Middle East seemed to attract more public interest. Allenby's arrival in Jerusalem was filmed by the War Office Cinematograph Committee and published as a newsreel the following year (p. 69). However, for the common soldier, as Kitchen shows, the war in the Middle East did not create the "bombastic rhetoric of a holy war" (p. 90) because for them, it was "not a glorious crusade, but a dirty, brutal and uncomfortable war in which spiritual solace seemed a long way off" (p. 92). In contrast to the image of crusaders, many soldiers saw themselves as oriental tourists, who glorified war as a way to see foreign and unknown places (p. 99).

In chapter three (pp. 101–121), Kitchen explains the role of command and control with regard to their impact on morale in the various Middle Eastern campaigns. The crisis of 1917 is seen as a crisis of leadership and not one of morale in the lower ranks. When Allenby was able to successfully use his cavalry to gain victory at Megiddo, he became a central figure of the campaign, and it seemed that great men were able to achieve something – in contrast to the Western front. Allenby especially was later seen as the man who was able to end the morale crisis of 1917, but following Kitchen's argumentation, there was no such crisis. It was the command levels which were yet to function, and it was Allenby who replaced the war staff in the Middle East, creating an army that was finally able to win battles.

The fourth chapter takes a closer look at the British citizen as a soldier in the Middle Eastern war (pp. 123–149). The territorial troops used their "civilian identity" (p. 128) to tie bonds with their comrades. Next to these connections, family ties secured contact with the home front, from where families sent presents to the Middle East. Furthermore, sporting activities were used to recreate standard civilian life (pp. 132–133), and war victories seen as a chance to shower the regiments with glory and honor (p. 149).

One dominant group in the Middle Eastern campaigns, the ANZAC forces, are the main topic of the subsequent chapter (pp. 151–181), which deals with their legend, comradeship and morale. The "EEF's mobile fighting arm" (p. 22) was useful because the vast expanses of the Sinai and Palestine campaigns provided a suitable theater for cavalry warfare. The bonds between the ANZAC soldiers and their horses remained strong, and both created their own legends during these war years, an experience which is still remembered in Australian national culture.

Another ethnic group, the Indian Army, also fought for the glory of the British Empire in the Middle East, and its role is discussed in the sixth chapter (pp. 183–213). Kitchen describes the process of Indianization in 1918 (the "imperial manpower reserve" (p. 183) mainly reached the Middle Eastern sphere in the final year of the war). Their participation transformed the campaigns in Sinai and Palestine into a global event that also underlined the effect of total warfare within the British Empire (p. 196).

Kitchen provides a highly recommendable account of the Great War in the Middle East and shows that "warfare in Sinai and Palestine in the First World War was a complex business; the armies that fought there reflected this complexity, as did the combat motivations of their soldiers" (p. 23). Even if it seemed to be a sideshow of the First World War, it had significant impact on the further development of the Middle East as a political and cultural region. He also underlines the various aspects that are important for understanding the development of soldiers' morale during warfare. Therefore, the account is recommended not only to military historians who are concerned with the Great War but also to those who have to consider morale and its determining factors in general.

Gavan McCormack / Satoko Oka Norimatsu:
Resistant Islands: Okinawa Confronts Japan and the United States.
New York: Rowman & Littlefield 2012.

Pedro Iacobelli

The Okinawa prefecture, Japan's southernmost region and once the independent kingdom of Ryukyu, was heavily militarized during the years of American administration (1945–1972), including the building of several bases throughout its territory. The Cold War period defense agreements between the United States and Japan perpetuated the military occupation of wide sections of the prefecture's land, adversely affecting the livelihood of the local Okinawan population in ways that persist even today. The authors of this volume focus on the struggle (resistance) of the local civil movement to oppose the dictates of Washington and Tokyo. As they put it in the introduction, this book narrates "the process by which, for the first time in Japan's history, grassroots democratic forces seized the initiative and over a sustained period became the key subject in determining the course of history" (p. 12).

Building on extensive Japanese and English literature, McCormack and Norimatsu present a new reading of the events and situations that have shaped the current position of Okinawa as a space of resistance against the governmental elites in Japan and the U. S. The book's main temporal focus is the years of Democratic Party (*Minshuto*) rule in Japan. In this sense we can observe a continuation and expansion of Gavan McCormack's previous book, *Client State*. There McCormack analyzed Japan's structural political dependence on the United States and the impact that this relationship, among other issues, had on Okinawa up to 2006.[1] But the volume under review is more than an update of McCormack's previous book. In *Resistant Islands* the authors bring to the fore Okinawa prefecture's past, before and after its annexation to Japan, and use recent history to convey the idea that the Okinawan people's most distinctive features are their sustained resistance, hatred of war, distrust of the military, and refusal to pursue 'national defense' agendas.

The book's first four chapters deal with the historical background of Okinawa. The first chapter outlines the annexation of the islands by Japan, in what was called the *Ryūkyū Shobun* (Ryukyu Disposal). The authors emphasize the nuance of punishment that the word also carries. In doing so, they convey the image of a country that has several times been punished by a stronger and more powerful one. The second chapter, the longest in the book, deals with the important issues of war and memory. The authors see the Battle of Okinawa as an 'ideological resource' for the postwar opposition to the military bases in the prefecture. For them, the horror of the war, a combination of the bloody combat experience with the discriminatory attitude of the Japanese army towards the Okinawans, is the source of the contemporary Okinawan anti-military identity. In the same vein, the war atrocities committed by the Japanese military against the civilian population in Okinawa, such as "forced suicide", rapes, and the establishment of comfort stations staffed with foreign and Okinawan women are an organic component of the social imagery of distrust against the Japanese government. For the authors, the ways in which these atrocities are remembered (or forgotten) are another chapter in the struggle over memory. Chapters 3 and 4 describe the process of U. S. militarization of Okinawa. McCormack and Norimatsu criticize the moral foundations of the bilateral agreements that allowed the establishment of the U. S. administration of Okinawa and the continuation of such control once the islands were reverted to Japan. They condemn the secret agreements (*mitsuyaku*) that permitted the massive U. S. presence in Okinawa after reversion. The authors contest that the reversion was not meant to unify the country but to strengthen the U. S.-Japan alliance.

The rest of the book tells how, while the U. S.-Japan alliance has deepened, a grassroots civil movement has emerged to oppose it. Chapters 5 and 6 provide an in-depth examination of the issue of the relocation of part of the U. S. base of Futenma from Ginowan to a new complex near Henoko. The new base building plan triggered a social backlash. The authors note that when Hatoyama Yukio and the Democratic Party seized power in the 2009 elections, Tokyo's elite supported the Okinawan

1 Gavan McCormack: *Client State. Japan in the American Embrace*. London / New York: Verso 2007, pp. 155–174.

people's position for the first time. Hatoyama opposed the relocation project. However, his position was rapidly discredited both at home and in the United States, making his government untenable and forcing him to resign. For McCormack and Norimatsu, "The Hatoyama Revolt" was swiftly controlled by the United States, a clear expression of Japan's position as the secondary state. The U.S.-Japan alliance, the authors tell us, could intervene in elections in order to achieve its purposes (more blatantly as "the importance of securing at least the appearance of local consent to major reorganization of the base system arises") (Chapter 7). After Hatoyama's government, the subsequent Democratic Party governments deepened the defense alliance with the United States (Chapters 9 and 10). But the imposition of Washington-Tokyo security plans in Okinawa has consistently been contested by local communities. Indeed, for the authors, the 2010 elections in Okinawa, when the anti-base position and thus the opposition to the defense alliance won an overwhelming majority, represents a turning point in history (Chapter 7). The book finishes well, with testimonies from well-known Okinawan activists and some speculation about the prospects for the islands (Chapters 12 and 13).

The dialectics in *Resistant Islands* shows us the confrontational position of Okinawa as an American Japanese military territory against the local communities' struggle to oppose the power play at work in their land. The synthesis of this confrontation is resistant islands: a place of ongoing antagonism to militarism, wherever it comes from, and constant reaffirmation of a unique Okinawan identity. In this sense, the authors should be praised for their ability to contextualize, in a well-written text, a local civil movement within the framework of the U.S.-Japan defense alliance. But in their quest to fit a local movement within a wider frame, they repeatedly generalize the different positions, making it difficult to fully embrace the proposed interpretation. The David and Goliath narrative obscures the more contingent disputes and differences within each of the groups. For example, there is no reference whatsoever to the different factions within the Okinawan movement nor of their different approaches and strategies. It gives the impression that the Okinawan resistance is homogenous against an equally homogenous enemy, and this is not the case. Nevertheless, *Resistant Islands* is an important book, one which does not merely introduce the current political tensions in a group of islands that are fundamental to U.S. policy in East Asia, but also (re)positions Okinawa as a third actor in the U.S.-Japan alliance.

Shinya Sugiuyama: *Japan's Industrialization in the World Economy, 1859–1899: Export, Trade and Overseas Competition.* London / New York: Bloomsbury 2012.

James A. Wren

On 1 March, 2014, Shinya Sugiyama stood before the Faculty of Economics at Keio University (Tokyo, Japan) to deliver his farewell lecture, ostensibly a summation of his life-long work entitled "The Economic History of Japan from the Viewpoint of Global History." As he brought his presentation to an end, he officially stepped down from his long-held post as Professor of Economics, as well as from his posts as Director of the Keio Information Technology Center and Head of the e-Learning Unit with the Research Institute for Digital Media and Content. In doing so, he signaled the beginning of his retirement.

Over a career spanning more than four decades, Sugiyama has been recognized for his succinct, concise, and undoubtedly groundbreaking research in the field of economic history, where he introduced the postwar generation of scholars, East and West, to innovative and compelling approaches to understanding the complexities behind the modern economic history of Japan and Asia. The final years of his leadership might best be characterized by a move beyond the relation between the development of the Japanese economy and the international economy, to venture with his usual expertise and meticulous attention to detail into the historical analysis of Anglo-Japanese economic relations. In turn, he pioneered the development of modern information and distribution networks across Japan and the environmental and economic history of the modern period. Coming full circle, he would ultimately re-evaluate and redirect attentions toward the importance of the socio-economic history of the treaty ports.[1]

It therefore seems only fitting that the Bloomsbury Academic Collections has brought out his redoubtable monograph, *Japan's Industrialization in the World Economy, 1859–1899: Export, Trade and Overseas Competition*, an important, still-relevant and influential analysis first seen in his 1981 dissertation at The University of London. Of great importance to the field, his work would urge a new breed of economic historians forward, as they would confront and challenge those long held, if disingenuous, assumptions of "modernization theory," namely that modernization is synonymous with the likes of westernization and any and all progressive visions of economic success (2012, p. xiv). Doubtless, it was his own strident disavowal even as he made practical use of his already finely-honed set of analytical skills, especially with respect

1 Almost simultaneously, Sugiyama's research led both to the development of a three-dimensional visual representation of trade statistics over the last 150 years – thereby allowing him to delineate and differentiate the primary historical trends in the trade in key goods between major countries – and to attempt to reconstruct from a large collection of old photographs a better understanding of the significant economic impact of coal mining in Hokkaido in the last century.

to the varying successes (silk and coal) and unanticipated failures (tea, for example) which characterized Japan as she began to compete within the international market. His work as a whole would become one of the first to lend credence to the absolute necessity of statistical data behind commercial competition (the volume provides a veritable treasure trove of data in its many tables, figures, and maps). With a remarkable understanding of the international historical and economic perspectives arising from the time that Japanese ports first opened to foreign trade,[2] he makes significant in-roads toward a reassessment of the discernible and seemingly unparalleled characteristics of – indeed, the importance of – foreign trade during the long Meiji period.[3]

Clearly, Sugiyama's volume warrants the highest possible recommendation for inclusion among the collections of public, undergraduate, and high-school libraries alike, however "dated" it might appear at first sight. The writing is clear, jargon-free, and possessed of a certain elegance without once distracting from the topics at hand. Furthermore, the sheer depth with which he covers certain heretofore ignored details from the economic histories heard across modern Japan – in particular his significant discussion of the export of three commodities which resulted in Japan's successful economic growth by the end of the nineteenth century – is reason enough to make the material available to everyone. Unfortunately, at this printing, this and other works are available only as hardcover or in eBook formats, both of which are extraordinarily expensive, especially if the volumes are intended to serve as textbooks. Certainly, this work has stood the test of time and academic scrutiny and will prove better suited and far more substantial for graduate students in any way interested in modern Japan and for those specialists who have dedicated themselves to the subject. Ideally, were the volumes much less expensive, then they might also serve undergraduate students well. But the price remains a significant obstacle, so prohibitive, especially during these (re)current economic crises, that it would be ill-advised to require the work as a primary reading. Instead, it might benefit everyone involved to place the text (or preferably several copies) on reserve in a central, restricted location.

2 Sugiyama at no point addresses pre-Meiji Chinese and Dutch trade through the isolated port of Dejima, a small island off the coast of Nagasaki; in doing so he misses an opportunity to emphasize two important points behind his argument. First, that Japan prior to the Restoration of the Emperor Meiji did not remain absolute in her insistence upon isolation from the outside world. Second, that the farmer class were in no way subservient to and powerless against central authorities. Put differently, Japan was never completely "homogenous," in the strictest sense. Economic historian Philip C. Brown has done an excellent job at teasing out specific examples of defiance among peasants who frequently and deliberately "redefined" their land holdings. In fact, even today, some large farms in Niigata prefecture – and they represent but one striking example – are known physically to move the very landmarks and cornerstones, time and again, by which tax assessors from Edo/modern-day Tokyo would rely upon to differentiate individual property lines, if for no other – or better – reason than to decrease the annual taxes levied against them by those in power. See his thoughtful, well-argued monograph, Philipp C. Brown: *Central Authority and Local Autonomy in the Formation of Early Modern Japan: The Case of Kaga Domain.* Stanford: Stanford UP 1993.

3 See also, Yamamoto Kozo: Japan: The Officer in Charge of Economic Affairs. In: A.W. Coats (ed.): *Economists in Government.* Durham, NC: Duke UP 1981, pp. 600–628.

That said, Sugiyama's work will remain that rare find, insofar as the material provides a fine example of historical and economic research and its presentation at its best, of certain benefit for students, instructors, and lay readers alike. It is hard to imagine a scenario in which a reader would not benefit from a thorough reading and rereading over a long course, an extended break or an entire career.

Table of Figures